WHERE THE WORLD WAS

Also by Rosemary Sullivan

Non-Fiction

The Betrayal of Anne Frank: A Cold Case Investigation

Stalin's Daughter: The Extraordinary and Tumultuous Life of Svetlana Alliluyeva

The Guthrie Road

Villa Air-Bel: World War II, Escape, and a House in Marseille

Cuba: Grace Under Pressure

Labyrinth of Desire: Women, Passion and Romantic Obsession

Memory-Making: Selected Essays

The Red Shoes: Margaret Atwood Starting Out

Shadow Maker: The Life of Gwendolyn MacEwen

By Heart: Elizabeth Smart/A Life

The Garden Master: The Poetry of Theodore Roethke

Poetry

The Bone Ladder: New and Selected Poems

Blue Panic

The Space A Name Makes

Fiction (Juvenile)

Molito

WHERE THE WORLD WAS

WAS a memoir

Rosemary Sullivan

Edited by Linda Pruessen.
Cover and page design by Julie Scriver.
Front cover photograph courtesy of Rosemary Sullivan. Background image by George Desipris, unsplash.com.
Printed in Canada by Marquis.
10 9 8 7 6 5 4 3 2 1

Library and Archives Canada Cataloguing in Publication

Title: Where the world was / Rosemary Sullivan.
Names: Sullivan, Rosemary, 1947- author.
Identifiers: Canadiana (print) 20230206050 | Canadiana (ebook) 20230206107 | ISBN 9781773102818 (softcover) | ISBN 9781773102825 (EPUB)
Subjects: LCSH: Sullivan, Rosemary, 1947-—Travel. | LCSH: Voyages and travels.
Classification: LCC PS8587.U483 W44 2023 | DDC C814/.54—dc23

Goose Lane Editions acknowledges the generous support of the Government of Canada, the Canada Council for the Arts, and the Government of New Brunswick.

Goose Lane Editions is located on the unceded territory of the Wəlastəkwiyik whose ancestors along with the Mi'kmaq and Peskotomuhkati Nations signed Peace and Friendship Treaties with the British Crown in the 1700s.

Goose Lane Editions
500 Beaverbrook Court, Suite 330
Fredericton, New Brunswick
CANADA E3B 5X4
gooselane.com

In loving memory of my dear friend Constance Rooke,
master of the essay genre

Rosemary Sullivan in Havana, Cuba, 1993 (Juan Opitz)

CONTENTS

PREFACE

"Live all you can. It's a mistake not to."
— Henry James

Once we only read about global pandemics. Now we have firsthand knowledge of what it is like to live in one. As I write, we seem to be in a moment of respite, but for two years we were under voluntary house arrest, isolated from friends and sometimes from family. Looked back at, it's almost impossible to believe it was actually two years, as if time only counts in relation to others. Without people, time collapses into non-time.

Space also emptied. The streets were vacant; the airports deserted. We were left only with space inside — a house, a grocery store, a mind.

All of us tried to find a solution to this sudden imprisonment. I discovered that what I most missed was travel. Out of a kind of nostalgia for something lost, I began to gather together the travel journeys I'd written over the years. I call them journeys, not travelogues, because I was always searching for something. There were so many of them — trips to Russia, Czechoslovakia, India, Egypt, and on. I ask myself now: what propelled me to undertake these journeys?

...

I remember reading somewhere that perhaps the memories that lie in the pools of our minds are what, cumulatively, make us up. With this thought rattling in my head, I turn to childhood with curiosity. For most of us, childhood is an accumulation of spotlighted moments that our adult selves have selected to understand who we are.

And so I begin. I was born in 1947, the second of five children, to an Irish Catholic family in Quebec. When my father was demobbed from the military, he was asked if he wanted a house or a university education. He chose a house.

Our four-room, two-bedroom house was on Bras D'Or Avenue (Arms of Gold) in the West Island town of Lakeside Heights, where the lake we were supposedly beside was at least ten miles away. The street had a post-war loneliness about it—everyone trying to live tidy lives behind closed doors. It would only occur to me years later that many of the men who had chosen houses on this street probably suffered from PTSD. So much had to be hidden.

When I dig down into my memories, the first one that surfaces is a traumatic incident that occurred when I was five.

The neighbourhood kids had gathered in the circular field at the top of our street to play Blind Man's Bluff. I was chosen to be the blind man. With my blindfold firmly in place, my sister led me over a slightly elevated manhole cover. I stumbled and fell, slicing my nose at the bridge. I ran home, my nose almost dangling to the side of my face, trailing a river of blood. A doctor was called—I remember his name was Dr. Sweet. I was laid out on our kitchen table where he sewed my nose back onto my face with black thread. Luckily, within a couple of weeks, I developed tonsilitis and was taken to Montréal General Hospital, where Dr. Cohen insisted that my nose would have to be broken again or "the child" would be disfigured for life.

That's when the nightmare began—I remember I was inserted between the jaws of a huge circular black machine. It was cold and dark inside. After the operation my wrists were tied to the hospital bed so that I wouldn't touch my nose.

My second memory is also traumatic. We attended a French Catholic elementary school run by nuns who wore white wimple-like headdresses that had the effect of obstructing their view of the world to each side.

It must have been late fall. We kids were waiting for the school bus at the stop at the bottom of our street beside a culvert that was roaring with white foaming water from a recent rain. Somehow my foot slipped, and I plunged into the ditch. I remember the water's rage, its gulping sound as I was driven towards the concrete tunnel under the pavement. I was certain I was going to drown when my sister grabbed my collar and pulled me out.

In retrospect we liked to joke: she defaced me; she saved my life.

I ran home to change my clothes and ran back in time to get the bus. But I had forgotten one thing. As I climbed the stairs at school, the nun below me, who was whipping us into single file, shouted my name. "Sullivan!" She was in a rage. "Where are your underpants?" she demanded. "Why do you have no underpants?" I was too terrified to explain. I would later understand how much the nuns feared and hated the body, a psychosis they tried to pass on to us.

Not long afterwards I carved my initials in black ink into my desk. It must have been satisfying—the deep repeated cuts with the black pen. What was I doing? Three decades later I would title my first book of poems *The Space a Name Makes*. I meant that while you arrive in the world with a given name, you must claim it, stretch out to the very edges of it, assert your identity, your authority to be you.

I also remember a ritual I developed when I was ten years old. At that time our street dead-ended at a forest. As darkness fell, I would run down the vaguely lit street into the woods. I knew mysterious dangers lurked in the underbrush, but I forced myself to keep going until I reached the swamp where the wild calla cowered beneath white hoods and the bullheads thrust up fists. On the edge of the swamp was a huge oak tree. When I'd circled the tree, I could go back. As I ran home in the dark, a monstrous phantom train was at my heels. I would rush into the house and lock the door just as a huge hand turned the knob.

When I look back, I think I know what I was doing. I was training myself to run into my fear. It was thrilling. I would confront the world head on, even if it was scary.

I turn back to this memory because it defines me as a risk taker, daring the mysterious dangers of the phantom train. I recognize a similarity to the anecdotes of other writers who speak of growing up with a sense of childhood loneliness, a sense of belonging somewhere else.

When I told two women friends who are writers about my ritual, they laughed. They both had similar stories. Linda said, "My ritual was long, long walks with my dog in order to get lost. These were town walks involving corners and sidewalks, but I got good and lost. Then I used a magic formula to get home: three to the right, turn left, turn right... et cetera." Barbara nodded: "It was a craving for the excitement of the unknown. The unknown, the unfamiliar, the 'other' has always drawn me," she explained.

In a collection of photographs from my childhood is one that is very odd. It's a photograph of the family, with a small hole in one corner. I'd cut myself out of the photo, out of the family. I have no memory of the moment, only the evidence of it. I don't even know how old I was when I did this, but according to my sister, I was the culprit. But why?

I don't remember myself as a timid or angry child, though I was certainly shy. When I reconstruct the act, it is done with resilience and a fierce attention. I believe I was removing myself from the scene; setting out to create my own world.

Barbara told me she also cut her face out of a photograph — it was the school yearbook — because she hated how she looked. But she explained, "That I actually went so far as to behead my image had to do with a desire to alter reality, and a belief that it was my right to do so."

. . .

Where were the books in my family? We had no books at home — it was an expense we couldn't afford — but my mother took us to the small library in the local town of Valois. There I found *Alice in Wonderland*, *Charlotte's Web*, Nancy Drew, and then "The Raven," *To Kill a Mockingbird*, and on. I fell in love with words and began to keep long lists of difficult words and their definitions. By the time I was thirteen, I was keeping a notebook — which, I'd read, is what writers do. But it would take a long time before I found the confidence to say I was a writer.

In high school I was in the A-stream with the other brainiac nerds, and we looked with envy at the popular girls who received all the boys' attention. It would turn out that not having to perform one's beauty was a gift. Many of the popular girls ended up with indifferent lives. Meanwhile, I was having a good time. I was elected student council president, participated in debates at McGill University, entered speech contests, and wrote a fashion column for the student newspaper, which had more to do with language than with fashion. In the summers I worked as a lifeguard, and from the age of eleven I took part in swimming competitions—I'd perfected the back crawl into my winning stroke. The external world seemed easy to negotiate, but inside I was still a shy, insecure child—though one with a will of steel and ready to engage the world.

In my final year the drama club mounted *The Sound of Music*, and I was assigned the role of Mother Superior. The nuns dressed me in their full regalia beginning with the underslip, and it suddenly occurred to me that they harboured the secret wish that I join the novitiate. But their costume felt like a cage covering my whole body, and I couldn't imagine ever wearing a nun's black habit. When the school year ended that June of 1964, I invited my cousin and my sister to join me as I made a ceremonial bonfire in the backyard and burned my school uniform. I was heading into a different life.

I had made it clear to my father that I was going to McGill University. I would get scholarships; I'd had a job in a bakery at age sixteen. I would pay my own way. My father said no. He insisted I must find a job to help support the family. He had done it; everyone in his family had done it. He spoke to one of his buddies at the Green Hornet Tavern who was principal of the boys' high school. This man called me to his office and told me that university would be wasted on a girl. My sister tells me that the rage I let loose in the house was devastating. Years later, the fact that all five of his children had university educations was my father's proudest claim.

University was the place I belonged. In those days it was a misogynist institution—in my four undergraduate years I had only one female professor—but I didn't care. Still, I couldn't say, out loud, that I wanted to be a writer—writers were people whose work you studied. When I met a young man in a Romantic poetry class who said he intended to be a writer, I was shocked. How did he have the temerity to make such a claim?

But then something happened to the risk taker in the child that, until then, I carried inside me. It was the dead of winter. It must have been ten o'clock—certainly it was dark—and I was about to take the bus home to the apartment I shared with a girlfriend during my last year of university when I realized I didn't have the bus fare. There was nothing for it but to walk. I started up over the Montréal overpass on Park Avenue and, suddenly, two hands pushed me down into the snow and a body climbed on top of me. He fumbled but then grabbed something from my purse and ran.

It was 1968—a time when a woman was expected to stand up for herself. I shouted every foul name I could think of and told him he was robbing a poor student. He stopped, came back, and punched me repeatedly in the face.

Afterwards, I could not say what he looked like; I only remembered his eyes full of hatred for women. I ran to the edge of the overpass and shouted for help into the mad frenzy of cars, noise, and lights below. I had never experienced gratuitous violence before, and it terrified me. The police came. I went to the station and looked at grotesque mug shots of rapists. I went to the hospital, where I felt only people's prurient curiosity. I kept repeating that I was not raped.

Experts say that most people who go through a traumatic event experience some period marked by symptoms like nightmares, anxiety, or headaches. This was my case. For a year after, I could not let anyone come up on me from behind. I recovered but the episode changed my life. Following the advice of a professor, I had decided to pursue my MA at the University of Connecticut and my PhD at the University of Sussex.

Six months after the attack, I married. He and I had been on and off lovers for four years, but now I was heading to another country. One day as we walked along rue St. Denis in Montréal, he grabbed me by the shoulders and said, "Are we going to get married? You have to decide." It was easiest to say yes. I think to be female on the receiving end of violence renders one passive. Now I felt I needed protection for the adventure I was embarking on.

During those six years, my husband and I had a good time. We were professional tourists traveling on $10 a day. He was a poet with time on his hands and meticulously researched our trips, which were mostly literary. In Sussex, we visited William Blake's house in Felpham and Henry James's house in Rye. We travelled to Shakespeare's birthplace in Stratford-upon-Avon and D.H. Lawrence's childhood home in Eastwood, Nottinghamshire. In Paris we dined at Les Deux Magots and watched Simone de Beauvoir and Jean-Paul Sartre eating sea urchins. We talked to Samuel Beckett in the café La Closerie Des Lilas and visited James Jones, author of *From Here to Eternity*, at his apartment on Île de la Cité on the Seine. It seemed we missed nothing. But it turned out this was neither the life nor the travel I wanted. It was too hermetic, too aesthetic.

In 1974, I was offered a job in Victoria, British Columbia. As my husband and I returned to Canada, I discovered we'd been protected from reality by our travels. The disparities between us surfaced. I had married the poet when I wanted to be one. When I showed him the poetry I'd begun to write, he dismissed it and advised me not to bother. I was the academic, and, luckily, society paid me a salary. When I told him I needed to take a year off to work on my own writing and he should get a job—he was shocked. He responded testily that I didn't believe in his art. I suddenly understood that he was one of those artists who expected his genius to be supported by a wife.

It's a rule: the easiest way to break up a marriage is to fall in love with somebody else. This I did, with the usual outcome. My married lover was not what he seemed. I was the route out of his marriage, but not a place to stop. In the end, though I thought I loved him, he was the route out of mine.

Deciding to leave my life in Victoria, I got a job at the University of Toronto. I bought a red Toyota Celica with my last $5,000 and drove across the country alone.

By now it was 1977. I was thirty years old. A friend had said, "There's a time when things change. You find you are no longer running from; you are running towards." I began to write my travel journeys. Often,

I was following a writer, or I was writing a book, or setting out to know another culture. I would try, like a chameleon, to take on the colouration of a place, carrying as little of my own baggage as I could. Some of the places I visited involved risk—it was unusual to travel alone to Russia or Prague in 1979—but my desire to encounter those worlds for myself outweighed my fear, just as it had when I trained myself to run into the woods in my childhood.

Organizing these journeys chronologically, I've discovered they describe who I am. I realize I have been a traveller all my life. My quest has always been to meet the world, to celebrate its richness, to face its darkness. I've wanted to encounter the Other, observing and recording the myriad different expressions of our human imagination.

SUFI SUMMER CAMP, 1977

In the summer of 1977 I'd fled a job, a marriage, and a lover on the West Coast of Canada and ended up in Toronto, where I knew no one. Those first months alone were like solitary confinement: like crawling into a hole and pulling the hole in after you. At first, I walked the city, trying this café or that one. Once I stumbled into the red-light district, then on Church Street. I still laugh at the barb one of the girls directed at a john: "Who are you, Bugs Bunny looking for a hole?" It was entertaining and depressing, like the underside of any big city. That August I spent my birthday at McDonald's as a kind of protest against being alone.

In search of human contact, I joined a yoga club. I'm not much good at physical discipline and I didn't last, but while there I read an ad on the notice board. It said simply: "Sufi Summer Camp, North Carolina." It provided an address and invited those interested in Sufism to phone.

For me Sufism meant the writers and the poets: Doris Lessing, Robert Graves, P.K. Page. I'd read Idries Shah's *The Way of the Sufi* and was fascinated. In Victoria, P.K. had become a close friend, and I knew she travelled in the summers to England to spend time with Shah and Lessing. I'd had what William James, in his book *The Varieties of Religious Experience: A Study in Human Nature*, called a natural mystical experience.

It happened in the small town of Falmer, Sussex, where I lived for three years while at the University of Sussex. In order to take a train to Brighton, you had to mount steep stairs, cross over the tracks along a corridor with a glass awning, and descend to the other side. I suppose it was the way the sun hit the glass, but one day, while crossing the tracks, the boundaries of my body just dissolved and I fell into a state of tranced ecstasy. When I talked with P.K. about this, she said simply, "We live within a kind of filter system that allows us to process the world. Occasionally the blindfold comes off and we experience the world in another way, perhaps even the world as it is."

And then she recounted a dream: she was in a formal garden walking amidst towering trees and green shrubs. There were two dogs in the garden, both Irish setters. Their fur was not red; it was a dazzling gold. They had two animal eyes and above these was a third eye, which was human. In the dream, P.K. asked herself, "If their third eye is human, what is our third eye?"

Why not Sufi summer camp? I wondered as I contemplated that ad on the message board. I phoned the New York number. The camp was very inexpensive, which I took as a good sign: $100 a week for room and board. I was told that when I got to Salem, I should take a bus to the Weatherly bus station and then to Deerlake and phone from there. Someone would pick me up. That's all the information I had.

I booked a flight to North Carolina. When we landed, it turned out the airline had lost one of my bags in transit. The sleeping bag came down the ramp, but the knapsack didn't.

. . .

Stripped, I think, in one of those moods to find everything emblematic.

I go to the baggage claim desk. "Don't worry," the clerk says. "Where shall we send it when it comes through?"

"To the Sufi summer camp," I answer.

He stiffens. "Where?"

"S-U-F-I summer camp," I repeat. He writes down the address, and I retreat outside to wait for a bus.

An airport attendant runs up to me. "You the one going up to that Sufi place? Doing your devotionals?" he asks in a heavy Southern accent. When I look blank, he says: "Oh yes you are. I've been up there. I'm leaving in an hour. Wait and I'll ride you." He looks me up and down. I imagine the airport cops standing against the wall and swivelling their holstered hips are also examining me. A taxi slides by, and I jump in.

"Take me to the Weatherly bus station please."

"Where are you going?" he asks.

"To Deerlake."

"I'll take you for twenty-two dollars," he says. "It'll cost you eighteen by bus, but you go round the long way."

I look at my driver. He's in his mid-fifties, wiry, with stubble hair and walleyes.

"Is that right?" I say, defeated.

"Cash in advance." He smiles. "I've had customers disappear through too many back doors."

We move off, and after a long silence he says: "Do you want to know about discipline? My congregation teaches discipline."

"Your congregation?" I say.

"You ever heard of the KKK?" he asks.

"No," I reply, and he believes me.

"When my daddy was dying last year, he said to me, 'Son, join the KKK, and stay in it if you can. Staying's the thing. No drinking, no women, no fooling around.'"

"Sounds hard," I say.

"Well, if you're going to discipline others, you have to discipline yourself."

"How do you discipline?" I ask.

He is suddenly excited. He speeds up to pass a Volkswagen van. A couple of teenagers are horsing around in the back seat. I mention they seem to be having fun. "Them's women," he says. "The men pick them up and take them into the mountains. They do what they want with them."

I look again.

"Them women get beat up and used like dirt, but we discipline them. That's one of our errands. After we get through with their lessons they don't sit down for a week. I know the one on the right. Can't see the one on the left though."

In my mind I see one thousand Ku Klux Klansmen raiding a Sufi summer camp. I go silent and wait it out.

"I'm a bachelor," he says, "fifty-eight. You've made me some time. On the way back I can take off an hour. Spend it with my girlfriend."

We pull up into Deerlake.

"Sure been nice talking to you," he says.

I think, What about the KKK's "no women" rule?

The letter describing the Sufi camp said simply: "Go to Deerlake terminal and phone. Someone will pick you up." I phone. After thirty rings and no answer, I look around me for the first time. The bus terminal is actually just a pull-in stop. The terminus is a window grill with a middle-aged woman behind it. On the right, there's a low-slung building—the sheriff's office—and big beefy men stroll in and out in the heat.

I notice a woman standing in front of the bus stop sign. She's about forty-five and wears a pale yellow cotton sack—two pieces of cloth sewn at the shoulders and down the sides and left to hang, unhemmed. She has straw-grey hair streaked with bright yellow, and she combs it compulsively with a large pink comb she's just taken from a white envelope.

"Ma'am, could I find a motel in this town?" I ask. "I was to meet friends here, and they haven't shown up. My luggage was lost at the airport terminal, and I'm stranded."

"What's their names, honey?" she asks, and her voice sounds like molasses dripping slowly into a bowl.

I think, Sufi? "Brown," I say.

"Which, honey? There's lots of Browns round here."

"Leslie Brown."

She pauses. "I know all the Browns, and there's no Leslie. Let's look in the book."

We make our way to the telephone booth. There are Lolas and Lornas but luckily no Leslie. "We'll call Audrey Brown and see if they's kin."

Before I can stop her, she dips into her white envelope for a dime and slips it into the slot. No answer. "I'd like to go to a motel," I say.

"Well, let's call the taxi man. He'll know."

We wait.

Her fingers are like little ferrets rooting in the envelope. She takes out her comb. The heat and dust are heavy and it's getting darker. Farm pickup trucks rip around the corner and a bus pulls in.

"Name's Beula," she says. "I have an idea, honey." She looks at me tentatively. "Why don't you stay with me?"

I think, I can put my sleeping bag just about anywhere. I tell her I'd be grateful.

"First, honey, I have to go to the supermarket." When the taxi arrives, we jump in. The driver knows her and says, "Night, Beula. Where to?" We taxi to the supermarket. Beula goes inside and I go to the phone booth. I try the camp and finally make a connection. Someone will come in forty-five minutes.

I go inside to find Beula wandering among the frozen foods, picking at ice packs with a disconsolate finger. I tell her I've found my friends. She winces, and her voice is sticky as flypaper. "You coulda stayed with me, honey. I would have been right glad to have you." My crumbled look evokes a smile. "Besides," she says, "I was buying you a TV dinner. You gonna miss your TV dinner."

I take the same cab back to the depot. The driver eyes me askance and his look is brittle. "Beula is certainly a kind woman," I say. "Is she okay?"

"Well, I tell ya," he says, "sometimes she is, and sometimes she ain't."

"Is she very poor?" I ask.

"No, she's got government money. She's got a retarded son who's twenty-two. She visits him in Layton." He says it with the tired kindness of a man who has driven up and down the same street all his life and is pretty sure he doesn't want to get off it.

I set up my watch at the depot again. It's getting darker, and the white pickup trucks are back. A man runs up to me and asks, "Have you seen a grey Ford?"

"No. No." I shiver.

The depot lady, finally closing down, comes up to me. "Honey, are your friends coming?"

"Yes," I say.

"Well, you'll be all right here." She pats my arm. "The sheriff's over there if you need help." I look through the window to see a roomful of men looking at me. Buses come and go.

Finally, a little white bug splattered in stickers pulls up to the depot. Inside, a vague and beautiful girl in white pyjamas smiles. "Have a good trip?"

I get inside. We set out in the dark, and I'm not even bothered when the car skips skittishly from side to side along the road. She apologizes:

"This work spaces you. What are roads? There's never one way." She pauses. "All you can ask is, has this road got heart?"

We drive through farm country until we reach a private estate. There's a huge iron gate stretching across the roadway, and she asks me to open it. She explains that we're entering a model farm constructed in the 1930s by some philanthropist who wanted to give the unemployed a place to live. There are about fifteen buildings, including an assembly hall, a kitchen, and sleeping quarters. In the summer the Sufis take over the premises. It's so dark I can't see much. I can only smell the woods, heavy with the scent of rhododendrons; the crickets sound like stones rolling in a jar. We drive past a cluster of deserted buildings until we reach one that is blazing with light.

We park and get out to look into a large assembly room. Through the screen door I see about one hundred people in various stages of undress swaying to Eastern music. The air is murky with the heat, and they look surreal. We enter and take up our places in the group, and for the first time I see the focal centre of the room. On a raised platform, a small man—firmly muscled and in bathing trunks, his entire body covered in black hair—leads the group in slow rhythmic movements and then begins to drum. As he strokes the drum, the group responds as if it were an extension of the instrument he plays. He looks fierce and solid and rather frightening as his eyes roll, exposing the whites.

A soft-eyed girl comes up and invites me to follow her. We climb stairs to a dormitory where eight mattresses with sleeping bags are spread out on the floor. There are homey touches, like a clothesline hung with underwear, and each bed seems to have its cache of personal goods—books, drums, hair dryers, finger cymbals. The girl, Tamara, finds me a mattress and then shows me the bathroom. The tap is running, and, indignant, she turns it off: "Think of that water wasted when people in deserts are thirsty."

"This is a good room," she says. "The people are nice." She looks at me, unblinking. Her eyes have the slow quiet of a still pool. I ask how she came to be here.

"I joined belly-dancing class and then became interested in the group," she answers. "I was a spoiled child. I like this discipline, when somebody actually says NO. It's hard, but it gives me something to measure myself against." I ask about the discipline. "We fast. There's a guy here who's lasted forty days."

"Jesus!" I say. She tells me her best count is ten. "It sounds like a competition," I say.

She's put out. "There's no competition here. How can you compete in being?" The others begin to return, and we settle in for the night. From time to time I wake as shadows slip in and out, going in search of their own mysterious encounters.

...

I wake with the dawn and walk down to the artificial lake. A man is there with his two children. He looks like a middle-aged sociologist searching for a community, and I think, What kind of man would bring his kids to a place like this? He says, "You one of those Sufi freaks? This is my place too. How would you feel if your relatives showed up with a guru?" I learn the estate is owned by four brothers and that the Sufis have been invited without the permission of the other three. There are very definite boundaries to this retreat.

I walk out into the open pasture, which is orange in the misted sun and still wet. The long grasses cool my legs. Only me and the flies. I pass a man bathing in the stream, his naked body brown against the orange-brown rocks. Another person passes in the distance. The way he runs is ethereal, springing on his feet in an undulant rhythm from which the tension of direction—somewhere to go—is gone.

For the first time I sense the mystery of this place. I walk up to a girl squatting beside the road, and I see she is talking to a butterfly. She looks up with her moon face and tells me how the butterfly selected her. It gentled beside her and began to secrete liquid drops. It has laboured for two hours, and she has protected it. I look at the butterfly, a large yellow monarch with charcoal shading and two blue eyes on its wings, and at the girl who wants to be nature's butterfly keeper.

People have begun to collect in the field and finally the Master as they call him here, though his name is Adnan, comes striding purposefully. He sits, and they gather round him in the sun, the women closest. He is completely quiet for some time, and the group responds. I realize he is a man of extraordinary consistencies—no highs and lows, but a well-paced self-control that speaks of a remarkable self-sufficiency. His eyes look through you and seem to make demands. I think of reflectors: when light is turned on them it bounces back.

He begins to talk with complete assurance.

"If you are here it is because you want to know who you are, where you have come from, where you are going. Most people forget these questions. Man lives in loss. What is life but existence. Form is death. Life is movement. The secret is concentration. Learn detachment and indifference, to live beyond emotions. Once out of worrying, you will be different. I will change you, but you must suspend judgment and follow because the mind is devious. Fear distracts people. Take what you need. One day you will move beyond the Master. Nothing will be asked of you. It must come from you."

This sermon worries me. "Indifference." "Suspend judgment." "The mind is devious." These words feel potentially coercive. Where might they lead? He seems to be asking for complete control.

The group disperses and a young man approaches me. His face is thin and fierce, and he is fastidiously groomed. He struts, cock-of-the-walk. Apparently, he is chief rutter in the camp. I've already been warned off him.

"God, it's good to touch," he says. He takes half an hour massaging the little bones in my hand. "Skin's beautiful. I was on drugs for eight years. Started as a chemist and then learned to push my own." I look at him. "Yeah, out of it every day for eight years. Used to lie in bed by the phone getting high. But I've got my will back with this work, and now I'm into astrology. I can do your chart for three dollars if you know the hour of your birth."

He dips into mental pockets for arcane trinkets. "What I want now is a non-chemical high. This work can really flash you." His fingers on my back seem to read the bone structure very precisely. There is much talk here of body language . . . deposits of pain in the bone . . . all parts of the body—eyes, feet, hands—encoding the body's life in psychic shorthand. Suddenly I feel exposed. I thank him for his work, and he moves on, holding himself stiffly as if he feared a sudden sabotage of his careful control.

People begin to gather slowly in the assembly hall. There's a ruckus, and someone grabs my arm and whispers, "A cat fight." I see a woman square off on knees and fists, threatening, like an animal. She says to someone, "You have my space." There is a locked tension and then the offender retreats. It strikes me as a primitive battle for dominance. I notice the Master has watched this carefully. With seeming indifference he says, "Form in three circles." Seeing that she has been defeated by this directive, the woman collapses like a toy, and two other women flutter over her, kneeling and comforting. She looks familiar. I think she's the one I saw earlier giving the Master a psychic rub.

The exercises begin. Hands, legs, feet, torsos raise and lower to the hypnotic rhythms of the music. Everything moves in waves of expansion and contraction, as if one organism were breathing. At moments the group dozes uniformly, like a child. Outside, the cicadas drill like pebbles on a beach drawn along by the retreating waves. The chanting begins.

I've never done anything like this before, but why come so far if I don't throw myself into it? You are meant to regulate sound and breathing, and so there must be an element of autohypnosis. After a long time, I see a kind of red dark and am in a domed space. Gradually I realize that it is my skull, and I'm looking through arched windows that are my eyes. Light floods in. With intense listening I see an image of the inner ear—the ear opening and sharp threads of liquid sound visibly pouring down the inner canal. Then the membranous beating of the heart. Slowly the membrane becomes a throbbing wall, until I am the wall throbbing. Finally, I have a glimpse through a circular aperture of a stone and green landscape, and I feel a flash of relief.

The group deflates in exhaustion, and we go out into the sun. A girl catches me by the arm; her eyes are dilated in a kind of fascinated horror. "During the chanting I saw images," she says. "I saw a female vagina out of which were born plastic dolls—all stiff arms and legs. Then I saw transparent skeletons, mainly leg bones, like a chain racing up and down. The vagina had a circular grate in the opening, as if anything entering would be sliced like an onion. What do you think it means?" Thankfully, she doesn't wait for an answer before she begins to tell someone else her story, and I think, If you create a perfect isolation, then alter the body through fasting, states of total exhaustion, and aural assaults, you alert the unconscious to articulate itself in images. Such ground can be very dangerous.

It is evening, and we go to hear the Master read a Sufi text. Some dance a little, each in their own private circle, and finally we eat for the first time that day. I begin to talk to a very fierce young man about the literature we've heard. "I found the tone didactic," I say.

"It is our ignorance that blinds us," he replies. "If we were more advanced, we would hear better. There's an Arab saying: when a pick-pocket looks at a saint, he sees only his pockets." He moves off with a mincing, pious step, holding himself stiffly as if he were brittle as glass.

The Master beckons me. "How is it?"

"Fine," I say.

"Well, just follow the diet. Your eyes have the depth and intelligence this work needs; there are so many crazies here. I would like a small core of people I can really train. Perhaps you would like to be one of them." He pats my knee.

The meal turns out to be salad. People disappear to the dormitories in groups. I lie in bed and when I think all is quiet, I take my flashlight and head down to the garden. As I root among the tomatoes and beans, I notice several other flashlights in the distance.

I wake early from a dream. Two people, a janitor and an old woman, wish to give me advice about the Master. They are his friends. They say he is a wonderful man, but he has two shortcomings. The first is money. In the dream I reply: "But they say he uses no money for himself." They respond that he is keeping the money for his basilica. And then, they add, there is women. I say I must leave to prepare a reading. I am to read *Anabasis*. I find myself in a university and a mad little professor scurries past like the White Rabbit, singing, "Nails, nails, nails, he was the blood of the lamb." I recall that *Anabasis* is an ancient Greek text about a successful military retreat. I'm getting as crazy as they are.

I decide to take an early-morning dip in the creek. The fields are beautiful in the low, heavy-scented heat that smells of cinnamon and red dirt. There are butterflies as big as hands settled on the ground. The crickets sound like Indian cymbals. People drift like leaves through the gentle landscape or run with the steady rhythm of fabulously whirling disks. The brook water is white and ice-cold. The speed of the water is the same as the speed of blood in my veins; even the sound seems the same, as if I could hear my blood beating. I have been fasting for two and a half days. I am to meet four other people who are escaping to town in a borrowed car. I sit by the road and wait without effort. To improvise one's life is a lovely thing.

Once outside the gate, we pull up to the first store for ice cream cones. Five men in overalls are sitting out on the veranda smoking in the lazy morning and passing around a sarsaparilla jug. One whinnies like a horse when we step out. It is then I notice the beer-bottle-cap lawn, thousands of metal caps wedged into the soil to make an aluminum lawn. Inside, an old man tells us they have only popsicles. He takes out five and, with a heavy meat cleaver, tries to separate them. They dance on the table like fish as he misses with each blow. Finally, he breaks them in shaky alcoholic hands.

We stop down the road for melons. The store is unpainted and dirty and again old men sit on the veranda. The owner gets up to serve us. He is impeccable in pressed pants, polished shoes, and white socks. He has a way of holding his Coke bottle with the last two fingers lifted delicately. He tells the boy who works for him to count out the melons. After a moment he says, "Junior, I can't hear ya countin'." As we drive away, I ask the others if they noticed Adnan's car parked in front of the Texas Ranger Steak House. "I thought the camp was vegetarian," I say with a smile.

We rush back to camp to be in time for what I, too, have come to call the work. After exercises, the chanting begins. This time it is breathing without words. We are instructed to take in the air through the eyes, send it to the top of the head, then to the solar plexus, and expel it. After a short time, this breathing creates in me a state of tranced suspension, another kind of sleep, with the mind in abeyance. I can see and hear but make no discriminations. When someone calls my name, I feel an electric current of panic. I would not be compelled from this indifference. I get up slowly and return to my room. My feet seem weightless; they touch the ground simply for information. I sleep a long time. In a dream someone says to me, "You will have to return." I wake inside the dream only to discover I am half alive. The people watching smile. "You have been for a short time in the city of Philadelphia." Brotherly love. They comfort me. I say to them they should be careful with spiritual power.

That night the Master drums and a feast of delicious Middle Eastern food is served. I am shown how to belly dance, and I almost get it. I discover that many of the people here, most in their twenties and thirties, are from New York and are survivors of the drug culture of the late sixties and early seventies, when brains were fried with LSD. They seem like lost souls bent on some kind of desperate exorcism.

After dinner the Master approaches me. "You are beautiful. For body, soul, mind, and face to meet in strength and beauty does not often happen. I don't do sex during the work, but this would be different." He smiles and drifts away. Am I flattered, or simply curious? After the disintegration of my life on the West Coast, I have stopped thinking of sex as making love. Now, it is simply the body pleasuring itself. Two girls take me to a room where the Master is waiting. We have sex. I suppose I expected some kind of Sufi sex—the *Kama Sutra* of desire. Instead, it's rather flat, unmemorable, over in seeming seconds.

When I return to my room, I ask the girls about sexuality at the camp. Does the Master have lovers? One girl looks appalled and says, "We all love him in a spiritual way." But another takes me aside. "Last year they had to petition the Master to lay off the women." That night I dream of a mouse ripped open by a cat. When I go to save the mouse, the cat eats it and grins. I awake exhausted in mind and body.

I pack my things. I buy some dried bananas from the girl who is running a small banana business in the women's dormitory. I am meeting a fellow Canadian who is also leaving and has offered to drive me to the bus station. I recognize that this is a human place like any other, full of falsity and some truth. I haven't understood it. To them I am simply one of the defectors, but in my mind, I hear an odd voice warning, "If you cannot be God, you just don't fall back to the rank and file." I wonder where that came from. But I realize whatever truth is here, it is not my truth. This place feels like a retreat from a world that is too painful, but

I am moving in the opposite direction. I want to encounter the world with appetite and attention.

On the path through the fields to meet my drive, I stop to watch four soaring hawks. I can see their fluted wings, almost diaphanous in the white light. They move with such pleasure and power, as if they enjoy their mastery. I feel their freedom.

TRACKING DOWN
ELIZABETH SMART, 1978

Over the last year I'd kept my promise to myself, and was writing poems that I was publishing in small magazines and also essays about Canadian identity. When I finally wrote about my experience at the Sufi summer camp, I sent the piece to a new British magazine called the *London Review of Books*. They wrote back saying they liked it but couldn't tell what was fact—what had actually happened—and what was fiction. I folded the letter away, not yet experienced enough to realize I should just have written back to assure them that everything in the piece had actually happened—dreams and all.

After teaching for a year at Erindale College in Mississauga, in those days a colonial outpost of the University of Toronto (which suited me, since they left you to your own devices), I packed my bags and moved to London, England. When I'd taken the job at U of T, I'd negotiated an unusual contract: I would work for one year and then be allowed to take the next year off in order to accept the Canada Council grant I'd just won. That fall of 1978, I was going to London ostensibly to write a collection of essays.

But in fact, to be truthful, I was blown there by the fatal wind of a romantic obsession. I was still mourning my West Coast lover, and I was putting the sea between us. Absurdly, Canada, the second largest country in the world, had become too small for me because it contained that one person. But bleak and lonely London matched my bleakness, with its subway ads of lovers selling the fulfillment of desire, a fulfillment that had eluded me. I had never felt so angry at the world for peddling love as a vehicle to sell things.

That fall, the name of Elizabeth Smart surfaced in the British papers—she had brought out a new book after a silence of thirty-three years. She was known as the author of *By Grand Central Station I Sat Down and Wept*, but that had always been enough. The book is a classic, like *Wuthering Heights*: the kind of book that enters lives and changes them so that everyone remembers when they read it. It is a story about romantic passion, about falling madly in love and then losing the gamble. Suddenly, I needed to know how Elizabeth Smart had survived that first book, for it seemed to me so real that I presumed she must have lived its story of loss.

I wrote to her as a fellow Canadian, requesting a visit. What I said I can no longer remember, but she invited me to her cottage, The Dell, in Suffolk. It was winter, and I can still remember how desolate the cottage seemed. It was adjacent to a vast empty gravel pit, the landscape strewn with standing pools of frozen water and interrupted by huge cranes rising like pterodactyls. She stood at the gate waiting for me, dishevelled in mackinaw and gum boots. She would have been sixty-five then. My first impression was that her face was ravaged, lined and lived-in, yet somehow as young as a child's.

Perhaps it was the effect of the shaggy blond hair framing it or of her eyes, blue and backlit in the way of the eyes of people who have lived. Everything about her seemed ingenuous, particularly her shyness, for she seemed shyer than I, who felt like an interloper into her intense privacy, though years later I would discover that her house was open to everyone, like Grand Central Station itself—the taxi driver was invited in with the passenger.

Inside, the cottage rambled, hodgepodge fashion, comfortable in all its discomfort as only an English cottage can be. It felt like the home of a woman used to living alone. I particularly remember the kitchen, which centred on a pulsing coal fire. The moped her children had bought her for her sixtieth birthday to negotiate the back lanes of Bungay sat on the stone floor (she complained she'd been stranded for days because its narrow wheels could not manage the snow). The curtains on the windows were William Morris prints, and there were books everywhere. She showed me the portrait of herself that dominated the sitting room: a young woman, wildly beautiful, looking like one's fantasy of John Fowles's French Lieutenant's woman with hair blowing stiff as sails against a rock landscape, her gaze fierce with romantic challenge. Standing beside this icon, aged and diminutive, she seemed to me to be amused and bemused by its ironic comment on life's capacity to deflate us, though the eyes with which she gazed at me were still candidly and fiercely blue.

The meal was exquisite and decorative: sole bonne femme. To tame our shyness, we drank heavily: white wine and vodka (she said if you didn't like the taste of alcohol it was best to drink vodka because it has no taste). After lunch we stumbled into her winter garden. She wanted a photo of me sitting in the garden chair amidst the snow—it would be so Canadian—but the chair collapsed under me. Years later, after Elizabeth's death, her daughter would show me the photo of myself, legs in the air, the inelegant record of my first encounter with Elizabeth Smart.

Though I was in pursuit of answers for my life, I cannot remember talking about myself that afternoon. I certainly never got round to asking her for a formula to survive obsessive passion. We talked about her first book. The one detail among myriad that sits as if under a spotlight in my mind was her answer to a question: I asked her why the man in her novel with whom the narrator was so desperately in love hardly had an identity. He seemed to me faceless. "Of course, he has no face," she replied impatiently. "He is a love object." I did not realize it then, but everything I needed to know about obsessive passion was in that phrase.

We drank so much alcohol that, by five in the afternoon, we decided we had to sleep if we were to make anything of the evening. I was placed upstairs in a narrow bed with a hot water bottle under layers of blankets. How can I explain what I felt then? It was as if there were a free-floating erotic intensity that sought no particular object but simply filled the air like oxygen. The energy was palpable, like a vortex sucking me down. Was it my alcoholic stupor? Yet it seemed like a force field of longing—the condition in which this woman lived. From her room I could hear Elizabeth flailing in her sleep, and eerily crying "Mother, Mother." She was still a stranger and I too shy to mention what I'd heard. Years later I would read her journal: "I am sixty-three. I still scream, cry out at night; heard throughout the house, through several walls, still wrestling with infantile anguishes and anxieties."

We trudged off to the local pub that evening. I left the next day for London. I would see her one more time before I set off on another of my search/escape journeys, this time travelling alone to Moscow. I placed that first encounter with Elizabeth on a recessed shelf in my mind. It would be a decade before I realized that, in one afternoon, she'd offered me all the clues I needed to understand my own quest.

For I had to pursue the conundrum of obsessive passion on my own. The curious thing about this kind of passion is that it's like an empty shell, a form into which everyone can fit their own experience. It has a formula—longing, ecstasy, frustration, grief—and the details range from the exquisitely painful to the ridiculous. You walk into that kind of love as into a labyrinth of mirrors: it is yourself that you see reflected back—heroic, raging with appetite against life's normalcies.

At the age of twenty-seven, I fell in love (amusing that we still say "fell"), danced the peculiar dance of compulsion and retreat for two years, and took another two years to resurrect myself. That year in London I came to see romantic love as one of the routes we take to construct the self.

The function of the lover, I now believe, is to crack open the defended self. For me, the first hook was his voice on a transatlantic phone wire, the second his body, the third his mind, and the fourth his pain.

If he had not been in pain, I would not have seen him. For romantic obsession seems necessarily to be built on frustration, the lusting after the unattainable. The lover seems always to be a frenetic trickster, a shape-shifter. In romantic love, if you are a woman, you always seem to be healing somebody. A man presents his life as pained, and you are meant to believe that you are his solution. You are the still centre where he will be able to come to rest. In my own case, I am appalled to think how familiar the lover's pain was.

He was unhappily married. Not that his pain wasn't real. I remember his account of a dream. He entered a room. There was a candlestick on the piano. He picked it up and began to cauterize his face with the flame. I believe he thought that were he to take off his mask, there would be nothing: no face. But I could never have been his solution. Like me, he could only find that in himself. Meanwhile, our collusive dance continued: he frenetic, approaching and then retreating; me believing I could heal him when I only wanted to heal myself.

What was I really doing in that collusive dance? I ask myself. I believe I fell in love with the version of myself that he reflected back to me. You find the one who can hear all your stories. You believe only they can recognize you. For the first time you can imagine what you might be. In this way, I started to take myself seriously as a writer. Romantic obsession is, ironically, purely autobiographical; the lover serves, as Elizabeth said, as a "love object."

Obsessive love is a training ground. My lesson was quite simple — how to say I WANT THIS, something I hadn't really been able to do before. In the end it didn't matter whether I got it or not. In the end, in fact, I was lucky I didn't, because I never really knew the man independent of the idea I had invented of him. As the Australian writer Christina Stead once said: "Every love story is a ghost story." When obsessive passion is over and the projections are ripped away, the person standing there is almost always a stranger. For romantic love is projection — of all that is most dramatic, indeed loveable and unclaimed in the self. I weaned myself of my obsession in London when, in my endless readings, I discovered the word *tolerance*. I had to tolerate the fact that life might have room for a different, larger version of me than the fantasy of a man I had constructed in my head. Love is not a life solution. I had fallen under the illusion that another had become so crucial to my life that without him I would be destroyed. I discovered life was much wiser than I was. Years later I would find myself back in Victoria where I'd fallen in love. I drove through the streets, and I laughed, uproariously. I felt a wonderful affection, laced with humour, at the intensity of that younger self caught up in all that pain and grief. As August Strindberg once said: "Ah, the agony of ecstasy and the ecstasy of agony. You look for love outside yourself when love is your very nature."

Elizabeth Smart had four children with her lover George Barker, though she never really lived with him. When I asked her why she kept letting him back in the door, she said, "He had such a good sense of humour." She always insisted she did not expect a husband. And the children were her idea. Of childbirth she would write: "This is work! Serious, gigantic, absolute . . . Love and all its flimsy fancies are rolled under this mighty event: crushed like straw conceits." Was that bravura? Elizabeth remained friends with Barker until her death. She always said she understood her collusion in "all that pricey pain."

Four years after we met, Elizabeth ended up living in Toronto for a year. When she invited friends to a dinner party, she always brought out Barker's *Collected Poems*. At table we were all required to recite a poem we had by heart. By the time she was sixteen, she'd already memorized most of Shakespeare's sonnets. It was "the poet Barker" she was inextricably attached to. Those were the days when there was little room for women writers, particularly in England. Elizabeth always said the poets would talk to her one on one, but she had no place at the literary table. Barker would go on to have a total of five "wives" and fifteen children, none of whom he financially supported. He was the model of the priapic poet of the 1940s — promiscuous, rebellious, the genius devoted only to his art.

I remember once walking with Elizabeth down Bloor Street. She turned to me and said, with an unaccustomed serenity, "I had my vision." She was right. She is remembered long after George Barker has been forgotten.

I did not know it then — it would never have occurred to me — but ten years later I would write her biography. It would be titled *By Heart*.

MOSCOW IN MARCH, 1979

Though it was wonderful to meet Elizabeth Smart, London in 1979 proved a closed circuit I couldn't penetrate. The only friends I made were an Australian woman and a Scotsman. I don't think the British are snobbish or inhospitable; it's just that the sanctity of privacy inhibits. I concluded they didn't want to intrude on my lonely privacy.

Almost every week I went to the West End to see a play at the Aldwych or the Old Vic. I moved digs five times (once because, on the way back to my apartment on Archway Road I encountered the outline of a body chalked in the sidewalk. Nobody could say how the person had died). It was a year of celibacy, though I did have one close encounter. I met a handsome Englishman in knee-high leather boots at the Institute of Contemporary Arts on the Mall just off Trafalgar Square, where I'd gone to hear a poetry reading. He invited me home for a drink, and I missed the last bus. He said, "Not to worry." I could have the guest room. We listened to organ music (which I detest) and drank cognac, and then, as he led me to my room, he confessed, "I'd like to sleep with you, but I have to sleep with the au pair."

One day I saw a large billboard advertising Intourist trips to the Soviet Union. (Intourist was the official Soviet travel agency.) I'd been reading Solzhenitsyn, Mandelstam, and Akhmatova, and the idea of visiting the Soviet Union piqued my curiosity. Even at -35°C, Moscow in March seemed preferable to bleak London.

I wrote Czech friends that I was going. Alarmed, they wrote back: "It's too dangerous to go alone!" It was, after all, the era of Leonid Brezhnev, which saw the return to state repression after the Khrushchev Thaw of the early 1960s. But I looked up Julia Somerville, whom I'd gotten to know a bit when I taught at the University of Dijon in Burgundy in 1972, where her husband was also teaching. She was now an anchor on the BBC World News, and I assumed she would know all the foreign correspondents. She gave me the phone number of Kevin Ruane, the BBC correspondent in Moscow.

I wasn't searching down literary heroes this time. I was interested in the regime and how it impacted ordinary people. One didn't just up and travel to the Soviet Union in those days. I knew that an Intourist tour was the closest I could get to meeting the real Russia.

I think my curiosity had something to do with growing up in Quebec, where issues of politics and power threaded through ordinary life. I was studying at the University of Sussex in England in October 1970 when a small cell of the FLQ kidnapped and murdered Quebec deputy premier Pierre Laporte. They also kidnapped British diplomat James Cross, whom they held hostage for two months. The government of Pierre Elliott Trudeau responded by imposing the War Measures Act. Hundreds were arrested and detained, many of them musicians, artists, and writers. Canadian students at Sussex held a forum to discuss the crisis, and wrote the Montréal newspapers to protest that, however tragic the death of Minister Laporte, it did not warrant the complete suspension of civil liberties. It was a sad moment in the province's history, one that stayed with me because the transition to the dark side was so immediate. Of course, this was nothing in comparison to the Soviet repression of dissidents, who were still being sent to prisons and psychiatric hospitals.

There were about sixty people on the tour — many devotees of Russian culture, several wearing Harrods furs, were hoping for an exotic adventure. Very few came to satisfy their political curiosity. I was on my own.

We disembarked at the Moscow airport at 7:00 p.m. on a Friday evening. After the good humour on the plane, all were suddenly sober as we passed innumerable heavily armed Russian soldiers (whether guards or travellers I didn't know) on our way to passport control. Our party divided into two lines and waited. A large group of Spanish-speaking tourists was waiting with us. Everything seemed under control until, from the opposite side of the barriers, we heard shouting. Our line of vision was narrow, but we could see a jacket flying through the air. Suddenly one, two, then five men from among the Spanish tourists leapt like birds over the turnstiles while the Soviet officials looked on passively. The Spanish women cried in panicked voices and tried to settle their men.

I moved up to one of the women and glanced at her Cuban passport. Suddenly the men came leaping back over the turnstiles, all smiles and good humour. No one among our group could figure out what was happening, but we speculated that perhaps the Soviet officials had tried to bar one of the Cubans from entry or to arrest and detain a returning Soviet national.

When we got to the other side of the barriers, the explanation was not one we'd anticipated. A member of our tour had become very drunk and abusive on the plane. Once through passport control, he'd started to shove one of the Cuban women, and the men had leapt to her defence. We waited for two hours in our tour bus while the Soviet officials decided what to do with the fellow and who would pay. They put him on the next plane back to London, at British expense. I'd had my first disorienting experience of trying to read the landscape and finding I was utterly wrong.

The trip into Moscow was uneventful. The city seemed a sea of high-rise apartments, lights ablaze in rooms without curtains, allowing a view into the frugal interiors. We were to stay on the edge of Red Square at the Hotel Rossiya, a huge modern structure much like any Western hotel, though a little the worse for wear. It was said to hold five thousand guests. Our rooms were pleasant, furnished in hotel Danish. Each floor had a "key lady" who took your key when you left your room and gave you a paper that assured you access to and from the hotel.

As I entered my room the key lady followed, smiling. My suitcase had been delivered and was sitting, open, on the bed. She gestured at my sweater and vest: "Roubles, roubles," she said, and added, "secret, secret," touching them. We'd been warned not to sell foreign currency and advised that we couldn't take roubles out of the country. I smiled at my key lady and said I couldn't sell. I gave her some cigarettes and she withdrew good-naturedly. There was a new key lady at the end of my corridor the next morning. I wondered if the other woman had fled because she believed I might turn her in. To whom? I thought. The landscape was getting ever harder to read.

We went down to dinner the first night at about 11:00 p.m. The dining room had a stage. Midway into the meal a rock band appeared. They set up their amplifiers and began some fifties rock tune. Suddenly women in miniskirts jumped up from their tables with their solid partners and danced furiously. When the song was finished the diners returned to their tables and the band disappeared. They never returned. I felt like I was in a Fellini film.

The tourist is free to walk about Moscow if she chooses. I suggested to the girl next to me that we walk over to Red Square. The night was crisp and moonlit. When we broke onto the square, I was dazzled by the beauty of St. Basil's Cathedral, a Byzantine fantasy with its turrets sprouting like fantastically painted mushrooms, and by the golden domes of the Kremlin secluded behind the fortress's high brick walls. Two men immediately sidled up to us. For cover, we directed our steps toward the soldiers on guard. When the soldiers turned their backs, we understood that two women do not walk alone at midnight in Moscow either; we retreated to our hotel.

We were given a program of trips and were free to choose what interested us: the Pavilion of Economic Achievement, the Lenin Museum and Tomb, the Kremlin, et cetera. I took a number of the tours and still had time for private strolls.

There was a group of five Irish people on the tour—one married couple, Anastasia and Peter, and three single men: David, whose father owned a tea factory in Belfast; Shawn, a nurse; and Michael, a hairdresser. They travelled together annually, and this time Anastasia had chosen a trip to the Soviet Union in the dead of winter in honour of the name her family had given her. I was quickly drawn into their circle. They were fun, voluble, even outrageous.

On the night of their arrival, they'd celebrated with a party in David's room. Apparently, things had gotten rather rowdy, and the chair David was sitting in broke. I was told he picked it up, opened the window, and threw it out in the snow. The next morning the menacing key lady confronted him in her gruff Russian-accented English. "Two chairs! Three chairs!" David smiled benevolently (he was very handsome) and directed her to the window, pointing to the broken chair ten storeys down, embedded in the snowbank. She laughed, as if boisterous alcohol-fuelled exuberance was something she, a Russian, recognized. There were no consequences. David wasn't even asked to pay for the chair.

What most attracted me to them was their instinctive disdain for Soviet officialdom. They never seemed able to produce the passes necessary to enter or exit the hotel and would simply walk by astonished officials who did not know how to deal with such effrontery. Together we took the troika ride—a sleigh ride through the woods outside the city that ended with vodka and caviar and a Russian dance band. The tour guides seemed amused by our efforts to imitate the high kicks of the traditional Russian dances. I noticed that our guide Dunya fancied the handsome David. We could expect special attention.

Dunya invited the six of us to visit the best Moscow tavern the following afternoon. We were delighted to be away from the group, and it wasn't long before we were having snowball fights and dunking each other in the snow. I watched the Russians watching us with a mixture of amusement and censure. On the trams, Dunya kept us quiet—there seemed to be a standard of decorum that called for sobriety. The tavern was so busy we had to line up outside while Dunya went to consult the chief administrator about our admission.

We checked our coats and entered the low, smoke-filled room of long wooden tables. The vodka and shrimp were excellent and Dunya was happy. Her gift to David that afternoon was a pamphlet on the Soviet Constitution. The next day, on the train to Leningrad, we learned from the English guides that when Dunya got back to the hotel she was called to the front office and told that one does not take tourists off the official route: she would be relieved of her position as tour guide and would undergo six months' rehabilitation as a typist.

When I asked our British guide what had prompted this, she speculated that one of Dunya's fellow guides, seeing the chance for advancement, had turned her in. The Soviet system, I discovered, was built on betrayal.

We now understood that any contact with Westerners could be compromising for the Soviet citizen. I was not particularly skeptical when one of our party insisted that he'd woken up the evening after the incident to find someone searching his room.

All the while I'd been trying to meet Kevin Ruane, the BBC correspondent in Moscow. He'd been busy on an assignment, but I finally reached him the last evening of my stay in Moscow, and he invited me to accompany him to a dinner party. He arranged to pick me up but warned that, without a pass, he wouldn't be allowed to enter the hotel, and I should come outside when I saw an Englishman gesticulating wildly beyond the glass. We drove by taxi to his residence (his car wouldn't run in the -30°C weather). He lived in the area assigned to foreign correspondents, the "foreigner's ghetto," as he called it. The guard checked us through; we picked up some music tapes and set off.

The apartment we visited on the outskirts of Moscow belonged to an artist. We were ushered into a sombre, candlelit dining room. Every inch of wall was covered with beautiful icons, and Russian folk music was playing in the background. There was a quality of nostalgia to the room, as if it were a kind of retreat. We were warmly received by the host and his guests, everyone speaking Russian, of course, as Kevin translated for me.

I could see that the Russians turned to us with a kind of urgency; we were their momentary vehicle for communication with the Outside. These were still the days of the Cold War and the Iron Curtain, when the Soviet Union was a closed universe.

No Soviet artist or sports figure travelled outside the country without a handler. In Toronto, in June 1974, we'd caught a glimpse of this world when the dancer Mikhail Baryshnikov, on tour with the Bolshoi, requested political asylum in Canada. The newspapers were filled with accounts of the cloak-and-dagger secrecy to which his Canadian rescuers resorted in order to orchestrate his defection.

Most of the evening the talk was of Russia and the future. Each of the guests had, it seemed, his personal experience of the Gulag. One was a militant Christian dissident who'd spent six years in the camps. He was on a prisoner's train in August 1968, heading to the Gulag when news arrived of the Soviet invasion of Czechoslovakia; the prisoners held a chess tournament in honour of the fall of that country. He'd been a member of a group of students who'd been hiding guns, believing that if they started the revolution the population would follow. They'd been betrayed. And I thought: the student protests of 1968 in Paris, London, Berlin, Rome, Prague, the United States, Mexico, and on had reached Moscow too, but word had never reached the outside world from this closed universe. I asked him if things would ever change in the USSR. He said he was hopeful: "The system knows how to deal with organizations, but it is vulnerable in that it cannot contend with the individual. The value of the person still survives."

Another guest was a young priest who'd spent four years in the camps. He'd been relieved of his preaching duties and could conduct only funeral services. He spoke of Solzhenitsyn and said that only a Russian can read *The Gulag Archipelago*, because only he can be moved to pity and love. In that room I was continually reminded of Solzhenitsyn's words that "under the cast-iron shell of Communism . . . a liberation of the human spirit is occurring." It was a shock to find myself in a culture that must deal daily with the problem of accountability, where people live on an edge and either turn their backs on conscience or must discover a morality that can cost them dearly.

We spoke much of literature in the Soviet Union, where writing a poem is a terrorist act. They said that they saw the poet as a vehicle of world harmony, and I remembered Nadezhda Mandelstam's comment that in Russia it was easier to save a manuscript than a man. In fact, in the profoundly human atmosphere of that room, it was her voice that was in my mind. I remembered her optimism in *Hope Against Hope* about the future of Russia. "We have tested the ways of evil," she writes. "Will any of us want to revert to them?" And yet when I placed this dark, clandestine room against the world of official Moscow, I was not optimistic. My key lady's words ran in my ear: "Secret, secret." How do you fight a conspiracy of control through silence? The Soviet Union seemed to me a closed society, and if it was not entirely monolithic, the spirit of conformity still seemed stronger than the spirit of dissent.

We took the eight-hour train ride from Moscow to Leningrad the next day. Standing in a passageway between two cars, I tried to imagine the loneliness and physical pain of those long journeys of deportation that dissidents endured through the northern wastes. The countryside was a white emptiness broken by occasional small villages, often of thatched cottages with chimneys smoking. A young man named Mihail joined me in the passageway, and we spoke in a pidgin English. He passed me vodka and told me of his desire to become a teacher. As I said goodbye, he gave me his junior Communist Party badge.

Leningrad was as beautiful as I'd imagined it, and unbearably cold. Here too it was the people we met who held my attention. I was coming down the corridor with the Irishman David one evening in the Hotel Leningrad when we encountered a group of young Russians who were partying. They swept us up in their midst and one of the girls offered me a cup of vodka. As I drank, we were carried in the ensuing euphoria into their room. Introductions all around — one of the men, Kostya, was a concert violinist, others were medical students, one girl was a linguist and served as our translator. They were anxious to hear about Canada and Ireland. We soon had to go, but they insisted on seeing us again.

The night before our departure for London I passed their door and, hearing them within, I knocked. It was two in the morning. We had to leave at 6:00 a.m., and I had no intention of sleeping that night. They were delighted to see me and kissed me with great Russian hugs: "Ah, Rosemarie. It's Rosemarie." Kostya was there and the young linguist, and there were new faces — a young man called Vladimir, who was introduced to me as the best rock star in Russia (to which he nodded assent), with his girlfriend, Anna. I sat beside the linguist, who would pat my knee affectionately and say with Slavic conviction: "Yes, we are women: we share."

After an hour I said I had only come to say goodbye and must join my friends, who were having a farewell party. They were so desolate that I suggested they join us. Kostya, Vladimir, and Anna accompanied me upstairs, but when they got out of the elevator, the key lady spotted them and sent them back. Vladimir and Anna managed to slip by. As soon as we were in the room, Kostya phoned to say he was afraid to come up, but could we shift the party to his room? With Dunya in mind, I warned him it was late. I could hear the disappointment in his voice.

The party broke up within the hour, and we all returned to our rooms to pack. Vladimir picked out David and me and demanded that we accompany him to his room to hear his music. We had become his "Western" audience and there was no way to refuse. Not without protest at the hour, we entered a room with a stereo and amps crowded in one corner. Two middle-aged women were in the twin beds, and with the sudden blaze of light, they groaned and pulled the covers over their heads. Vladimir turned the music high, and there was an immediate telephone call from the key lady. He turned down the volume and looked to us for our approval, which was not hard to give. He was very good. We listened to his music and embraced and parted friends. In the lobby an hour later, just before departure, I encountered Vladimir again, roaming the halls with a friend, looking for his audience. I did not find it easy to leave Russia.

I returned home to my flat in Belsize Park and the next night walked up the hill to my favourite pub, the Flask, in Hampstead. A very handsome young Russian assumed the seat next to me at the bar. I found myself talking about my recent trip to Moscow and Leningrad. Perhaps I said I was a writer. His questions were probing. He asked me if I was going to write about my trip. I said probably—in a small magazine I wrote for in Canada. He talked about his travels to various countries, though it was never clear what his work was. I looked at him more carefully and wondered what this world traveller was doing outside of the Soviet Union. It was impossible to travel in and out of Russia so easily unless one was working for the firm.

He was very seductive and finally suggested we go back to his place. I said I might consider it but there was too much of a chance he was KGB. He replied: "And you are CIA." (I laughed, because he should have said RCMP.) It was absurd to think I would be of enough interest to be tracked down by Russian intelligence, though tracking passengers returning from a trip to the Soviet Union, especially one who'd visited dissidents, was not unthinkable. I remembered reading somewhere that one in every ten Russians was forced to become an informant for the secret police. Still, I reminded myself that I'd probably brought home some of the paranoia that, sadly, pervaded the Soviet Union, where ordinary activities could feel resonant with menace since someone was usually watching.

It still feels as if I lived a bizarre eight-day fiction, at moments comic, at others tragic. It may simply be that Russia is a poignant, eloquent, and terrible country where life has a starkness of definition, unknown to us in the West, which forces everything, good and bad, into fierce relief. I stood as an outsider, puzzled, pained, sympathetic, amused, and even frightened, and yet understanding evaded me. There were too many camouflages and deliberate mystifications.

What can one comprehend in eight days, anyway? What I want to remember is the wonderful warmth and generosity of the painter, the violinist, the linguist, the rock star—all of them—but these figures flicker in my mind through the dark clandestine rooms with their burden of the past and their spiritual claustrophobia, and that remains the closest I came to touching the heart of Russia.

A SANDCASTLE IN PRAGUE, 1979

When I returned to London, I found myself writing poems about Russia.
They were disheartening accounts of loss, which, I suppose, was accurate
to my experience.

HOTEL LENINGRAD

Kostya I am sorry
our words could not cross
but only stared blankly
with the eyes of hurt animals

I would have liked to hear your violin
only the woman at the end of the corridor
was listening too

You kissed my hair as if you touched
your mouth to foreign soil
and I was a freedom
that would leave you
in the small hotel room
where five people looked across language
and did not understand.

Outside the wind is bitter
along the ice-locked Neva
I was less than I should have been
because I did not understand.

Since my experience of the Soviet Union seemed so bleak, I wanted
something against which to measure it, and so I decided I needed to visit
another Communist country. The Czech author Josef Skvorecky was my
colleague and friend at Erindale College. (I make a cameo appearance
in his 1977 satirical novel *The Engineer of Human Souls* about Erindale
College.) Josef had debuted as a major writer in 1958 with the publication of *The Cowards*. The book was soon banned in Czechoslovakia.

He was forced to flee Prague just before the Soviet invasion of his
country in August of 1968, and ended up teaching in Toronto where
he and his wife, Zdena, founded Sixty-Eight Publishers, dedicated to
publishing banned Czech and Slovak authors.

I wrote to Josef, telling him about my trip to the Soviet Union and
asking whether he thought it a good idea for me to visit Czechoslovakia.
"Yes, of course," he said and gave me the name and number of a close
friend, with a proviso: I could refer to Toronto, but I must never mention
his name. It would be dangerous — not for him, but for those who might
know him.

I decided to go by train. Three months after returning from the
Soviet Union, I took the ferry to Belgium, crossed through Germany,
and landed in Prague. The trip, over a thousand kilometres, lasted
about twenty-three hours. I slept in my seat.

I was reading a collection of essays about the Soviet invasion of
Czechoslovakia and hadn't noticed that we'd crossed the German
border until I looked up to see that the landscape had changed. In a
panic, I realized I needed to get rid of the book. It wouldn't do to be
found by the Czech border guards carrying dissident literature into the
country. I scurried to the washroom and shoved the book down behind
the sink, wondering who might find it and what they would make of it.

We had left behind the well-groomed fields and tidy forests of
Germany and entered another territory. The farms with their mangled fences were simpler, less exacting. We passed innumerable small

stations, their bleak concrete structures filled with family groups and soldiers parting from their girlfriends. Nothing of the usual barrage of billboards that are the emblems of Western stations. I had the sense of stepping back into the relative austerity of the 1950s.

I arrived in Prague at eight on a Sunday evening and felt utterly lost and alone in the confusion that takes over when suddenly nothing is familiar. The station was large and modern but empty, except for a few travellers. There was no tourist bureau offering advice about accommodations. I speak neither Czech nor German, and my feeling was one of panic. I might think I had successfully trained myself to run into my fear, but it didn't always work.

I had talked with a Czech passenger on the train who told me, in answer to my question about hotels, that if I knew anyone in Prague, they would take me in. "Prague is a city with heart," he'd said. I had the phone number of Josef's Czech friend.

Unable to find a foreign-exchange kiosk, I went to the telephone booth and inserted German coins into the coin box. Unexpectedly the phone worked and was answered by an operator who spoke a garbled English. When I explained my plight, she rang me through. I mentioned to the voice on the other end that I was a Canadian from Toronto. He said immediately, "I would love to see you," and we arranged to meet. When he learned I had not yet booked into a hotel he insisted that I stay at his home, warning that they were a little crowded but if I didn't mind this, they would love to have me. I accepted gratefully, though with some trepidation; after my experience in Moscow, I assumed it was difficult for Czechs to invite foreign visitors into their houses.

The taxi driver spoke minimal English, so I indicated the address on my map.

"American?" he asked.

"No, Canadian."

He laughed and pointed to a Team Canada hockey sticker on his dashboard and a small Maple Leaf pin stuck in among other national emblems. "Good," he said. I was to learn that Czechs love Canadians. There is even a Jack London cult, and the Yukon and the Klondike gold-rush loom large in their imaginations. The driver took me far out into the suburbs in the grey rain and dropped me at the address I'd given him. He was halfway down the street when I remembered my bags in the trunk of his car and ran after him. He was embarrassed, thinking, I suppose, that I believed he was stealing my luggage. I walked back in the rain, wondering where I was. I couldn't find a bell and banged on the door for ten minutes before anyone came.

The house was a simple two-storey stucco structure with balconies, and very nice inside. It was tastefully furnished, with plants everywhere. Many people lived in that house, including aunts, uncles, a grand-mother, and a son-in-law. I was made at home on the divan in the living room, and indeed I did feel almost immediately that I was part of the family. He was a surgeon and had a modicum of freedom since he was valued by the state. She was a professor of English. She told me she'd been invited to a conference in Ireland, but the government refused to give her permission to go. Perhaps they'd assumed she would be critical of the regime. She showed me a samizdat copy of Josef's latest novel, which was being passed around among his friends. Holding the handmade, makeshift publication felt immediately subversive.

In a very short time, I came to love old Prague, with its narrow streets, its cathedrals and castle, its cafés and bridges. It is a beautiful city, having the largest collection of baroque buildings of any city in Europe. Everywhere the impression is of black and red stone and of the golden patina of cathedral spires. The river Vltava flows through the centre of Prague and is crossed by eighteen bridges. The labyrinthine streets run like arteries through the city, which is geographically the heart of Europe. There were tourists, especially German tourists, but they mingled casually among the Czechs and were hardly noticeable. It was the Czechs themselves who filled the cafés at night and could be found ambling along the boardwalks by the river in the daytime.

My understanding of the city grew gradually, subject of course to the simplification that comes from a short three-week visit. From the outside life seemed good, the city prosperous. People dressed simply but with flair and seemed relaxed. I spoke in English and French and was greeted with warmth and courtesy, though occasionally I felt the rudeness of an ideological snub. My experience of official life was lim-ited to coping with the bureaucracy. To change money was an ordeal that involved several stages of documentation, buying a train ticket took several hours, booking a hotel involved identity checks. (I had left the home of Josef's relatives, anxious that I might be compromising them, though they were too courteous to say so.) When I decided to change my train reservation for Vienna, I could only feel the deepest respect for the young mathematician who negotiated this transaction. Suddenly I understood the fatalistic patience I could hear beneath Czech humour.

Certainly, this did not feel like the Soviet Union; it was more like a vassal state squirming against the empire's constraints. People talked freely of the government. Those to whom I spoke, often in casual encounters on the street, seemed committed to socialist principles but worried about the corruption and hoarding that are a consequence of the scarcity of goods. For instance, because of the shortage of apartments, some people pay rent for two, keeping one empty so that their children will be assured a home when they grow up. People also worried that Czechoslovakia was becoming a consumer society. They spoke freely and bitterly of the Russian occupation and their resentment of Soviet imperialism.

So it seemed from the outside that compromises had been reached in the process of "normalization" since the 1968 Prague Spring. Public life was tolerable and private life reasonable. Walking the streets and feeling a degree of calm, I thought of the imprisoned dissidents, like the television journalist Jiří Dienstbier or the playwright Václav Havel, who'd recently been arrested as members of the human rights group Charter 77. I had to wonder: is the sacrifice of personal liberty worth so much when ordinary life seems to have achieved a kind of equilibrium? But I had not yet heard enough.

Perhaps on a trip there are always small moments of epiphany that seem to illuminate the whole landscape. On my last evening, I walked through the city in the warm summer air. The road beneath St. Nicholas Church was being repaired, and a huge pile of sand had been dumped beside the new paving stones. As I passed, I stopped to watch a group of about ten university students building a huge castle in the sand. A girl spoke to me, and I replied in English that I was a visitor and didn't understand Czech. "Play," she said, and I got down on my knees. With the shadow of Prague Castle looming over us, we built an elegant and elaborate sandcastle and carved sandstone sculptures for its ramparts.

One of the students took coins from his pocket and threw them into the moat, and people passing by followed his hint. He then gave guided tours of our "baroque" structure. We scooped up the coins and went off to the nearest wine cellar and toasted our patrons. To me it seemed a wonderful flight of fantasy, and I read it as a gesture of free spirits. And then I spoke with them—in French, as that was our only common language.

I told them I was from Toronto, and they were curious when I announced I was a writer. We talked a little about literature, and then I asked if they knew of Josef Škvorecký. To my surprise they threw back their heads, laughing, and said, "Ah! Josef Škvorecký, il est parti"—he left. I was taken aback and wondered if they were angry at those who had gone into exile in 1968. I asked, "Do you not think he is a good novelist?"

"Oui," they said, "il est très bon. Il est parti." They explained to me with the patience one uses addressing a child: "The good here cannot stay," and they laughed with their Soldier Švejk humour. I asked if they had read Josef's books. "His books, they don't exist," was the reply. "Yes, we have read them, but they don't exist in libraries."

One member of the crowd was a young painter, and I asked him how it was for artists. He smiled and said, "The good here they are very low; the bad, they are very high. La vie ici n'est pas bonne. Nous ne sommes pas contents."

To relieve the gloom I said, "Well, you must come to Canada to visit me."

They smiled. "When we come to Canada, we will be dead." It was impossible to travel, they explained: no money, no permission. Beginning to catch their black humour, I asked what places they had seen. "Well," they said, "we have been to Bratislava [thirty miles away], and we have been to Bratislava, and we have been to Bratislava." But soon they admitted they had also been to Moscow, Budapest, and Skopje.

I told them I had to catch the midnight train to Vienna. They would not let me go. They demanded that I stay; I could go home with them. But I thought of Dunya in Moscow, who was fired from her job for fraternizing with tourists. Two of the students walked me through the deserted streets to the train station. We had about an hour to wait. While Viri (who spoke French) went off to get us a drink, I stayed with

Ales. We had no common language and sat in silence until he turned to me, smiled and said, "William Blake, good?"

"Very good," I replied, and we traded the names of painters and paintings for about twenty minutes. I kept thinking: I've seen the originals, which he may never see. My train arrived. We hugged and said goodbye and I blew kisses from the window as the train shuddered out of the station.

...

Wanting to understand what was really happening in Czechoslovakia, on my return to Toronto that August I joined a committee for the Defence of the Signatories of Charter 77, the document that dissidents had produced after the unwarranted trial of members of the underground rock band the Plastic People of the Universe. The dissidents were demanding that the government respect the United Nations' covenants on human rights and the Helsinki Accord, a diplomatic agreement guaranteeing fundamental freedoms, which the government had signed.

Two months later, on October 22, six leading charter activists were tried in Prague. Their official offence was to have published statements documenting judicial proceedings against members of the civil rights movements, facts which are in any case supposed to be in official court proceedings open to the public. Their real offence was to have sought to penetrate the secrecy that surrounds political trials in Czechoslovakia.

Gordon Wright, a Canadian civil rights lawyer from Edmonton, went to Prague to attend the trials as an impartial observer. He was refused admission, of course, but he was able to interview Czechs who had attended. On his return he stopped in Toronto, and it fell to me to house him, though I had not met him before. He was a man of fifty. British-born and trained, though a twenty-three-year resident of Edmonton, he was the best product of the British legal tradition: a humanist, articulate and sophisticated, and deeply committed to the principle of fair play. He was exactly the person to attend that Kafkaesque trial, because instead of reacting with disgust to the parody of justice it represented, he proceeded rationally and scrupulously to recount how the Czech government violated the principles of its own legal system.

Immediately after the trial Wright talked with eleven relatives of the defendants who'd been admitted to the court, and their account was unnerving. The defendants had been refused the lawyer of their choice, and the lawyers appointed by the state were biased or otherwise compromised. For instance, the lawyer representing Václav Benda, a Catholic layman and philosopher who was spokesman for the group, began his client's defence by congratulating the state on its indictment. He told the judge he was a good socialist and that he regretted his client's insistence on entering a plea of not guilty. He then read an automobile magazine throughout the proceedings.

The trial was closed to the public on grounds that there was no room, though five or six seats were empty. One of the defendants' wives was ejected from the court for taking notes. The judge informed her that she must have his permission. When she asked for it, he said no. She then asked for a "confidant" to replace her. In "closed" trials the accused is allowed one confidant or observer. The judge replied that that wouldn't be possible as this was an "open" trial. The wife was arrested, interrogated, subjected to a body search, and finally released thirty-six hours later into the cold night without coat or money, her coat and purse having been left in the courtroom.

The trial lasted two days of eleven or twelve hours each. The sentences delivered against the defendants ranged from a suspended sentence to five years. Relatives to whom Wright spoke said they were relieved that the sentences were so lenient.

One of the members of the Plastic People of the Universe was, in fact, a Canadian named Paul Wilson. He'd moved from Canada to Czechoslovakia in 1967 and had performed as a singer with the Plastic People until he was expelled from the country in 1977. He was devastated, of course, at the fate of his fellow musicians. When I met him, he was living in Toronto and working for Josef Škvorecký as his translator.

It was lucky that Gordon Wright was sent from Canada. There were three foreign lawyers in Prague that week. One, a Belgian woman, was harassed and arrested, supposedly for trying to sell foreign currency to undercover agents; circumstances forced the other to keep a low profile. Only Wright was able to assess the legality of the proceedings, interview relatives, and offer them some sense that their plight was being recorded. Their courage was remarkable; he said they had a European stoicism that we could not know. Wright noted, as I had, the black humour. He remarked that relatives pointed out the secret police watching them with the comment that it takes eighteen men and two cars to watch one person, three shifts round the clock. The person himself may be unable to find a job, but he has a legitimate function: to keep other Czechs employed. Wright also came back with Czech jokes of the following variety:

A policeman goes home for the weekend to visit his mother. It is mushroom-picking time, and the mother asks her son to gather some mushrooms for her in the woods. He takes his basket and sets out. When he gets to the forest, he can locate only one mushroom. He grabs this by the neck and demands, "Where are your comrades?" The mushroom shakes in terror and is too frightened to respond. The officer takes out his truncheon and repeats his demands. The mushroom replies: "I am alone. I have none." In a rage, the policeman beats the mushroom into little pieces. Still, he can find no other mushrooms. Finally, he puts all the pieces in the basket and goes home to his mother. She asks, "Did you find any mushrooms?" He nods and points to the basket. She looks and asks, "What happened to this mushroom?" The son looks dumbfounded: "Uh! It slipped and fell on the bathroom floor."

This against the backdrop of the trial! There is something daunting about a culture that makes such black laughter the force of moral outrage.

That fall I often thought of the students I'd met under the shadow of Prague Castle. Would they feel forced to declare publicly their opposition to a government that punishes, with five years' imprisonment, individuals who simply demanded adherence to human rights? A thousand people signed Charter 77. When I was in that mood, I kept seeing the sandcastle under St. Nicholas Church and imagining the puzzled faces of the workers who arrived the next morning and must have wondered who built it as they swept it all away.

Addendum, October 1981

I had carried home from Czechoslovakia a commitment to do something. In addition to the Charter 77 committee, I joined Amnesty International and soon, with the input of others, I and two graduate students came up with the idea of organizing an international congress called The Writer and Human Rights in Aid of Amnesty International. I turned again to Josef Škvorecký and asked him what he thought. "Let's get the writers on side," he said. "Make sure they'll come." And we flew to New York to attend a National Writers' Union meeting (NY chapter). I was mostly intimidated by the august company, but Josef knew everyone. When he spoke about the congress, the writers seemed enthusiastic. The idea was to gather together writers who could use their prestige and access to the media to fight for political prisoners.

By the time the congress was launched, we were a committee of ten volunteers, including a lawyer, an administrator, a secretary, a fundraiser, a publicist, and the two graduate students. We had gathered financial support from federal, provincial, and city governments to the tune of more than $100,000.

Most of the writers we wrote to said yes. We ended up bringing writers from Argentina, South Africa, Taiwan, Chile, India, Japan, Czechoslovakia, West and East Germany, Israel, Palestine, Poland, Russia, El Salvador, Sweden, Vietnam, and Uruguay. Among them were Susan Sontag, Joseph Brodsky, Nadine Gordimer, Eduardo Galeano, Jacobo Timerman, Margaret Atwood, Allen Ginsberg, Alan Sillitoe, Carolyn Forché, Chuong Tang Nguyen, Romesh Thapar, Fawaz Turki, Per Wästberg, and many others.

We wanted a pragmatic edge to the congress, something more than words, so we followed Amnesty's practice of campaigning for political prisoners. We chose seven symbolic cases that would represent all people imprisoned and tortured for their beliefs. These included: two writers from the Eastern bloc (the Soviet Union and Czechoslovakia); two from the Western bloc (Argentina and Chile, where thousands of people were disappeared); two from Africa (north and south); and one from Taiwan (Amnesty had no names of Chinese dissidents). We collected works by these writers, which were then read on stage at the University of

Toronto's Convocation Hall by some of Canada's best actors, including Martha Henry and R.H. Thomson. The capacity audience was 1,730, and the amphitheatre was full every night.

Our visions were grand. As soon as some human rights abuse became public, hundreds of writers would rush to publish letters of protest in the international media. They would have the world's ears.

Unfortunately, two writers arrived with their own political agenda. At an in-camera session exclusively for the writers (as coordinator I was the only congress member attending), the Russian poet Joseph Brodsky stood and challenged the congress's selection of the seven political prisoners. Where was the case of Armando Valladares of Cuba? Then Susan Sontag stood up. "Who are these Canadian organizers to tell the writers who they should campaign for?" she asked. "If one examines the Canadians' list, it is anti-American. Five of the writers are under America's hegemony, and only two under the Soviets'." Suddenly we were in the old Cold War game, with the added element of a US takeover. It would become clear, from Sontag's later editorials in the *New York Times*, that her mission was to expose how the Left had become soft on Cuba.

That night I found myself on a couch in the lobby, sitting next to Joseph Brodsky. He put his hand on my knee and asked conspiratorially if I did not think Amnesty International was a terribly wealthy organization. Where did I think their money came from? "From the KGB," he said triumphantly. I looked at him. He is a wonderful poet. I knew that he had suffered much, and it could not have been easy to live with his paranoia. But, however much I shared his disgust with Soviet human rights abuses, I would not let the congress be part of his political agenda. The worst cases of human rights abuses were the disappeared in Argentina and Chile. And we did include Valladares's name on the list of all imprisoned writers supplied by Amnesty International, which was waiting in Convocation Hall for people to sign. During the in-camera session the next afternoon, the majority of the writers confirmed our selection of symbolical cases.

In the end, the congress was exciting, powerful, and produced a wonderful book published in the United States and Canada by Doubleday, but it didn't do what we'd hoped — there was no network of writers, united beyond ideological differences, to fight for the imprisoned.

Still, for me, the congress had been a baptism of fire. After it was over, I joined the editorial board of a small progressive journal called *This Magazine*. The board included writers such as Rick Salutin, Ian Adams, and Carole Corbeil. I also became a close friend of the great Uruguayan writer Eduardo Galeano, who had written the seminal book *Open Veins of Latin America*, and of Carolyn Forché, author of *The Country Between Us*, poems about the horrors then being committed in El Salvador, to which she was a witness. Because of them and other factors, my attention turned to Latin America.

But not before I travelled to India.

A PASSAGE TO INDIA, 1982

When the congress was over, I decided the only way to come down was to do something amazing. A notice went round the English department at the U of T from the Shastri Indo-Canadian Institute, inviting faculty to apply for an exchange program to introduce Canadian literature to young professors at Karnatak University in Dharwad, India.

India — so exotic, so mysterious. What could be more exciting? I applied. When I learned that I'd been accepted with three other professors, I decided I would go for an additional three weeks, travelling, as usual, on my own.

When you set out on a voyage, it seems that the logic of the drama is invented for you. The plane I took to India was called the *Sir Walter Raleigh*, a nice twist that also offered a note of caution: my impressions of India would probably be as much an invention as Raleigh's had been of the New World. India is so vast in size, history, and psychological scope. It is comprehensive in a way few other countries are: modern and ancient, rich and poor, sophisticated and backward, pragmatic and mystical. Every project of the human imagination seems to have been enacted there. What would I find?

I began my initiation in the state of Rajasthan, the "land of kings." It is a dry desert area north of Delhi, stretching to the Thar Desert on the Pakistani border. The landscape is made up of hills of black slate and brown valleys, except where irrigation has created oases of green. Yet in the midst of this natural austerity, you find the most elegant palaces of pink sandstone with interiors of marble and inlaid mirrors and gardens imitating the intricate patterns of carpets. Contrasts and paradoxes: India always imposes conundrums on you and demands an integration.

In Rajasthan I met Lala Ram, who became my guide to India. I had set out one morning for the Johari Bazaar, the market centre of the capital Jaipur, city of pink sandstone, intending to take a bus tour of the city. Inevitably, the information I had been given proved imperfect—one learns quickly that Indians, following an ancient tradition of courtesy, will tell you what they feel will please you, intoning "Accha, accha," with a bend of the head, a generous gesture, as if your ideas were being slowly sifted like flour. When you get used to this you learn to share the ceremony, for time and fact matter less and less the longer you are in India.

It turned out that I should have purchased my ticket the previous night, and the bus was full. I was offered a spot on the floor beside the driver. A small man of about thirty in mud-spattered dhoti (so thin that his body seemed to hang limply from his shoulders) imposed himself between me and the driver. In imperfect and hurried English, he offered me the best personal tour of Jaipur on his motor-rickshaw, a motor scooter with a makeshift cabin attached to its rear. Grabbing me by the arm, he displayed his credentials, a book of comments by satisfied customers. His importuning manner annoyed me, but I felt I had no option; it was him or the floor of the bus.

As soon as he saw he had won me over, Lala dropped his slick obsequious pose and introduced himself. I recognized that his aggression was the desperation of a poor man who needed my rupees to survive in his snakes-and-ladders world. Lala had a dignity that impressed me in the three days I knew him. He gave me my tour of Jaipur—the Palace of Winds, the exquisite City Palace, Jai Singh's observatory, the Gaitor Cenotaphs—but he gave me much more. I visited his friends, met his brother who drove a lorry, and learned something of the homiletic wisdom that sustained him in his world, for the one fact that describes India is its constant poverty. As one Indian friend put it, "We live on top of poverty here, like on the back of an animal that is always moving slowly beneath us."

We were sitting on the scarred battlements of Jaipur's famous Tiger Fort. Lala offered me a cigarette, assuring me that its buzz was mild, and then he asked me the perennial question: "Why aren't you married?" I demurred and asked about his wife. "Ah," he smiled, "a wife is life and life is a wife." I asked why he had only two sons. "India," he replied, "cannot sustain more people"—this an act of faith when so many children die.

He took me down to the Amber Palace where we visited the Temple of Kali, The Hindu goddess Kali (which translates as black one) is depicted with blood in her mouth. Around her neck she wears a garland of the severed heads of evil demons she's vanquished. Although she incites fear, she is actually a celebration of female power and of just vengeance. Lala believed that in life, the goddess sometimes offers you her dark face and you must accept her rhythm.

With his acquiescence before the expected prospect of disaster, and yet his capacity to survive on nothing by sheer wit and native intellect, living by his rickshaw that he rented from an overlord for thirty rupees a day, Lala came, in my mind, to stand for India. He was courteous to me, but he was proud of his country and willing to castigate any affront on my part. Once, when I stopped to take a picture of street urchins playing among the hogs in a pile of excrement, he was offended: "Madame, mine is a poor country. That is not a good picture."

One of the highlights of my tour of Jaipur was the visit we made to the cinema, done up in red-and-gold drapery with little Buddhas in the niches. Lala guided me through the crowds, obviously amused at the curiosity we aroused—I the only White. We took our seats and the film began with a long preamble of advertising clips offering all the luxuries of the West—boats and cars, jewellery and beautiful women—clearly a form of theatre for the audience, who could not hope to own such things. The merit of Indian films escapes a Western aesthetic. They are often sentimental melodramas with an archetypal plot. Although I don't speak Hindi, I could understand the story of the orphaned hero, a sort of urban Robin Hood (this time on a motor bike) who defeats the robbers and the forty rapists who would violate his loved one, discovers his lost family, is reunited with his beloved in an apotheosis of dancing and singing in a temple ceremony that seemed to include hundreds of thousands of Indians, and lives happily beyond forever after. Yet something of the truth of India is in such films: the Indian genius for synthesis and the urge to capture the whole of reality in a myth of possible fulfillment.

Outside, we drove to my hotel in the dark, I in the back of the rickshaw, my teeth rattling over the stones of Jaipur, past the few rich houses secured behind stone fences, past the vigil of strikers sitting all night by oil lamps in a plea for a sixty-cent raise, past the camel carts drawing stones from the quarry. The peacocks gave their long, thin, plaintive wail, and everywhere I could smell the sweet scent of jasmine.

The desperation, resilience, and tranquility of Lala was for me the strongest first, and indeed, lasting impression of India.

Before I left Jaipur, a young Indian writer I met had invited me to a traditional wedding. I felt a bit odd accepting, but there were so many people at the ceremony that I was hardly conspicuous. The bride and groom were university students of the affluent upper middle class, and a foreign professor's attendance at their wedding was a gesture of respect.

The ceremony began at six in the evening. I waited at the tent that had been erected for the ceremony. In the distance a parade was approaching; hundreds of people dancing and singing, the men in kurtas and dhotis or Nehru shirts and Gandhi caps, the women in colourful, ornate saris trimmed with gold braid and with jewellery on every possible appendage.

The groom approached on an elephant decked in red brocade and bells and then changed to a frisky mare, arriving like a Rajput warrior. He wore a brilliant silver turban and blue Western suit with checkered tie. The bride wore a red sari and her hands were painted in intricate patterns with red henna. While the crowds gathered in glee, he placed a wreath of jasmine over his bride as the priest offered incense to Krishna. In the yard a canopy had been erected, and the priests sat cross-legged beneath it in front of a pentangle drawn on the ground in rice. A small table to the side held loops of marigold and coconut, symbols of good fortune. When, with elaborate ritual, the couple had circled the canopy seven times, they were married.

The groom seemed shy but pleased as I took my flash pictures, and the children scurried to be photographed. But he was also apologetic for the archaic ceremony and turned to his friend: "I am only doing what you did before me." It was a typical example of how the present in India sometimes sits uneasily on the shoulders of the past. Modern Indians are caught in a predictable vise: to be too modern is to ape Western ways and to deny one's Indianness, and yet, for the well-to-do at least, ritual has often become formulaic, a nostalgic invocation of a meaning that is fast fading.

The feast was wonderful, a garden party for 150 people, although Indira Gandhi's government had recently legislated the numbers that could be served at weddings because it was famine time. And weddings had been notoriously lavish. When the chief minister of Narayana married off his daughter, ten thousand were invited to the reception. The son-in-law received a Mercedes, ten air-conditioners, and a video camera. His six brothers received Fiats.

Curious about Indian spiritual traditions, I visited several of the ancient religious shrines or caves. To enter those cave mouths is to enter a primitive and mystical part of the human imagination that we have, for the most part, lopped off. I went first to Ajanta, fifty-five miles by bus from Aurangabad. It is a complex of twenty-nine caves built into the steep face of a rock gorge, overlooking a forbidding ravine and the swirling waters of a mountain torrent. The caves were built by Buddhist monks (200 BCE–650 AD) who literally carved the inside of the mountain, apparently hacking out these holes from the top down to the floor, removing thousands of tons of rock, and in the process shaping pillars and walls. Many of the temples (some one hundred feet long and thirteen feet high) have monasteries attached to them that consist of cells arranged around an inner hall, each containing a stone bed. At the end of the great hall is always a colossal statue of the Buddha, just visible by torchlight between the massive stone columns—as if the Buddha had been revealed in the body of the rock. I thought I had begun to penetrate the profound interior of Indian spirituality—the inward search, shrouded in darkness, total, indiscernible, unknowable, the journey to the motionless centre of movement. But perhaps it was a seductive illusion, for it was destroyed by the sunlight and tourists the minute I emerged from out of the stone.

The Ellora complex is similar, but the caves include Hindu and Jain temples. One of the most dramatic and impressive is called the Kailasa Temple, named after Shiva's Himalayan home, and the temple represents that mountain. I walked over the bridge, past the two massive stone elephants flanking the exterior pavilion, to the interior stone shrine. At the core of the shrine, as if all paths of energy pointed to this centre, the sacred lingam (phallus) rose out of the waters of the yoni (vagina). The slit of the yoni led to a hole in the temple wall. When I traced this hole on the outside, I found a stone bowl where water, pouring over the lingam and travelling down the narrow channel, was collected for the worshippers to drink. As I crouched on my knees and looked back through the hole, I could see the massive stone phallus rising in all its power. The *Rig Veda* describes Shiva's symbol as a flamboyant pillar with the brilliance of a hundred fires, capable of consuming the universe, without beginning, without middle, without end, incomparable, indestructible. It was overwhelming: sexual mysticism, mystical sexuality, and the mystery in which these two planes of consciousness meet. Modern Indians are somewhat reticent about the symbol: in a puritanical society it has become totally abstract, and no one wanted to talk much about it. Yet that pillar in the core of the cave, so primitive and so mysterious—Shiva, the destroyer who generates life where multiplicity reigns—offers a vision of reality that is at once static and dynamic, apparent and hidden, human and cosmic, infinitely complex and minutely precise. My Western consciousness seemed narrow and constricted in comparison.

These ancient images seem to live sporadically in the present, especially in the more backward areas of the country and among the poor for whom the sacred and mundane mix easily. I took a side trip to a small village near Belgaum in the state of Karnataka, one of the many villages I visited. It was like entering another kind of consciousness.

As I approach the town, the holy goddess Lakshmi appears on a billboard advertising offset printing. A cow, sacred to Lakshmi, stares from a poster on a cafe door, and inside garlands of jasmine are hung above the goddess who sits beside the till. The sun leans on its elbow, and I watch the children playing volleyball and flying kites and the boy cobbler mending shoes. I pass the sacred tank, where men dive like fish to wash their sins at the underwater shrine, and the smell of cow dung hangs in the air. An old man in orange dhoti poses for my camera. His golden trumpet announces the penitent's approach to the temple.

I and a few others enter the Mahalakshmi Temple. Lakshmi is the goddess of wealth, and her temple is a labyrinth of dark stone. I look down the long corridor to her golden shrine at the bottom and pass through the great brass doors. A circular corridor surrounds the shrine: you make a round first before you enter, touching the wall at the back of the shrine affectionately. This contact through three feet of stone is the closest you come to the goddess of wealth. An usher joins his palms and wishes me well, then directs me with a whistle. It is dark and intimate here. The drums beat and the worshippers watch the priests attend to Lakshmi. Below, a boy priest prepares a fire of camphor and oil on a golden disk and sets out cups of holy water for the supplicants to drink. Everyone is pleased with the ceremony and strains to see.

I also visited the sacred city of Varanasi, holy city of the Ganges, which is the focus of one of Hinduism's most beautiful myths. In former times, Ganga, the goddess of the Ganges, washed only the sky. One day the Earth had become so cluttered with the ashes of the dead that there seemed no way of cleaning it. A sage thought of bringing Ganga down to purify the world, but the sacred river was of such size that her descent would have destroyed it. Shiva allowed Ganga to fall on his head and, after meandering in the god's hair, she divided into seven torrents and flowed smoothly over the Earth. Varanasi is the city where the tributaries of the Varuna and Assi join the Ganges, and here Hindus come to await death. At dawn, priests gather along the ghats (wide steps that extend four miles along the banks) on small platforms under brown umbrellas. They wear white dhotis and sacred threads around their chests and prepare libations for the worshippers who come for purification. Several of the ghats are reserved for the burning of the corpses, whose ashes are dispersed in the river. And here the beggars, eternal as the river, come for baksheesh.

Yet the beauty of this idea, this peaceful accommodation to death, was inaccessible to me in this city that seemed a terrible portrait of the poverty in India. I took a drive through the city one morning on a bicycle rickshaw. We began at the railway station in the early dawn. Hundreds of bodies were stretched out on the station floor asleep. Are they waiting for a train, or is this the only shelter? We passed the open field by the hospital compound where the poor relatives of the sick were emerging from their tents to prepare their meals over open fires. Young rickshaw wallahs slept cramped on the seats of their bicycles and people were bedded on charpoys (the portable rope bed) anywhere there was a free space in the narrow streets.

Impressions assault me, to my Western eyes surreal: the sharp scream of an injured dog—I turn to see it holding its mangled paw; the painted prostitute, her face powdered a pale white; the naked children, bottoms bone-thin, pressed to pavements—they look through me. Suddenly the whole street is shouting and running—a bicycle has been snared by the wire cargo on the back of a truck and the cyclist is dragged along around the corner. He is hurled from the bike, and the bike is dragged on. A funeral procession approaches—a jagged sound of whistles and drums. On their shoulders they carry a sedan chair in which sits a dead man in turban and silks. His head lolls from side to side with the rhythm of their walking. A man pushes past with a cart that contains the small body of his child garlanded in flowers.

As I approach one of the ghats, I see a boat, more like a skeletal wreck, beached on the shore. Sand is needed for the cement factory and must be carried by boat from a sandbar through twenty yards of water. A line of people, perhaps one hundred old men, women, and children, forms into a chain to carry baskets on their heads, down to the steps where they fill them with sand and remount. They move like a human clock in endless rounds. Another group, already exhausted, sits to the side waiting to replace them. In the shallows of the river, on a rope bed, the corpse of a young man lies staring at the sky. He has flowers in his hair. Beside the river a funeral pyre is burning.

Death is casual here. The dogs squat among the ashes of the cremated and my driver insists—"Look! There, the feet sticking out of the fire." The body of a child floats on the water, a bird sitting on its chest. My mind cannot take this leap into death that is so enfolded into the process of living. I require a more careful decorum. I can see only the terrible poverty of this city where the listless rickshaw wallahs move endlessly as if through circles of hell and faces are empty with the exhaustion of hunger. And I wonder what I am doing here, the tourist-voyeur, witness to such suffering.

...

It was now time to turn my attention to the town of Dharwad in Karnataka state, where I was meant to take up residence at the University of Karnataka, spending six weeks in a workshop discussing literature. Of course that, in itself, seemed surreal—to talk of Canadian bush gardens in an Indian hill station among the eucalyptus trees.

The person I became closest to over that time was a young man called Bankim Rudra, handsome, fiercely intelligent, and with a gentleness that bordered on diffidence. He looked at the world ironically and with a perpetual smile that masked a kind of despair. He had that remarkable Indian courtesy and self-control, and a self-mockery that to me was disconcerting. One habit I particularly liked: he always carried a silver box that contained cloves and cardamom seeds, which he passed around with ceremony.

One Sunday afternoon we rented bicycles and cycled through the town, in so doing breaking a taboo I was vaguely aware of: a young married Indian with a white woman. (I assumed this hadn't been an issue with Lala Ram at the cinema because he was from the lowest class.) Bankim took me to visit the offices of a local publisher, revered in the area as a promoter of Karnatakan literature. He was not home, so we stood on his balcony, smoked a cigarette, and watched the crowds below stare up in amusement at this spectacle, since only working-class women smoke.

Bankim spoke excitedly of writing, of the myths and people and images of his culture that found their way into his poetry. We spoke of relationships in India: he talked of the wife he loved, whom he recognized when he first met her as the one he would marry, as if their souls had encountered each other in a former life. He spoke of his alienation from Indian society. His history was unusual in that his parents had separated when he was a child, something that was frowned upon. He grew up without relatives, casteless and footloose, in a rigorously structured society. Perhaps this accounted for the aura of isolation he carried with him everywhere. "Yet I am class-conscious," he smiled. "Look at my Western dress."

He tried to describe the caste system to me. There are not five castes. There are thousands, like a tree with endless branches. Or it is like a grammar, and there are as many castes as there are possible sentence structures. It defines you: you are the barber and no one else can be the barber. He explained that people cling to caste because of the shared rituals—the bullock ceremony, the leaf ceremony. The caste is your moral structure. You know caste by name, dress, dialect. When a person crosses caste he is lost. Bankim complained that caste rigidifies and conventionalizes everything and Indians live life abstractly. Life is an illusion to get through, though you accumulate as much money as you can in the process.

We cycled our way back through the Karnataka hills in the dusk, along the dirt roads, past small huts, lamps swinging in the wind. The fields, with their regular strips of plough marks, looked like the folds of a black sari. We passed the women walking with their copper urns on their heads, singing in high, piercing voices. This rhythm of life seemed eternal and unchangeable.

Mansure, one of the professors attending our lectures, is a musician, son of one of the most famous singers of Urdu poetry. He invites me to a concert where he will be performing, in a small town called Kolapur. We start out from the bus station. It is one hundred degrees. You feel as if you are walking through a hot bath, which challenges your instinct for survival. People swarm over the buses. You cannot imagine so much humanity: everyone walking, digging, selling, or simply sleeping on charpoys out in the street. Squeezed on the bus, I sit with my knees under my chin, sacks of garlic at my feet, and contemplate the monsoon rain beating against the window, feeding the tired rusty earth. The vegetation is beautiful—the lavish bougainvillea, the bo and tamarind trees. Life swarms outside in stark images. In one town I see a fakir with his legs behind his head, a steel bar through his throat, and a snake at his feet. He is begging.

The theatre in Kolapur is a remnant of colonial days, an imitation of the Old Vic, dark and in elegant tatters. A black rag doll draped with peppers and lemons hangs from the archway to ward off bad luck. The floor of the auditorium is draped in a white sheet, and we sit cross-legged to listen: music masters in the front, men on one side of the room and women on the other. This is Mansure's first public concert.

The musicians take the stage—the blind tabla player, the harmonium player, the two female sitar accompanists, and Mansure, thin, elegant in his brief beard and Nehru shirt. The music starts, and immediately the audience and musicians are climbing the musical scales together, following the involution of the voice with their bodies, punctuating the ends of phrases with expansive gestures of open hands.

Mansure's elegant, articulate fingers move in complicated arabesques through the air, taking the notes for a walk. The audience exclaims when he returns to the root rhythm of a familiar raga in unexpected ways. The interdependence of musicians and listeners is marvellous and complicated; the music carries us out of ourselves, the smell of jasmine producing a languor that is wonderful.

I met Veena Bose at Karnataka University and travelled with her to her hometown of Agra. We started by train at midnight, and the porter came to check that we had locked ourselves in against the thieves. We bought our chapati and rice from the hawkers through the window and began our conversation.

Veena is twenty-seven. Her arranged marriage had just fallen through, and she is afraid that she is becoming too old to marry. I try to convey my incredulity at the idea of my parents choosing my husband, and she says, "You do not understand the power of the family here. I have never been outside Agra, except to come to this workshop, though I have the possibility of going to the movies with my sister. The man my family selected was from Agra, a doctor, handsome, from my caste. Your romantic attachments seem to fail so often. We are more pragmatic. Marriage is for children."

We talk of women in India and she explains that women are considered inferior to men. Her brother was always more important than she. "You see," she says, "India is conventional." She has never, for instance, worn a bathing suit and couldn't imagine doing so. "And saris," she remarks, "you think them beautiful, but for me they are a constraint. You don't know the codes—so many. The sari worn after marriage is a fertility symbol. I would feel ridiculous in too bright a sari at my age. I prefer pants, and I hope my husband would accept that.

"There are many constraints on single women, you know," Veena adds. "An unmarried woman is watched. She could never invite someone to stay overnight. And she could never drink or smoke in public. She would be accused of trying to ape Westerners. Of course, you must

understand, it is the middle class that carry these obsessions, these constraints for the culture — purity, pollution. Wealthy women can do what
they want, and the poor, they have the freedom of poverty. They can't
afford status symbols."

She describes the bride-examination ceremony to me. "You know,
when a marriage is arranged, the groom comes with the priest to examine his bride. It is a ritual. The priest examines your palms and your
ankles, the symmetry of your toes, and with the Shiva string measures
your fingers and palms and compares that to your height — from feet to
saffron dot on the forehead — and you must read to show your voice. Yes,
it is ridiculous. It didn't happen to me, but it does happen in traditional
families."

When I ask what the saffron dot on the forehead means she smiles
and says, "It is simply a sign of beauty. In ancient times when two men
fought for a woman, the one who won dipped his sword in the blood
of his victim and placed a dot on the woman's forehead as a sign of his
conquest. But people have long forgotten that meaning."

"What happens," I ask, "when things go wrong in a marriage?"
There's divorce, but it is rare. A friend of Veena's is divorcing, but it
took her a long time to tell her parents that her husband was beating
her. They had arranged the marriage, and she didn't want to hurt them.
But when she finally told them, they took her away and were very hard
on the husband. A man is expected to act honorably.

We visited Fatehpur Sikri together. It is one of the ancient Mogul
cities, built by Emperor Akbar in 1570. The legend is that Akbar had
no male issue and made a pilgrimage to Fatehpur Sikri to consult the
Sufi mystic Salim Chishti, who foretold the birth of a son, Jahangir. In
gratitude, Akbar built a new and splendid city, but he lived there only
fourteen years due, it is said, to difficulties with the water supply. An
inscription over the gateway to the city reads ironically: "The world is a
bridge, pass over, but build no house upon it. He who hopes for an hour
may hope for eternity."

Akbar was a good politician, an intellectual, and a great sensual-
ist. Apparently, he invented a new religion called Din-i Ilahi, which
attempted to synthesize elements from all the major religions. The

architecture of his city, which is six miles in circumference, combines Hindu columns and Muslim cupolas; and he kept Christian, Muslim, and Hindu wives. His city includes a palace for his favourite Hindu astrologer, his doctor's house with its fine Turkish bath, and the palaces of the court poet and of each of his important wives. The house of the Turkish sultana who was Akbar's favourite adviser is a single chamber surrounded by a veranda divided into rooms by portable stone screens. Victor Hugo described it in his India travelogue as either a very small palace or a very large jewel box, so intricately is it carved with figures of birds and animals.

Akbar's own private apartment is called the Khwabgah, or House of Dreams. Its walls are carved with frescoes of poppies, pansies, tulips, and roses, and ornate gold-lettered Persian verses. Water channels under the floor keep the rooms cool in the hot summers. Outside his chambers, across a large courtyard, is a water pool spanned by a marble dais on which the court musicians played, surrounded by floating lights; and in a second courtyard, a pachisi board is laid out on the ground in the form of a cross with a low red sandstone stool in the centre. Akbar would sit on his stool and direct the movements of his dancing girls, who played the pieces.

There is the House of Hide-and-Seek where he played with his concubines, and the Five-Storey Palace surrounded by marble-latticed screens through which the ladies of the harem viewed the world without being exposed to its vulgar gaze. There the emperor and his wives would retreat to enjoy the moonlit summer nights.

Veena and I play the pachisi game and the "hide-and-seek" and conjure the great Akbar directing his silken dancing girls. And we imagine what it would be like to be the young concubine, her hands painted with red henna, her black eyes two kohl stones, listening as the emperor passed her door.

...

"I don't know what to do about my poor India," Pandey said. "It will take one hundred years to make a dent." We were standing at a kiosk munching pan, a betel-nut aphrodisiac that turns the teeth bright yellow. Pandey had just come from a demonstration—a march where the Kannada Action Committee, a lonely group of fifty members, wore black bands over their mouths to protest being silenced.

The opposition in Karnataka is trying to pass a language bill to make Kannada compulsory in the school system. There have been riots and hunger strikes, and already two have been killed in Bangalore. India is of course a babble of languages—five hundred dialects, sixteen official languages, with English the language of education and bureaucracy.

At first it seems to me insanity that in a country that has no government relief program because 43 per cent of the population would qualify as destitute, language reform should be a major issue and one for which people die. But of course the issue is rooted in politics and economics—what the official language is determines who gets the jobs.

Nothing is simple in India; for a reformer like Pandey, despair is the daily bread. When the government introduced a local food program, a kind of community soup kitchen, the poor Brahmins refused to eat with the untouchables. As Pandey said: "In India, the common man is everyone's hostage."

Pandey is a poet, a man of about forty, cosmopolitan in his socialist ideals and, it seems to me at least, in his agnosticism. He has collected a few of the local writers and students to talk with me.

Like many Indian intellectuals, having studied in England, Pandey is ambivalent about the British. He speaks in swaths: "The British left bureaucracy and a civil-servant mentality that hasn't helped. And the caste system is a system of exclusion that undermines change. But the young Indian is a new product. We are seeking a new consciousness, approaching our India as an unknown entity that it is our responsibility to name. We live in a continual crisis of conscience because stark social injustices confront us as unsolvable."

Pandey was imprisoned during Prime Minister Indira Gandhi's state of emergency in 1975, which he felt was the stratagem of a dictator and destroyed any illusions about Indian democracy. He complains that the legacy of British education has left Indian intellectuals abstracted and divorced from their country. Only those who were illiterate and are now becoming educated can see the new potential in India.

At the end of the meeting, I jump onto the back of Pandey's motor scooter, and we scurry away. He will drop me off at the compound on his way to his next agitation.

...

I ended my passage to India in the beautiful Himalayan Vale of Kashmir. I stayed in the capital, Srinagar, a canal city on the edge of Dal Lake. Like most tourists, I rented a houseboat, one of those elegantly carved flat-bottomed boats whose interiors are imitations of Victorian drawing rooms, a legacy from the days when the British sahibs vacationed here. The only mode of travel is the shikara, a kind of Indian gondola that is used to transport everything from hay and goats to vegetables and wood through the intricate maze of islands in the lake. Some are canopied and cushioned for the vacationers, Indian and foreign.

One day I took a ride through the channels to Srinagar's gardens. The ferryman who rowed me was like a watery Caliban, his ancient face lined with ripples, imitating the wind on the water. He was a skilled oarsman and guided me past the floating gardens, literally rectangles of sod floating on the water and seeded with tomatoes, through the beds of white lotus blossoms and past the many ramshackle waterside pavilion stores and tea shops. Every so often, merchants would pull alongside in their boats offering their wares. Like conspirators, they would slowly lift the cloth from a selection of silver jewellery, or gemstones, or ivory carvings, and smile broadly. We floated tranquilly on the water most of the morning beneath the astonishing blue Kashmiri sky, smoked on hookahs, and drank tea.

It was the month of Ramadan. One morning I awoke to hear the whole valley resonating with voices. I went out on the balcony. In the pale dark, the lake was misted and a few shikaras moved silently like shadows over the water, kingfishers diving in their wake. The mountain loomed like a black lingam in the distance, and from the mosques all over the valley came the sound of chanting: "Allahu Akbar! God is Great." It was a low sound, as if the mountain were breathing, and it built slowly as the light lifted, as if the light were spreading a message. When the red sun broke from the crest of the mountain, the valley was suddenly shining, and the sound of prayer reached a crescendo of praise. I felt a peace that moment that I have rarely known and that I will always associate with the Vale of Kashmir.

Though I am an inveterate traveller, India exhausted me because I saw the frustration of the traveller's vignettes, which are such crude approximations in the effort to understand. In retrospect, I found my India was encounters with people rather than landscapes or places, though the latter were spectacular backdrops to these meetings. When I left India, it was with conversations ringing in my mind, conversations that grounded me and threw me back into myself.

The words for *yesterday* and *tomorrow* are the same words in Hindi, and it is as if all time is present, layered in fantastic juxtapositions that are tragic and comic, beautiful and grotesque. It was hard to leave India. It had teased me with its beauty and mystery and shocked me with its pain. I knew I would return home with my memories, with the photographs I would shuffle uselessly like a deck of cards, since they would convey so little, and with, in my mind, the voices of the friends I had made. Initially, home would seem thin and bland in comparison to India's challenges, though I would lose that soon enough and settle back into my life. But India would always point out to me a profound human failure: that I, that we, could see and continue to see, and change nothing. In India you come to doubt that man has earned the right to consider himself human since he has found no solution to such poverty. The animal moves slowly beneath us all, but we have come to accommodate its motions.

CHILE: THE PHANTOM COUNTRY, 1985

I remember the way the clouds moved like waves and then broke open as the plane descended. The jagged peaks of the Andes looked like the spine of an ancient crustacean lumbering towards Santiago under the sea's weight.

Juan and I had been together three years. I met him in Toronto on the Danforth at a café the poet Gwendolyn MacEwen had opened called the Trojan Horse; the metaphor was clear — the café carried exiles into the secret belly of the city, bringing their entrancing and subversive music. First the Greek exiles and then the Chileans while the police sat outside in their cars with their electronic listening devices that occasionally cut into the stage microphone. We would laugh. What subversive conversations did they expect to hear?

I knew what Juan had been through, at least intellectually, but could I really comprehend it? In 1973, he'd been working for the Department of Culture in Salvador Allende's government while completing a degree in theatre. He told me that at that time, everyone in Chile expected civil war but not a coup d'état. On September 11, at 6:30 a.m., he woke to the noise of gunfire in the street. When he went outside, he saw tanks and soldiers marching. A few wore uniforms that came only to their elbows; he concluded they were gringos.

That night, Juan gathered with friends in a safe house near the central train station. They'd all cut their hair, shaved their beards, and changed their clothes to appear inconspicuous. The next morning, in the pre-dawn darkness, twelve carabineros carrying machine guns invaded the apartment and arrested the foreigners and a Jewish student. When it came to Juan, the capitan said, "Leave him." He'd recognized the name Opitz. Juan's grandfather had been a German general hired by the Chilean military to whip Chilean soldiers into shape. The name Opitz was risky—the capitan didn't want to make any mistakes.

One of the people who disappeared that night was Juan's close friend Carlos, an Argentinian who had taught him the magical art of making and manipulating puppets.

This wasn't Juan's first experience of loss. He'd already lost his wife, Luz Maria, to whom he'd been married for a brief eleven months. Luz Maria was the daughter of a general who'd died years before. Her family was rich and at one point had owned much of the resort town of Viña del Mar. The general's widow despised her pro-Allende "socialist" son-in-law and was fiercely against the marriage.

It was July 8, 1971. Juan's sister Elizabeth was visiting from Talca. That evening, they'd gone to dinner at the restaurant Il Bosco on the Alameda. As they were eating, a magnitude 7.8 earthquake struck in nearby Valparaiso and violently shook the capital. In panic, everyone ran from the restaurant, followed by the waiters waving their unpaid bills. Seeing nearby buildings collapse, Juan was terrified for his wife, but when he got to their apartment, the building was still standing. Once inside, he called for Luz Maria; there was no reply. He searched every room, and eventually looked in the closet. To his shock, all her clothes were gone.

He phoned every friend he could think of, and finally one friend told him that Luz Maria had been taken to a psychiatric clinic run by nuns. It was past midnight by the time he got there. He knocked repeatedly until the mother superior opened the massive door. When Juan asked for his wife, she turned on him: "Get out of here. You are not allowed here." When he asked why, she said, "Orders." Desperate, Juan went to the police, but the family was too well connected to the military, and they refused to do anything. Eventually, Juan received a letter from the Department of Justice informing him that his marriage had been annulled.

He saw his wife again only once. He was about to cross the Marga Marga Bridge in Viña del Mar when he spotted Luz Maria and her mother in the distance. When the mother noticed him, she turned her daughter around and exited the bridge. There was nothing he could do. These were the days of Pinochet.

...

Juan went back to Talca, the city of his birth. Having to figure out a way to survive after the coup d'état, he turned to his friend Jorge and taught him puppetry. They travelled through the Maule region like itinerant players, doing puppet theatre for children, using the puppets to tell the story of Augusto Pinochet (the only safe way to tell it): the bullfrog had a chest full of medals; a female puppet carrying the scales of justice had pockets full of garbage.

In late 1974, he was invited to teach theatre at the Catholic University of Talca. The rector told him that he had to mount the annual theatre production, but whatever he did, it would be on his head. How to speak? Impossible to say nothing when so many had been killed, but also impossible to say something. He decided to stage a play about the history of theatre. Oedipus was on the stage. At the end of the play, he plucked his eyes out. The generals in the front row clapped. But the next week the reviewer from hell asked: "What did he really mean?" The play was a defamation of the military. There was so much blood. He called for Juan's arrest.

Juan went underground, travelling from safe house to safe house, but when they began to harass his mother in Talca, he surfaced. He was shrewd: he reported to the police, not the military. When the police said they had no record on him, he went outside and smashed the windshield of a police car and was arrested. Had he ended up in the hands of the military, his fate would have been much worse. He was soon moved to the section for political prisoners where he was held for nine months. Unlike in the military's secret detention centers, there was no torture, but the guards took a sadistic pleasure in marching the political prisoners out into the courtyard to stand for hours in the broiling sun until many fainted.

The Catholic Church was just starting its office, La Vicaria de la Solidaridad, to help political prisoners. The young auxiliary bishop of Talca took up Juan's case and secured his release. He then advised him to leave the country as soon as he could. It took time to collect the money, but eventually, with his brother Fernando, Juan took the bus to Peru. They were given eleven days to cross the country, or risk deportation back to Chile.

Juan carried little, but in his jacket pocket he had a copy of Hermann Hesse's *Steppenwolf.* At the border of Ecuador, a woman approached. She had seen the book in his pocket and asked him about it. Her name was Fatima Lachporia. She had just spent two and a half years in Colombia working for CUSO. They had a conversation. She left for Brazil and returned to Canada. It was she who, as a South African with strong connections to the anti-apartheid movement's elite exiled in Toronto, was able to find a lawyer for Juan and secure him a visa for Canada.

What drives a life? Luck? Bad luck? Serendipity? A willingness to take whatever life sends you and survive it? After spending a year in Ecuador and eight months in Jamaica, Juan arrived in Canada in the dead of winter in his summer suit to begin his new life.

...

That was the story in my head as, together, we made our way back to Chile. Juan had spent ten years in exile. So strange to think that one's country can be amputated like a severed limb. Replaced by a phantom country. He carried it with him everywhere, but it would never be recovered.

We'd come back to pick up the pieces of his life. It was 1985, and the dictatorship of Pinochet was, if anything, more secretly repressive than it had been when Juan left, the dictator afraid of losing power as opposition mounted.

One of the things I'd arranged before leaving Canada was to interview Fernando Paulsen, founding director and editor of the opposition magazine *Analysis*. The previous editor had been killed by a car bomb planted outside his home. I thought, This man walks to death like an office. Every day! My first question when we met was how did he cope with the fear?

He said that in Chile there were two levels of law: the visible and the invisible. If you were not visible you could be taken at any time. But he was visible. He received phone calls from international journalists every day to ensure that he was safe. The secret police mostly kept their distance.

Then he told me there's a trick about fear. For the longest time fear isolates you, but eventually things turn, and fear becomes a strength. Eventually, there are hundreds of thousands of people in the streets confronting their fear together. And they are more powerful than the repressors.

Juan and I took the train to Talca (which means *thunder*), the colonial city where the constitution was signed and where most of his family still lived. It was a very conservative town — in the first days of the coup d'état so many people were arrested that the only place large enough to confine the prisoners was the empty municipal swimming pool. Juan's mother lived not far off the main square where the jacaranda trees with their violet flowers crowded around the large gazebo. The old men still gathered there to play chess.

The Spanish colonial house with its fifteen-foot ceilings, where Juan was born, was in three sections, one behind the other, each with its own patio; an earthquake had shattered the third patio. Juan's mother was like a barnacle — very small, unmovable — as she sat in her store at the front of the house selling snack and treats.

Across the street, two sentries with machine gun stood in boxes in front of the governor's house. At the end of the street was the jail where Juan had spent those nine months — his mother used to bring him lunch. I tried to imagine what she went through; she was so stoic, so enduring. But the grandchildren crowded the house with their cries of Juan's nickname, Tio Chiche (Uncle Little Rattle in the Baby Carriage), which sent them rolling with laughter.

Christmas was approaching. We went to the central square to buy the Christmas tree. There I watched poor Santa Claus sweating in his winter suit beside his reindeer and Joseph pacing in his life-sized manger. It was great fun — Juan, I, and the grandchildren carried home the tree horizontally, ten feet shuffling beneath green fir as we headed down the plaza.

Juan's mother refused to give us a key to the house. She hoped to keep us in. For good reason. At night the police vans scoured the neighbourhood. But it was high summer, impossible to stay home. One night we went to a café in the central square. When the café closed at 1:00 a.m. and the doors were locked, a young guitarist came on stage to sing the illegal songs of Victor Jara. Twelve years earlier, Jara had been murdered in the national stadium in Santiago. The legend was that the guards had cut off his hands to prevent him from playing his music for the other prisoners in the stadium. In fact, they had broken his fingers.

A group of young people at the café invited us to their home. They would have been as young as twelve when the coup d'état happened. As we slunk through the dark streets, military vans circled; soldiers shoved the people caught out after curfew into the backs of trucks.

At the house we drank cheap wine, and as the atmosphere warmed, one young man suddenly left the room. He returned carrying some objects carefully bound in satin cloth. When he unwrapped them, I saw they were books. One was by Oriana Fallaci; I don't remember the title. Another was Eduardo Galeano's *Las Venas Abiertas de America Latina (Open Veins of Latin America)*. These were banned books. To be caught with them would mean immediate imprisonment. The young man turned to Juan: "We were kids at the time of the coup. We live in a dictatorship, but we don't know how it all happened. You are the first person we have met who has come back. What can you tell us?"

There was silence. All Juan said was, "Who do you think I am?"

I remember how, at that moment, the air froze as solid as ice. Cold, cold fear. Terror. Suddenly the young people realized they had revealed themselves, given away their secrets, and they had no idea to whom they were talking.

Juan immediately put them at ease, but he'd delivered his lesson in the most dramatic way possible. He was saying that his generation had been too trusting, too innocent. In 1973, the government of Salvador Allende was a democratically elected government. The students were demanding reform, not revolution. After the coup they discovered that the watchman at the university was an informant for the secret police, as was the woman in the cafeteria, and the student who sat beside them.

For me, that moment—when the world turned from amicable comfort to terror—grafted itself onto my mind, permanently.

We ended our trip in Isla Negra at Pablo Neruda's house. The poet died there, on September 23, twelve days after the coup d'état, just hours after leaving the hospital. The official cause of death was cancer, but many believed the military had had him murdered.

His homes in Santiago and Valparaiso had been ransacked, but the house he'd built on the sea in Isla Negra was not vandalized. Juan had been there once with his fellow theatre students and described to me the dozens of ship figureheads that Neruda had collected and scattered through the house. As we approached the gate, we found it padlocked and bearing a sign that read: Closed by Order of the State. A woman shouted through the slats: "Prohibido!" Forbidden.

We walked down to the beach. On the fence that surrounded Neruda's property, visitors had left messages: "Neruda, despite Fascism, your steps still resonate." "With Neruda in your heart, advance the rebellion." The rocks on the beach were painted with symbols, one with a portrait of Neruda. An artist had carved a clenched fist from a huge bolder rising above Neruda's beloved sea, and painted the words "Yo acuso"—I accuse you.*

---

* On February 15, 2023, it was reported by the *Globe and Mail* that forensic scientists in Canada and Denmark had found toxic bacteria in Neruda's exhumed remains, a result consistent with allegations that he was poisoned. Further tests are needed for final proof.

ELIZABETH SMART: BASHING ON REGARDLESS, 1988

Whether by luck or serendipity, the travels I had made in 1979 to turn myself into a writer bore fruit, but in a way that was surprisingly complex, reminding me that one should always take the risk of entering the "unknown," as my friend Barbara put it.

My visits to the Soviet Union and Czechoslovakia had prompted me to organize the international congress The Writer and Human Rights in Aid of Amnesty International. One of the volunteers who worked with us was a young woman called Catherine Yolles. We assigned Canadian minders to international writers, and she took on Alan Sillitoe. They became good friends. Around that time, Catherine was working as an editor at Penguin Books. In 1987 she approached me with the idea of writing a biography of Elizabeth Smart.

My story with Elizabeth Smart had picked up towards the end of her life. In 1982, after pressure from the poet Patrick Lane, the University of Alberta invited her to be writer-in-residence. Living on the prairie had been a rather harrowing ordeal for her, since she was really a creature of London's Soho, but the next year she accepted the position of writer-in-residence at the University of Toronto.

We resumed our friendship. I found her a charming apartment in an old house in the downtown Annex, though it escaped me to take into account her age, sixty-nine; she had to climb three flights of rickety stairs to get to it. I had moved in with Juan. We saw the same stars from different hemispheres—was how I thought of it—and we needed to build up years of trust to align our perspectives. When Juan and I flew at each other in a temper, I would run to Elizabeth. She would say, "Rosemary, it takes a lot of imagination to love a man."

Elizabeth Smart died in her son's London apartment in 1986 at the age of seventy-two. She was in the midst of a telephone call. I wrote a memoir for *This Magazine*. I called it "Muse in a Female Ghetto" because, for me, the mystery of Elizabeth was her silence. How, after writing her masterpiece *By Grand Central Station I Sat Down and Wept,* had she fallen into a writer's block that lasted thirty-three years before she wrote her second novel, *The Assumption of the Rogues & Rascals?*

Perhaps it had been this article, which won a National Magazine Award, that prompted Catherine Yolles to invite me to write Elizabeth's biography. When she asked, I immediately said yes.

In order to write the book, I knew I would need the family's permission to quote from Elizabeth's published and unpublished work, as well as from her letters. I headed to London to meet Elizabeth's children. I met Georgina Barker in Soho. Over lunch, Georgina, as beautiful as her mother, with the same romantic swath of red-blond hair, told me: "Yes, write about my mother, but don't sentimentalize. The book will be useless unless it's the whole picture. Put the hard bits in; my mother would have wanted that." I met the rest of the Barkers and soon discovered that none of the family was afraid of exposing secrets. They had been brought up in a madcap bohemian world of books and writers. They were only afraid of banality and bad writing.

My next trip was to Ottawa, where I sublet Al Purdy's rundown apartment in the city centre for two months. I headed to the National Library, which housed Elizabeth's papers. There were ninety boxes of material. She'd kept a trunk in her basement and stuffed everything into it. All the chaos of a lifetime was there: passionate love letters; her own lover's letters of betrayal ripped into tiny shreds in an agony of jealousy but saved; the journals she'd crafted lovingly by hand for her children; fan letters; the ring and miniature horse of her dead daughter Rose burning my fingers—the detritus of a lifetime. Why had she saved all this? It was not simply ego, that she had lived a life she knew was worth recording,

though there was that. It was as if she were saying, poignantly, that everyone leaves behind only a confusion of details. In those boxes was joy,
passion, anger, the whole thing. *Don't be afraid of it. This is what you are
writing about.* As a person Elizabeth always had enormous guts, "bashing
on regardless," as she put it in her journal. She thought only appetite
mattered. She used to say that it takes enormous desire to live, with all
the attendant risks.

And take risks she did. I discovered that Elizabeth, newly pregnant with Georgina, had managed to secure a job with the British
Information Services and embarked for England in 1942, at the height
of the Second World War, on a ship called the *Tyndareus*. In the naval
archives I discovered that the *Tyndareus* was part of a convoy of sixty-
seven ships sailing to England, protected by an anti-submarine escort of
thirteen gunships. On the fourth night of the crossing three ships were
torpedoed and sunk; the following night the escort drove off thirteen
attacks. The *Tyndareus* was torpedoed but survived.

I soon travelled to Boston to meet Elizabeth's sister Jane. When she
opened her door, I did a double take: she looked exactly like Elizabeth.
As we sat in her living room, she told me she'd written her autobiography
from the ages of two to ten, but the only one who could corroborate
it was Elizabeth, and she was dead. She told me stories of Elizabeth
"collecting babies." She kept huge scrapbooks of photographs of babies
and babysat for everyone. Her schoolmates spoofed her in the school
magazine—while the careers imagined for other girls were an ambas-
sadress, a swimming champion, a world-famous surgeon, and a London
fashion designer, Elizabeth, like the Pied Piper, leads children trailing
behind her down Ottawa's Laurier Avenue.

Jane struck me as a very bright woman, but her rivalry with Elizabeth
was extraordinary. Finally, she sat up on the couch, back straight, and
said to me in a fierce voice, "I survived them all!" It was a memorable
performance!

She advised me to check the actor Peter Ustinov's memoir *Dear Me.*
The "Canadian Betty" he refers to is Elizabeth. By chance (or fate)
Ustinov soon came to Toronto to promote a new book. I lined up with
the rest to get an autograph, and when I reached him I told him that the
Canadian Betty in his memoir was really Elizabeth Smart, author of *By*

Grand Central Station. He was astonished. He invited me to come to his hotel the next morning for breakfast.

I showed up at the hotel at 9:00 a.m. and asked the receptionist to tell Peter Ustinov that Rosemary Sullivan had arrived. Intimidated, I assume, by calling the great man on the phone, he said Rosemary Ustinov was in the lobby. When Ustinov came out of the elevator his scowl turned into a sigh of relief. He said he'd thought one of his long-lost relatives had tracked him down.

Ustinov had attended Michel Saint-Denis's London Theatre Studio in Islington. One of the other students was a young woman named Elizabeth (in *Dear Me*, Ustinov refers to her as "Poor Betty") who was always on the receiving end of the "coaxing reach of lascivious poets." She stomped around like an elk from her native woods and was, according to Saint-Denis, a terrible actress.

He was shocked to think that this secretive and insecure Poor Betty was the author of a book he so deeply admired. "She must have been in training for something," he told me. "If one is ambitious, one does things of that sort to stimulate senses one knows are there but dormant." He imagined her as "very romantic, a kind of Charlotte Corday in the secret service of romantic love."

"If I'd been what I am now," he said, "I probably would have been absolutely fascinated by this strange creature, though at the time I would have been frightened by her intensity." He added that he didn't understand all this fuss about copulation (he was referring to Elizabeth's book). "Copulation takes only a few minutes," he said, "but it did result in my four wonderful children."

Following Elizabeth's footsteps was always entertaining because, as she admitted, her book is largely autobiographical. In *By Grand Central Station*, the lovers are arrested at the Arizona border (just as she and George had been) and imprisoned under the Mann Act, designed to counter prostitution. If an unmarried couple crossed a state border and the woman was under twenty-eight, they could be arrested. As Elizabeth put it: "You could fornicate in any state, but not cross a state line for the purpose." Elizabeth spent three days in prison before her father rescued her, while George, whose papers were in order, was allowed to go free.

It suddenly occurred to me that there were no checkpoints at US state borders. She and George must have been followed. I wrote the FBI to inquire if they had a file on Elizabeth Smart. Indeed, they did, but they could not release it. Citing the Freedom of Information Act, I demanded an explanation. I was told that Elizabeth's file was cross-referenced with another individual who was still considered a threat to national security. The only explanation I could imagine was that there must have been exiles from the Spanish Civil War at the writers' colony in Big Sur where she'd been living. After almost fifty years, the FBI still didn't want its secret surveillance operation exposed. I thought Elizabeth, the most apolitical of creatures, would have been amused.

There were many entertaining episodes such as this in writing Elizabeth's biography, but others were much more dramatic. One encounter sits in my mind as the most extraordinary. When Elizabeth met him, George Barker was married, and, after his relationship with her, he would go on to have three other wives (though only two marriages) and fifteen children. I needed to meet the children of his first marriage, who had been lost to him fifty years ago. I needed their permission to quote from the letters to Elizabeth written by their mother, Jessica Barker, whose place Elizabeth had usurped in Barker's life.

I finally tracked down the woman I was looking for, Anastasia Barker, and found myself travelling to a remote farm district in the blue hills of Kentucky to meet this complete stranger, carrying to her stories of a father she had never known. Her mother had told her in her childhood, "'Your father was a poet. He went to a poetry reading at Harvard and never came back.' This was stated in such a way that you knew the conversation was over," Anastasia said. "You weren't allowed to ask anything more." She and her brother had grown up in Greenwich Village in New York. Though they lived in England for a year when she was a teenager, it had never occurred to her to look up her father, so effectively had her mother erased his existence. George Barker was only a poet they had read in school.

I gave Anastasia photographs I had brought of her father—she had never seen them. There I was: an outsider, the carrier of her family history, at that moment the only one who could, however awkwardly, pull the threads together. Had I come to visit a few years earlier, Anastasia told me, she probably wouldn't have been willing to meet me. But her mother was dead—Anastasia had nursed her through several years of Alzheimer's. Giving care, in a way that one must, to someone so sick had been the most moving experience of her life. It had transformed her. "I'm tired of secrets. Secrets destroyed my mother's life." Her mother had remained embittered about George Barker, locking that rancour in her heart. She never spoke of him, but her children lived under the weight of his unspoken existence. And their lives became a geography of lost and missing pieces. Anastasia wanted everything told. "Publish anything you need to tell the story." What she was saying to me, I understood, was profound. It is the secrets that keep us locked inside private agonies. But the secrets turn out to be ordinary lived experience. George Barker's mistress, as Anastasia called Elizabeth, had been freer than her mother. She had spread her life generously.

I still needed to travel back to London to finish my research, but I knew it would be impossible to live in that city; it was so expensive. Until this time, I had been doing my trips intermittently, always heading back to Toronto. But now I suggested to Juan that he come with me. I wrote to Jeronimo Gonzalez Martin, a Spanish friend in Canada who had an apartment in Granada, Spain. He offered it to us cheaply. It was located in the Arab district called the Albayzin, with a patio that looked across a valley at the distant Alhambra.

When Jeronimo took us on our first tour of the Albayzin, something bizarre and unexpected happened. As we walked through the main square admiring the multiple cafés lining its edges, he gestured towards a large multi-storey house and said, "An Argentinian puppeteer named Carlos has moved in there. He's just arrived from Paris."

Juan responded, "I used to know an Argentinean puppeteer named Carlos. The last time I saw him was on the morning after the coup d'état when the police raided the safe house where we were hiding and arrested him. I never knew what happened to him."

Just at that moment, from out of the trees in the central park came Carlos. He and Juan did double takes and then embraced. Carlos said that on that terrible morning fifteen years ago, he'd been taken to prison but was eventually released to the French embassy. They'd flown him to Paris, where he'd been living ever since. He'd just moved to Granada with his girlfriend. The Spanish were getting ready for the five hundredth anniversary of Christopher Columbus's discovery of America and were offering jobs to Latin Americans. "A bit colonial," said Carlos, "but it's work."

It was winter in Granada, and the only heat in our apartment was the brazier under the table in the living room, pulsing at our feet, and there was no hot water. But I managed to write the Canadian part of Elizabeth's story, using the research I'd gathered in Ottawa.

Once every week I visited the Alhambra, one of the most exquisite buildings in the world. The reception hall is grand and ostentatious, but the rooms become increasingly intimate as the palace turns inward; its capitals are carved on only three sides, with the inscription "Despise the praise of admirers." In the Hall of Sisters, the inscription over the window reads "How often has that which was once very distant come near. Happiness! Happiness!" The ceilings of the rooms are carved like honeycombs of stone and painted blue, as if the firmament had been brought inside. The Alhambra's romantic intensity brought Elizabeth to me. One night she appeared like a wavering phantom at the bottom of my bed, giving me permission to write her story, as long as I got it right.

Four months later, Juan returned to Canada, and I headed back to London to pick up the British side of Elizabeth's life—a life precisely bifurcated into the Canadian and the British years. I visited her friends and fellow writers, drank copiously among her Soho crowd, and met some of her lovers (for indeed she did have other lovers than George Barker).

When I contacted Barker's last wife, Elspeth Barker, with whom he'd been living for the last twenty-seven years, she generously invited me to stay the weekend with them. They were housed courtesy of the National Trust, a government institution that provided heritage homes for artists. Once while reading the *Times* (a moment of synchronicity, Barker told me, since he never read that Tory rag), he'd found an advertisement soliciting applications from poets with children to occupy an old house on a country estate. It was gothic, a collection of excrescences that had been accumulating since the eighteenth century. Each Saturday night the Barkers were at home to family and friends. The night I was there, a number of the fifteen children, some from as far afield as Rome, had gathered. (One had gone into publishing, another into film, another into painting, etc.) The house shook with laughter and generosity, and no woman, I am glad to say, cooked.

I tried to imagine Elizabeth there. Would she have been happy? Would she have felt wisps of regret? Perhaps, but she was on to other things: to her beloved Soho, to her writing, to her particular destiny. Elizabeth and Elspeth had been profound friends. They even looked alike. Once, Elizabeth told me, when Barker was being particularly obstreperous, Elspeth had asked her if she would take him back. She said NO.

Barker was as witty and intellectually seductive as ever, but from his treatment of me, I recognized his technique. First, he found some way to make fun of me, then he commented on one of my brilliant remarks—take her down and then build her up. Elspeth had been a young poet when she met Barker, but he had discouraged her; her role was to nurture his talent. After bringing up five children, in 1991 she wrote a prize-winning first and only novel to critical acclaim. She had a heart as rich and seasoned as the house.

Elspeth lent me the Barkers' car to search out Elizabeth's old cottage in Bungay. At least twenty-five years old, the car was held together by the driver's will. It took me hours to find the right road. When I asked for directions in the village, people had only a vague memory of a woman writer having lived somewhere about, though her name was still listed in the local phone directory when I looked it up in a phone booth. As I approached the brickyards, with a sinking feeling I heard a tire hiss. I got out and found that a stake, an inch in diameter, had punctured the aged tire. Like a stake in the heart, I thought.

When I reached the cottage, a little man came scampering out. "Who are you?" he demanded. When I explained that I wanted to see Elizabeth's garden he looked skeptically at the metal heap I was driving. Clearly anyone with any kudos worth cultivating would not be driving such a car. That it belonged to George Barker rang no bells for him. He sent me packing, saying, "Phone me at my office for an appointment. It is not convenient now." And I mourned Elizabeth, and the days when the cottage was open to all and sundry, the days of the generous heart.

Her errors were never stinginess before life's mysteries. I thought of her words in her diary: "Oh to leap bellowing with jungfreud into the arms of the infinite." I was almost glad not to see her cottage—it would have been squeezed small by that tidy little man.

CHILE: WHO KEEPS THE LID ON DEMOCRACY? 1992

By now Juan and I were returning to Chile almost every year. I don't know why, then, that the year 1992 felt different in a way that compelled me to write about it. It was December, edging to Christmas, and very warm in Santiago.

The dramatic heart of Santiago is the Palacio de La Moneda, the presidential palace, on Morandé and Avenida Bernardo O'Higgins (named after Chile's Irish founding father). This was the palace that was bombed in the coup of 1973, but it has been rebuilt so cleverly that you can't tell the old from the new, unless you were here in 1973. Perhaps that's the point: it's hard to get a clear perspective on Chile from the outside. The streets I walk have for me three layers. I walked them in 1985, and I felt the fear of dictatorship in the faces I watched. I walked them in 1990 and saw relief: Chile had reverted to democracy; General Pinochet was probably the only dictator to be voted out of office. And I walk them now.

We begin at the beginning, as if learning an elementary school lesson. In Latin America there are twenty countries, each with a different history and culture, and multiple languages. It's a profound mistake to lump them all together. When I visited the novelist José Donoso, he told me Chile is a square country. "Bound by the cordilleras, by the ocean, by the desert, and by the icebergs. There is no way of squeezing out of it."

It's a sophisticated, intellectually complex country, with a transplanted European identity. As in Canada, the Indigenous populations—there are ten different Indigenous groups—were decimated. So far, they have not been given a voice in the official record of Chilean history.

When you look back to the late sixties and early seventies, one hypothesis is that the revolution that surfaced around the world—in Paris, in Mexico, in Czechoslovakia—surfaced in Chile, too, but here it stuck. Salvador Allende was elected with a socialist program. Did he think social revolution would be easy, benign? He hadn't calculated for the backlash of a social class that would react brutally when it saw its privileges eroded. It was a classic tragedy: he selected Pinochet to lead the army because Pinochet was the man he trusted most among the generals. Pinochet was his Iago. Could it happen anywhere? Maybe, if there were enough alienation between rich and poor; if there were a tradition of militarism; if there were a legal system that was easily corrupted, offering no stay to the breakdown of the principle of law; and if there were a superpower nearby that wasn't squeamish about getting its hands dirty.

The question is, what is figured on these streets as I walk them in 1992? Perhaps presumptuously, I would say that what I feel is a vacuum. All the old ideas are dead and something new is in the process of inventing itself, something we are all living. Chile is a blueprint of our postmodern world. It has happened so fast.

Everyone wants to know what Pinochet is up to now; what has happened to address the grotesque abuses of human rights; is President Patricio Aylwin's democratic government going to make it? Those aren't the right questions, but one can begin there.

Here they call Aylwin's government a caretaker government. Its function is to keep the lid on. Most believe this is the only solution, since it is remarkable that this country is on its feet at all. The key is economics. Economists have evolved a phrase in Chile: solidarity capitalism. What it means is that the country must generate wealth at the top through foreign investment (particularly Japanese, Pacific Rim, European), and the wealth will trickle down naturally. However, there must be some modest social programs: housing, health, schools, and the like.

In Chile the poor are marginally better off than they once were, although five million of a population of 13.7 million are still classified as living below the poverty line. The poor themselves feel, of course, that the promises of democracy have been betrayed. But it's working for the moment: unlike in Canada, there is a sense of economic optimism in Chile in 1992. Chileans feel proud that they have survived economically and are now the most stable market in Latin America.

I am in Chile to write an article for *This Magazine*, so Juan has left me to my own devices while he visits family.

I've set up some interviews.

My first is with the novelist Jorge Edwards, who tells me that few Chileans think Pinochet still poses a real threat. He explains that while what he calls the Establishment remains menacing, even it didn't want Pinochet back. As well, there have been too many scandals.

When the army was caught selling arms to Yugoslavia the previous December, contravening the United Nations embargo, it was noted that the bill of sale recorded a contract for $200,000, yet the Yugoslavs paid $6 million. Who got the money? On an earlier occasion, Pinochet's son, the owner of an arms factory, was found to have received a cheque for $2 million that was never explained.

No one expected that the judicial inquiries set up to investigate the arms scandal would ever clarify any of this. But the scandals opened up the opportunity for constitutional debate: it was obviously impractical for the army to act independently of Parliament, as the constitution Pinochet drafted before leaving office in 1989 stipulated. How could Chile keep face before the world if the army could contravene international law? Parliament had to be able to scrutinize the army's activities. When Pinochet was asked about revising the constitution, he replied, "I don't give a damn for your constitution."

As to human rights, the issue is whether to pass a new amnesty law, closing the books on the past, saying that no one will be prosecuted for crimes committed before 1989. That will pacify the army. Pinochet's hold on the officers is the notion that only he can protect them against retribution. If fear of retribution goes, so would Pinochet's power. Some on the left want this. There are revolutionaries who have been rotting in jail for years, accused of violent activities; if the torturers get off, they would also be freed.

But there are also those whose children disappeared. And though they don't believe in the possibility of justice, they want to know what happened. If the past is not exorcised by truth-telling, it could be repeated.

Once, on the train back to Talca, Juan and I sat beside a man who began a conversation. Out of the blue. It was a confession. He said that the army had recruited him at age sixteen and that he had participated in tortures before he quit the service in 1989. "It had gotten too much for me," he said. "No one will ever know what really happened." I was appalled. Was he seeking expiation? How human the compulsion to confess.

Who will win the amnesty debate is an open question. In the newspapers it is reported that an ex-CNI (Central Nacional de Inteligencia) officer, isolated, in debt, killed himself in his own taxicab. Francisco Zuniga was reputed to be one of the most repressive officers in the secret police. Though he had been tried for human rights abuses, he got off for lack of evidence. His victims had been disappeared. After that, nobody wanted to have anything to do with him; they knew it was dangerous to be around him.

Many tell me that all the old ideas are dead. Chile has been betrayed by the left and the right. Both systems are discredited intellectually. One assumed that the right in Chile and the ideology that fuelled dictatorship would be dismantled by the downfall of Pinochet; that the issue to be discussed would be how that debacle, that brutality, had been unleashed; what institutions malfunctioned to make it possible. But the pro-Pinochet faction is still having a field day. The ideas of the left have failed too.

On the beach in front of Pablo Neruda's house in Isla Negra, where one used to see affirmative messages honouring him, students from the University of Santiago have painted on a rock: "We don't need any more ideologies. We need ideas without ideology."

It seems to me Chile has moved into the pragmatic future. Now only the politics of economics fills the gap. It is as if Chile has awakened from a nightmare and nobody wants to look back. Rather, everyone is waiting passively to see how the economy plays out.

The main issue, discussed endlessly, is la delincuencia. As soon as the dictatorship was dismantled, what one might call free-enterprise criminals arrived on the scene. Assaults, robberies, murders escalated dramatically. Sometimes, the perpetrators were disaffected and out-of-work former secret police or family gangs of known criminals who had been paying off corrupt police for decades.

Sitting in cafés, I had conversations with people who expressed nostalgia for the days of Pinochet. At least there was law and order then, and you knew who the targets of the military were: extremists who somehow deserved it. Today anyone can be a victim. The fears of dictatorship have been replaced by different fears.

Curiously, dictatorship cushions against reality. With censorship lifted, the truth about pollution (Santiago newsagents dust off the newspaper before selling it to you, so thick is the pollution), about ozone depletion and CIDA (AIDS), about the menaces of modern technological life, are now subjects for the daily press, and anxiety is mounting. Cholera has arrived in Chile; cases of skin cancer are increasing in the south, where one hears of the birth of two-headed goats; and the penguins are going blind in the Antarctic. I want to say, "Welcome to the postmodern world."

Chile no longer fits the world's version of what it was. And in a way that's good for the country. When I interviewed him, José Donoso told me, "The gringos always wanted us to be colourful, wanted us to be passionate, wanted us to be revolutionaries, wanted us to kill ourselves—do all that for the gringos." The bitterness is understandable. Chile was a kind of morality drama for its neighbours to the north.

Jorge Edwards looks back at those years:

> We know now that the revolutionary option didn't work.
> This makes it so different. Then, we were fighting against
> repression, dictatorship. It was a very clear case. We knew
> what to fight against. In those days, we would go to the
> cathedral because someone said there was something

happening. I went to many masses during the dictatorship
though I had long ago rejected my Jesuit education. Those
ceremonies—they were partly religious, partly political
—were very moving. And then you went out from the
church, and you saw the police with their shields. I always
thought we were primitive Christians fighting the Roman
legions. This was subjective. It was a fantasy. Now people
are trying to survive to make a living. The people in the
cathedral are now in government. They have had to adapt,
to compromise.

Many North Americans do have to ask whether solidarity with Chile
was, as Jorge Edwards says, morally comfortable.

...

Juan and I stayed briefly in a small barrio called La Legua, a poor,
rambling suburb of Santiago. Under dictatorship the neighbourhood
had held together in its way. We sat around the table and talked about
the famous incident in 1985 when the Frente (Frente Patriótico Manuel
Rodríguez) captured a colonel and spirited him to Brazil. As ransom,
they demanded $1 million in food for the poor. Much of the food came
to La Legua, in huge trucks, and we laughed at the memory of people
chasing live chickens through the streets, running with bags of rice to
hide in their houses.

There are still small shrines on the street corners to commemorate
the places where people were killed. But everything is different now.
"People," I am told, "are learning to look out for themselves." Under
democracy the issues are rights and how to get them: to education, to
work, to housing. But the first instinct is rampant individualism; how to
meld that instinct with a collective good is harder to fathom.

Culturally, Chile is also changed. No musicians in the streets, at least
that I saw. Not many listening to Andean music; it belonged to another
age. At Café del Cerro, they are featuring a rock group called Sexual
Democracy, who are actually very good. Chilean artists, deprived of a
focusing idea, are like Canadian artists. Survival is the issue. Chile is not

an exotic third-world space. This is modern culture, and Chileans have as much right to its ambivalences as we do.

It's the passivity that feels so strange. We are all told of an abstraction called "implacable" economic forces, international markets. All we can do is keep the lid on, the deficits down, and wait. As we were leaving for the Toronto airport on our way to Chile, I'd noticed a sign on the Queen Elizabeth Way: "Don't Sit on the Lid of Progress. If You Do You Will Be Blown to Pieces. INGLIS." Who is it who knows what this progress is and, if we don't accept it, will blow us up? There was another sign too: "Discover the Results of Positive Thinking."

Who are these voices shouting at us? Perhaps the point is that we are under the same lid now, on the same timeline, and *here* feels ironically like *there*. If we are to survive the extraordinary self-destructiveness of modern culture, we will have to do it together.

HAUNTING HAVANA, 1993

Going to Cuba had been a whim. It occurred to me on a Wednesday; we were there by Sunday. Getting away: an ordinary miracle many of us take for granted.

The last time Juan and I were in Cuba was in 1983. The food was bad and the plumbing didn't work, but the price was right. The price is still right, only now, that same peninsula of Varadero is host to luxury hotels for the middle-class tourist. The Cubans have gone into fifty-fifty partnerships with the Italians, the Spanish, and others and have built tropical palaces. Our package deal took us to Sol Palmeras. We arrived at sunset.

Cuba is a country for the body. Even the air is soft, buffing the skin, kneading it open. We had our own bungalow, facing a brace of vegetation—ramon palms spinning like pinwheels, bougainvillea, giant cacti, and flowering shrubs that spanned the colour spectrum. From our porch that first evening, we followed a tight path through the brush till the sea broke on our vision. The sudden green and white foam hauled our eyelids up. Such beauty almost seemed fiction.

After two days of lying in the sun till we turned the red of nail polish—you can never remember ozone levels in paradise—we rented a Jeep and ventured out from our hotel refuge. Real news of Cuba had been so scant in northern papers that we felt we were on a reconnaissance mission.

It was 1993, two years into the Special Period in Cuba after the dis-integration of the Soviet Union, when the Russians cut off aid. With no money to buy gasoline on international markets, there was no traffic—everybody walked or cycled, and Cuba's buses run unreliably. We picked up our first hitchhiker on the way to Matanzas. She was young and blond, and I thought for a moment she was a foreign tourist, but her name was Esperanza (Hope). She told us she was training in tourism and would be taking her exam the next day. Her specialty was Canada, and she asked if I would test her. Her face broke open into a shy smile, and with concentrated intensity in faltering English, she began to recite: "Canadians are a friendly and affectionate people. They love their country. They all celebrate together on St. Patrick's Day, when everyone wears green. Is that right?" she asked.

"Yes," I said, "we love our country, but we celebrate on Canada Day, which is July first."

It was our turn to ask how things were in Cuba. "Things are bad," she replied, "but we have hope." As we passed a church, I asked her if Cubans went to Mass these days. "Oh, yes, many do," she said. "But not me. I am not religious, but I am a devotee of the Virgin." She had made a pilgrimage to the shrine of the Virgin of the Caridad del Cobre in Santiago de Cuba, on the south end of the island. "The Virgin has made me a promise. She will keep it, though I don't know when." We inquired what she asked for—love, wealth?

"I asked for the health of my son," she said. "That she will always keep him well."

Esperanza jumped out as we reached the end of the peninsula of Varadero. You could feel the change immediately—we had left the bunkered paradise of tourism, where they were still constructing new luxury hotels and everything was prosperous and bustling, and entered the real Cuba.

We were looking for the stalactite caves. There were no advertising billboards, beyond the old signs and slogans like "Restistir, Luchar, Vencer" (Resist, Fight, Overcome), now faded along with their once-passionate rhetoric. It took us a long time to find the discreet marker for the caves. As it was, we got it wrong and steered our Jeep through a railway tunnel as narrow as the vehicle, only to find ourselves in a rock pile with the highway twenty metres to our right. We did find the site in the end, with a restaurant full of lunching Cubans and a bar that felt like something out of a Humphrey Bogart film, only with a languor that was electrifying. They identified my companion as Chilean at a glance by accent and style—so many Chileans found refuge here from Pinochet's nightmare—but we did not talk of history. Our conversation was about the "magnificent" Blue Jays, Los Azulejos, winners of the World Series. They wanted to know what it felt like to sit in the SkyDome. "What a marvel." They smiled affectionately as they sipped their beer. "The greatest stadium in the world."

With four Italian tourists, we entered the caves. Our guide Maria, an athletic young woman who borrowed our halogen flashlight, preferring it to her own, led us down one hundred narrow steps to the cave floor. In 1910, she explained, a Chinese worker lost a hammer—it seemed to disappear into the earth. When he went down to hunt for it, he found the caves. They are magnificent—the calcium blue of stalactites and stalagmites looming down damp, claustrophobic corridors. Maria read the formations of the rocks for us. Her narratives were either romantic—the tower of love, and so on—or humorously scurrilous. On the surface again, we found that another guide, José, had decided to take us under his wing. What did we want to see? "A baseball game," we said immediately. "Ah, me encanta el beisbol," he said, and we were off.

The rundown stadium was on the outskirts of the city, identifiable by its floodlights, but from the outside it hardly looked occupied. There were no cars parked on the streets, no ticket wicket, no vendors. Yet it was full, mostly of men and young boys, with only an occasional cluster of women. And bicycles—many leaned on those they'd carted into the stadium.

It was 3:00 p.m., and the game was already into the sixth inning. We were ushered past an iron gate and into a front section. No one asked who we were, but by a code of questions about modern baseball heroes, they located us as Torontonians and the conversation was soon back to the marvellous Azulejos. The teams were national—Matanzas versus Santa Clara (I would see them later on the evening news)—and they

were excellent: batting averages flashed on the billboard in the neighbourhood of .300. The home crowd was like any other, furious when an
umpire's call went against their team: "Hey, they bought the umpire!"
Or screaming out the score: "Tres bolas, tres strikes. Eh, el es OUT!"

Everyone stood in unison when the team and managers filed onto
the field to high-five the player who got the home run. The Matanzas
ballboy was about seventy years old and had been the team mascot for
decades. It was almost painful to watch him hustle after a stray ball,
but this was his park and the crowd loved him. When the ball flew into
the stands, whoever caught it threw it back. Not because they had to,
it was explained to me, but since you got in for free, it was only fair
you returned the ball. At one moment, there was a disturbance in the
stands, and the crowd hooted. "No te preocupes," my seat companion
said, "probably just someone caught selling black market."

I thought of these players—they all had jobs apart from baseball,
but you could see that their bodies (and minds) were honed with the
sternness of athletes. They would never play their peers outside the
country, because the United States does not recognize Cuban teams.
And I thought, If the Blue Jays are a Canadian team, why don't they
play an exhibition game with Cuba's best? Then I remembered how
the team had once tried to hire two Cuban players; the Americans had
come down hard like a ton of bricks—they only approved of defectors.
But I was soon back to the game, and it made me nostalgic. It felt more
real somehow than a SkyDome game, like how I imagined baseball to
have been played in the fifties, when you knew the players intimately
and everything focused on the game. I missed the popcorn and hot dog
vendors, a luxury Cuba could not afford, but I didn't miss the commer-
cialism of the game we play, where the biggest stake is the money.

We drove back to town with José and walked the city streets. It was
obvious that José knew everyone. He had to. People depended on each
other for survival here. The streets were poor, the store windows empty:
a single dress, a pair of shoes. The state gave coupons for one dress a
year, a pair of shoes every two years. Otherwise, a dress costs six hundred
pesos; an average salary is four hundred pesos per month. Everywhere
there were lineups, people waiting resignedly for bread or with their
cups for ice cream rations to take home to the kids. Apparently, there

were not even the traditional rum and cigarettes to lift the spirits. "At least this is the tropics, and God, not the government, gives the heat," our guide commented laconically.

Over dinner, José declared himself apolitical these days. He had been a musician, but he'd walked off the tour for a few days in Czechoslovakia to rendezvous with a love interest. When he returned to Cuba, he found himself blackballed from the musicians' union for five years. "This is a country of regulations," he said. "Castro was right, in the beginning. After all, the Americans wanted to destroy our revolution. If Castro had retired in the 1980s, he would be remembered like Nelson Mandela. You have to be able to change. Now that Russia is gone, we are like a child without a mother." While we ate, an old musician came to play at our table. He sang a song he said his grandmother had written: "Such a cost to get this experience, and when you get it, you are too old to use it, and you die."

As we were saying goodbye to José, we reached into our pockets for money. He seemed genuinely indignant until we insisted: "A gift for your child." My eyes followed him as he retreated into the dark, and I wondered how problematic this contact had been for him, since I assumed there were watchers everywhere. (Every block, it seemed, had its appointed "neighbourhood watchers.") On the road out of Matanzas we stopped to inquire the way from an old man on a bicycle. "Varadero," he said bitterly. He pointed: "That way. You're going where they eat meat. Here we eat candles." ("Se come candelas" is the Cuban expression for starvation.)

Back in our bungalow, we turned on the television to a Miami station. (Cuban television has a budget to broadcast four hours a day; only the hotels with satellite dishes get the foreign channels). It was a commercial for Time-Life Books, a new series on serial killers: to understand the twisted motives of the serial killer, you'd get one book a month. Ted Bundy and company—one killer had buried his victims in the crawl spaces of houses. Why, I wondered, do we North Americans do this to our minds?

Two days later, we rented a second Jeep and headed for Havana. Just outside Matanzas, we picked up a family sitting patiently on the side of the highway—a father, mother, and child. From their dress and demeanour, I assumed they were farmers, but when we arrived in Havana and invited them for a coffee, we found he was an engineer and she was a lawyer, visiting a mother in the country. I was impressed by them, but we felt strange, sitting in the café—for tourists only—with the locals craning over the foliage to watch us. They explained apologetically that in Cuba, the envy of tourists these days is often strong, and not pleasant.

Our personal mission on this trip was to investigate a new medication Cuban doctors had discovered to control cholesterol (Juan had been diagnosed with dangerously high levels). It was called PPG, but because of the US embargo, Cuba could not export it. We stopped at the local pharmacy for tourists but found that the drug cost sixty dollars for a month's supply. That seemed a bit high, so we decided to wait.

As we walked into the street, a young man came running up to us, whispering behind a discreet hand: "PPG. Only seven dollars." We had to laugh at this drug trafficker. Not cocaine. Not marijuana. PPG was the drug of choice on the streets of Havana.

His charm was too strong to resist, and soon we realized we had another guide. Lazaro said he wanted us to see the real Cuba, not "the cosmetic version," as he described it, invented for tourists.

We followed Lazaro down the labyrinthine streets into an ancient colonial house. It was clustered with families, how many I could not tell: an old woman cooking on a Coleman stove in the hallway, two men carrying in pails of water. We entered a small room, curtained off from the hall, filled almost entirely by a bed and a night table with a cheap cassette player. Courteously, they invited us to sit on the chenille bedspread while a runner was sent for the PPG and the Cohiba cigars, and a second left to find change for our American dollars. Lazaro asked us to keep his share of the money until later.

Back on the street, we invited Lazaro for a drink. He brightened: "I will show you a real place, one you would never see!" And again we were off. We stood outside a colonial building that must have had great elegance once but was now graced with wood girders and looked so fragile I was reluctant to enter. No one paid us much attention, and I was free to watch the commerce on the sidewalk arcade.

It was an improvised market; a barber had draped a child in a sheet and was cutting his hair with electric clippers, plugged to a portable power supply by a cord so frayed it almost danced with electricity. Someone else was selling a few battered tomatoes. Inside, we climbed three flights of stairs braced by wood struts, along a corridor, and then up a narrow ladder in the dark (I thought, only in Cuba, where there is so little violent crime, would one risk such a climb). We emerged onto the roof, chickens scurrying underfoot, and entered the penthouse apartment.

We laughed. Lazaro's personal apartment was the best bar in Havana. The living room was white, sunny, and pleasantly decorated with maps, photos, and personal souvenirs. The young man who emerged from the bedroom embraced Lazaro and brought out several beers. We all sat down to talk, like old friends. I was about to refuse, thinking I didn't want to use up their drinks, when I realized with relief that we would be paying. When we had been identified as coming from Toronto, the subject turned not to baseball but to geography, Lazaro's passion. He pointed to the map of North America on the wall and said, with palpable longing in his eyes: "Un dia me voy a Medicine Hat. Un dia me voy a Thunder Bay." Knowing that except for musicians and politicians, most ordinary Cubans couldn't travel, we replied enthusiastically, "Yes, one day you will go to Thunder Bay."

Lazaro wanted our opinion of what had happened in the 1992 Los Angeles riots. For him, LA had been a kind of dream, but being Black, he identified with Rodney King, the American taxi driver violently beaten by members of the Los Angeles Police Department. The acquittal of the four policemen on trial for the beatings, even in the face of videotape evidence of the savagery of the beating, led to six days of protest riots. Sixty-three people were killed, 2,383 injured, and more than 12,000 arrested.

Lazaro understood that were he ever to reach the United States, he too would experience racism. "I know Cuba is a more just society," he said. "We have education and public health for everyone, but this poverty doesn't feel like justice. What can you do?" He smiled sadly.

We paid for our beer, picked up our contraband PPG, and said goodbye to Lazaro's friend. As we walked back through the streets, we met his girlfriend as if by prearrangement, and Lazaro instructed us to give her the money for the cigars. We discovered that it is illegal for a Cuban to carry American dollars. Were Lazaro to be stopped by the police with our bills in his pocket he would immediately be arrested. His demure girlfriend was more likely to pass unnoticed.

The red sunset was breaking on the harbour, and the stars had begun to splatter the sky as we left Havana. Again, we played the local guagua (the Cuban word for *bus*) — our first riders were two soldiers, then a family of seven squeezed into the back seat that comfortably held two, with me holding a little girl on my knee in the front. When we let them off beside a bus depot and yelled out "Local guagua for Varadero," another four jumped in. One was a young computer student returning to Matanzas, another an engineer, and the last a doctor and her twelve-year-old son. The doctor was a skin specialist at the largest hospital in Havana. Several of her patients were children from Chernobyl. "There is not much we can do, other than to relieve their pain," she said. We told her about our experience with the black-market PPG. She laughed, saying that people steal it from the dispensaries, but that it is in fact very effective for cholesterol.

"How are things in Cuba?" I finally asked.

"It is interesting for a doctor," she replied. "There have been so many new advances: vaccines for cerebral meningitis, new treatments for AIDS and cancer, new procedures for burn victims." We talked about the phenomenon of health tourists visiting Havana for cures. "But daily life is not good," she added. "There is such a shortage of food. All we have left is patience and hope." (I remembered Esperanza.) When we reached Varadero, it felt strange to leave her, too, at the side of the road, with her son, her bag of food, and tiny suitcase. On an impulse, we kissed goodbye, and she said to me, "Buena suerte." So generous, I thought. As if I needed luck as much as she did.

The next day as we gathered for the tourist bus to the airport, I found myself speaking to a fellow tourist of the doctor I'd met on the road. She replied: "They're used to it; after all, it's the system Castro wanted." I thought how hard ideologies can make us.

What can a casual tourist say? Only that beside the degradation that hemispheric politics have dealt Guatemala, Haiti, and El Salvador, Cuba remains impressive.

As we travelled to the airport, the bus slowed down each time we passed over a speed bump. Cubans call them "sleeping policemen." Their favourite verb is *resolver* (to solve). With their humour, their resourcefulness, they are a resilient people. As I looked out the plane window, I wished them buena suerte. Viva Cuba!

A TOURIST IN EGYPT, 1995

From the air at night Cairo looks like a celestial spider web, a dazzling son et lumière, a hieroglyphic of roadways and buildings that cluster and sprawl in accumulations that began thousands of years ago. There is nothing geometric about Cairo.

The day I booked my flight to Egypt, without buying cancellation insurance, was the day before al-Gama'a al-Islamiyya, Egypt's most militant fundamentalists, begged tourists to get out of the country. The fax they sent to Reuters read: "The coming operations, God willing, will be extremely violent."

I was travelling with the Canadian archaeologist Donald Redford, a professor at the University of Toronto and the world authority on the New Kingdom pharaoh Akhenaten. He was leading an expedition of five of his patrons on a tour of Egypt's ancient sites.

At the time, I had begun to research a biography of the remarkable Canadian poet Gwendolyn MacEwen. She'd been passionate about Egypt and had written a novel called *King of Egypt, King of Dreams*, which told the story of Akhenaten. I'd made an appointment with Redford, bringing him the list of articles and books she'd consulted during her research. I wanted to know if there was anything she'd missed. He responded that the list included everything available to her in the 1960s, when she'd written her book.

Then he told me she'd come to his office all those years back to consult him. He'd been a cocky young professor and had dismissed her for writing a novel. He said he'd always felt guilty about it. Why didn't he make up for this slight by inviting me to Egypt, where he would soon be leading an expedition. I wasn't really clear about what this would involve, but I said yes. How could I pass up Egypt? Several months later I was at the airport, not having spoken with him again. I simply gave my credit card to his secretary, who organized everything.

I barely recognized Redford at the airport, except that he couldn't have been anything but an archaeologist. He had a large florid face, a white beard, and a friaresque fringe of wispy white hair; he also had a charming habit of crooking his elbow at a right angle above his head and covering his bald crown with his hand. I imagined that his brain was so volatile that he was trying to keep his thoughts in. Skittish, like the White Rabbit, he was constantly distracted by the trivialities of keeping himself together—his passport, his wallet, and the Fort Knox of a suitcase that never left his hand, containing the money he was carrying to his various Egyptian employees. Beneath the disarray, he had a ferociously organized and passionate mind. I liked him at once.

When he asked me if I was worried about the violence in Egypt, I suddenly plunged into panic. Panic is a sensation of the body—as if, from your normal equilibrium, you free-fall, and the world comes into manic focus. You feel it in your blood. The professor, I realized, was playing this by ear. His measure of our safety was that all the archaeologists in Egypt were still hanging in, except in Middle Egypt, where two stations had closed. I wondered if I was ready to put myself in the hands of this stranger. Inshallah, God willing, I thought.

The Western tourist arriving in Egypt enters a dream framed by all the nineteenth-century tourists who have gone before. Everyone has been to Egypt and written about it: Flaubert, Oscar Wilde, Sir Arthur Conan Doyle, and all of those Victorian women who found romantic liberation in the East. Even if you haven't read Amelia Edwards, you've heard stories of marvellously batty women sleeping out in the desert between the paws of the Sphinx, burning the scattered remains of mummies for fuel. We have raided Egypt since the time of Napoleon, trying to cart her magic back to European centres, and Egypt, unwittingly, has shaped us more than we think. What is thought to be Egypt's cult of death has dug into our minds. So many old films with mummies terrorizing the living. I wondered if I would be dreaming of mummies. On the plane, the video screen played the American sitcom *The Beverly Hillbillies* with Arabic subtitles. So this is the enviable sophistication we give back in return.

My head an anthology of travellers' exotica, I spent my first night at the Mena House Hotel just below Cheops's great pyramid. Built as a royal hunting lodge in 1856 and expanded into an elegant hotel thirty years later, it is a Victorian fantasy of gilded Islamic mirrors and carpets, vaguely illuminated, a chiaroscuro. A piano played softly in the background as we drank the red hibiscus juice with which all hotels welcome tourists. That night, still awake at 3:00 a.m., I listened from my balcony to the recorded voices of the mullahs in what felt like a thousand minarets all over the city calling the people to prayer. It was Ramadan, and all Egypt was fasting. The volume was deafening. It is impossible to describe how strange that ancient sound is to the Western ear — a whole city crying in unison for God. The shadow of the great pyramid loomed as a backdrop to my thoughts, which were unnerving: the idea of a people united by one communal mind in which the individual seems to dissolve. Stretched past clock tolerance (I'd been more or less awake for thirty-two hours), I was thinking of al-Gama'a al-Islamiyya. But in one corner of the garden a man had spread his prayer mat on the ground. Alone in his prayer, oblivious to his surroundings, he was calling to Allah. Though we often focus on its hard, fanatical edges, the Muslim religion is a gentle religion. It occurred to me that our monolithic version of Islam is as distorted as those Victorian fantasies of Oriental exoticism.

The next morning our Egyptian tour director, Nasir, left us in the care of our driver. "Tell him what you want," he said. "Take his head between your hands and mould it with patience. There is no danger. CNN has given us bad press. People, you will find, will be very helpful." He shook my hand formally and then touched his heart.

We were only six in a small tour bus, with a driver and a young guide called Assa. Redford had briefly left us to attend to problems at one of his dig sites. I found myself sitting beside an American called Dr. Joe, a man of eighty-one on his thirtieth trip to Egypt. "For me," he said as we gazed at the Nile beyond the window, "there are only two rivers in the world: the Ohio and the Nile." We watched the strange human parade:

women in chadors washing the morning's dishes in the river, a shepherd tending his sheep, a group of villagers butchering a water buffalo,
endless people on mules carrying gardens on their heads. In ancient
Egypt the god of the Nile was a creature called Hapi: hermaphrodite,
with a green-blue body, one breast, bulging belly and phallus, he represented fecundity, the river that gives all life. Here the phrase "to ride
upon someone's water" still means to be loyal to them. Dr. Joe spoke of
the people's health, what could be done about the polluted water. He
had travelled all his life, and his face was lived-in. "You must keep life
in disequilibrium," he said. "If you ever settle, life stops and you stop.
Equilibrium is death."

I leaned back and read the few billboards on the roadside: IN EGYPT
YOU WILL FIND LIFE, IMMORTALITY, AND HAPPINESS. And just
beyond, a sign that amused me: FACTORY FOR THE REPARATION
OF PICKLES.

Ours was not to be a conventional tour, since we had passes that permitted us beyond the barricades of what people normally see. The first
stop was the great mausoleum complex of Saqqara and the Mansion of
the Spirit of Ptah, who was the city god of Memphis, the capital of the
first dynasty that united Egypt around 3150 BCE. At eight o'clock in the
morning my imagination feebly attempted to span those five thousand
years. Rule one: proportion. The Egyptians used two building materials:
brick for the ephemeral, the palaces, the administrative buildings, the
houses, for everything that was not eternal, that crumbled and could
be replaced; stone for the tombs and the temples and pyramids that
housed them. We have to imagine a civilization when we only have its
cemeteries, as if all that remained of Paris were Père Lachaise. But it
is magnificent, this civilization that began its internments at Saqqara,
and then moved north and south to include twenty miles of monuments
encompassing the great Giza Plateau, home to the pyramids. Rule two:
the Egyptians were preoccupied with death because they loved life. On
the head of Queen Tiye, the hieroglyphics read: "Ye living ones on earth
who love life and hate death."

It is hard to get one's mind around the Egyptian idea of death. That
we survive is clear — there were so many parts of the self to survive.
These include the hat, or corpse; the ba, or personality; the sheut, or

shadow that, like our ghost, flits among the living; the ka, or the cosmic double; and the akh, or glorified spirit. After death, one's ka lived on in the tomb, returning to the mummified corpse, or, if the corpse was destroyed, to a statue precisely crafted to resemble the living self. Relatives or employees, usually priests, were.paid to leave daily offerings of food and drink for the ka. And the deceased buried his furniture, jewels and amusements with him to occupy his time in the tomb. This tradition became so elaborate over time that the dead eventually had whole tableaux — miniature replicas of women making wine, men sorting cattle, building ships, whatever they valued in life — buried with them. Every culture has its mausoleums, but Egypt seems unique in burying the things of the living with the dead. It was a fetish for life, not death, that drove them, and a shrewd understanding that our personality is filtered through our senses. What is human identity without the body? When we later visited the mummy of Ramesses II in the Cairo Museum, the face and the imperious character of the man were still evident beneath the shroud. One could almost detect a new grimace of disgust on the tightly drawn mouth — being spread out in a glass case three thousand years later for the great unwashed to gawk at was not what he had in mind for eternity. But then perhaps he has abandoned the ba and become the ka, the cosmic double, or even the akh, the glorified spirit that could wing its way freely through the universe.

I do not pretend to understand the involutions of ancient Egyptian metaphysics. Over the hill we found Ramesses's entire cabinet, and a beautiful sarcophagus carved in the shape of a man with a child, his ka, held tenderly in his arms. How did they get this monumental piece of granite down a shaft one hundred feet deep? One theory is that they laid the sarcophagus on the sand and then removed the sand from beneath. In a distant part of this necropolis were found the mummified corpses of cats, dogs, baboons, ibises, falcons, and the Apis bull, the latter given a burial with the full royal pomp appropriate to a god when it died. Each animal was the living form of a god. In our desecrated modern world, such a "primitive," sacral relationship to nature seems compelling.

The next day we visited Abusir and the temple of King Sahure of the Fifth Dynasty (2465–2325 BCE). It was a chaos of stones, but one could make out the causeway that led from the now non-existent river to the monumental forecourt that would have been open to the sky, and behind that, room after room, until one entered the final inner sanctum where the god's statue was housed in total darkness. The temple was still standing in 625 BCE when ancient tourists first visited and wrote their commentaries. Adjacent to the temple is the tomb of Ptahshepses, described in the hieroglyphic inscriptions as "unique friend of the king, palace manager, the chief lector priest. He is the one who oversees the secrets of the morning hours [the king's toilet]." He was allowed to kiss not just the ground beneath his majesty's foot but his majesty's toe. He had touched the God. Beautiful pillars mark the door, now sealed, and we climbed a rickety ladder up and then down into the structure, finally crawling on our knees down the mouth of the tomb into the place of the great sarcophagus. Some of the ancient tombs contain curses. "All ye who come to the tomb, do not use it for the following purposes: to quarry, to take food, to defecate."

Over dinner, we discussed our flight to Luxor and whether it would be a good idea to have a military escort while we were there. Assa, our guide, advised me not to worry: I might be going south to where the troubles were, but she would pray for me. The desk clerk recorded my 5:00 a.m. wake-up call and told me to have a good dream.

In Luxor, our professor was like a man coming home. They embraced him and greeted him at the airport, in the taxi, at the hotel, always with a dramatic flourish, as if he were a long-lost relative: "Doktor! Doktor!" We headed for the Karnak temple complex. Nothing prepared me for its colossal magnitude—austere, aggressive, and very beautiful. It has survived in Upper Egypt (or the south—geography reverses itself in Egypt) because the Christians here were too poor to dismantle it and build their own temples, so they merely defaced and chipped away the exposed skin of the pagan figures and made do. Karnak is a perfect processional temple; from here the three resident gods—Amun, Mut, and Khonsu—were carried in their sacred barques or solar boats to Luxor temple a few kilometres away, in that journey reproducing the act of creation itself. Reliefs carved to commemorate the procession show it to have been a great party—with darbuka drummers, people clapping along the banks of the Nile, army men with castanets, acrobatic dancers, chariots, kiosks, libations of wine, slaughtering of animals, and the inevitable shaved priests with their red ribbons dangling from the backs of their bald heads. Generation after generation of pharaohs have built accretively onto Karnak Temple's core. There are Amenhotep's Avenue of Sphinxes, Hatshepsut's obelisks, and the magnificent pillars of the Great Hypostyle Hall—they rise one hundred feet above you like a forest of stone trees, carved to imitate the lotus and papyrus plants, and the squabbling birds have now reclaimed them. I couldn't help but think that in this place architecture is a sacred art—the human instinct for form and beautiful proportion expressing the mind's highest aspir- ations for order. That humans are capable of such beauty!

Later, in a kiosk beside the sacred lake, the professor regaled us with stories of the old days of archaeologists as eccentric gentlemen rather than bureaucrats. A gay art expert was found murdered in his hotel. Was he killed by his lover? Was he dealing in the illegal export of antiquities? Was he a spy for the British? The anecdotes had all the intrigue of a crime novel. Two of the artifacts from the professor's own dig site were stolen a few years ago. It was discovered that the locked storage shed had been built in such a way that the iron window grill could be slipped out; the stolen objects, the best of his discoveries, had been conveniently placed under the window ledge. "A local job with international criminal ties," the professor said, and added that the theft of antiquities, a skill inherited from tomb robbers thousands of years back, is still considered an honourable profession. I think of the reliefs of the different pharaohs mostly carved with a god at their backs. All protection is behind. In life, since time immemorial, another lesson: always watch your back.

On my balcony at dusk, the night fell in a blue haze over the Nile. The rhythm of the palm trees, their leaves swaying like fans dangling in the fading light, felt like hypnosis. Perhaps that's why only the pharaoh's most trusted official was assigned the task of holding the fan on his majesty's right side. The shops, stuccoed in a soft salmon pink, seemed to shift toward the dying sun. I watched the children come in and out of the Mossy Bazaar across the street. What I noted was the noise—the voices of men as they shouted, fought, and greeted each other with kisses. The electronic sound of the chants of Ramadan from radios and loudspeakers blared forth, mixed with the clip-clop of the horse-drawn calèches, the traffic and the jockeying of horns. On the street under an awning, men were preparing the sunset meal that breaks Ramadan. During Ramadan, you eat at 6:00 a.m. and again at midnight, stuffing yourself as much as possible, especially with sweets. The whole nation was on a sugar high.

At 7:00 a.m. we took the five-minute ferry across the Nile to the Valley of the Kings. That is a misnomer: it is also the Valley of the Queens, of the nobility—over six hundred tombs are here. We selected a few of the famous: Ramesses, Hatshepsut. They were beautiful but sanitized, their reliefs now covered in glass, so that it is hard to feel the mystery of these great funerary exercises. But we were invited to the professor's two new tomb digs, concessions the Egyptians have allotted to his wife, who is also an archaeologist.

We picked up three guards who led us to an indentation in the cliff-side. They had to lift away the pile of huge stones stacked to dissuade vandals. The first tomb belonged to Ria, chief herald to the king in the mid-eighteenth dynasty. Ria stood there carved into the wall, his head hacked away but clearly facing outward in greeting. He was with his four sons at the offering table, where relatives were meant to bring fresh food for the dead. In a cardboard box in a corner were hundreds of inch-long shawabti figures, little carvings that Ria had taken with him to work as servants in the afterlife. Centuries of dust filled our lungs until we were almost choking as we gazed at the vague remains of reliefs of golden figures against the bituminous black walls. We scrambled down a shaft barely lit by the thin strobes of our flashlights—luckily, it turned out, since the bats were everywhere. We could smell their guano. At bottom was only a hole, the sarcophagi long removed or never interred here. I watched with some anxiety as a small bat negotiated its way up the professor's jacket.

The second tomb belonged to Parennefer, first tutor and later butler to the pharaoh Akhenaten. On the wall inside was a sun disk, from which the sun's rays descended in spokes ending in minuscule hands. We could just make out what seemed to be the figures of Akhenaten and his wife, Nefertiti. The professor was brimming with excitement. His wife had discovered a false wall concealing another connecting tomb, and a hole had been dug, beside which lay the unearthed remains of several mummies. One was in full form—we could see the narrow feet and toes, the nose, the mouth, the ears like delicate flowers. The hands had caved into the rib cage. All around lay pieces of bone, scraps of mummy cloth, and then the tiny mummified form of a child. We felt these deaths as real and oddly personal, death itself as aggressive and also mysterious—to be with humans 3,200 years old. At moments archaeology must be a strange, humbling profession.

That night we went to the professor's dig house on the edge of Karnak Temple—by taxi through dirt roads where the legs of colossi lay exposed as so much rubble in people's backyards, past the square where the young men, gratefully relieved of history for the moment, played soccer. We were greeted by the immense form of the professor's head-man, Farouk. The professor dumped out his bag of keys, hunting among dozens for the one that fit, and showed us around. The building was a compound of rooms encircling a courtyard, primitive in the extreme, with plaster crumbling from the red vaulted ceiling over the potsherds room, the storage rooms, the bedrooms, and dining hall to house all the scientists needed in the archaeologist's trade: the osteologist, the physical anthropologist, the magnetometer team, the sedimentologist, the pottery expert, the epigrapher. We climbed to the roof and sat watching the planes pass like silver birds overhead and take a right angle for Cairo, beneath us the ripening fig trees, the interminable dust, and the East Gate of Karnak that had stood for thousands of years. Sipping our brandy, we listened to the sounds of the mullahs reciting the Koran in monotonous chants that layered the air till it was a din of competing voices, and the pink sun set.

We travelled for days: once by van into the red desert, down the wadis covered with the skeletons of white desert thorn, to the ancient quarries where the pharaohs got their limestone as far back as the Sixth Dynasty. The organizational genius of this ancient civilization is breathtaking. Expeditions of soldiers and huge corvées of forced labourers working off their tax obligations—the largest recorded group was nineteen thousand—were sent into the deserts to fill the king's orders. They chipped the monstrous granite blocks out with small bronze chisels and left their graffiti all over the place: drawings of gazelles and boats on the rock face, hieroglyphs with names and images of the gods and kings. We found the graffiti of Roman invaders—"Demetrius was here and in the time of," but Rome was new, a bare two thousand-odd years old—not to mention the graffiti of a tourist from 1852.

Another day to Dendera, a late Ptolemaic temple dating from the third century BCE. For me this is perhaps the most mysterious temple, dedicated to Hathor, the cow-headed goddess of fertility, love, and maternity. Her head graces the four sides of huge pillars as thick as a forest; the later Christians carefully hacked away each face. On the ceilings are magnificent reliefs of Nut, the sky goddess, arching like an inverted U over the universe, only her fingers and toes touching the Earth. At night Nut swallows the setting sun, which then travels through her star-studded body to emerge from her womb at sunrise.

Dendera is a mythic map. There are female mysteries here. In one scene in the "birth" room, the god Amun speaks to Hathor: "I have already impregnated the Queen. Make me a child." Khnum, the potter, fashions the child on his wheel, and Thoth the scribe records its name. There are stelae of the placenta, which was the twin of the self, and of the goddess Isis on the birthing stool.

Led by a guide, I crawled into a cavern under the floor of the cella, the inner sanctum where the goddess sat to impersonate the creator, and my flashlight revealed a magnificent gold serpent on the wall. Apparently the crypt also housed the statue of Hathor's ba. Outside was the sanctuarium with magic texts and the sacred lake where people came to be healed.

We were travelling to Aswan and the ancient south, down the inevitable Nile, the ibises clustered like white flowers on the mimosa trees, the morning light diffuse and rising with the smoke, the hypnotic peace of Egypt. The scarecrows in the fields were wearing galabeyas. We passed through Armant. It was Monday, market day. To our embarrassment, we found our driver Mahmud had taken us barrelling through the market, trading insults with the oncoming carts, scattering wagons and stalls and the women in black, seated on the road before their clusters of vegetables. The town's Temple of Montu, the god of war, is only rubble now. It was dismantled in the mid-nineteenth century by the local council as a strategy to keep the foreigner out. But we still come. I could see that the professor's head was full of images of the hieroglyphic stones that could be found in every foundation and back lane here.

Aswan is the capital of the south, or Upper Egypt, and at its heart sits the Old Cataract Hotel, with its avenue of phoenix palms leading to marbled portico and red carpet. This is Victorian Egypt—everywhere burnished copper, Persian carpets, stained glass, and elegant waiters in black galabeyas and white turbans; the open box elevator is scented with rose water. My room—thirty feet long with fourteen-foot ceilings, green satin curtains, paisley chesterfield and mirrored armoires—was meant for the tourist who came for the season. A little dowdy now, the hotel is still haunted by the shadows of its Victorian occupants. We gathered on the veranda looking out over the cataract, drinking our Stella beer and talking of Agatha Christie and *Death on the Nile*, which was partly filmed here. Needing to place me as other than a solitary woman, the waiter asked which one of the men in my party was my husband, my "big boss."

We drove up the Nile to see the quarries of Silsila and the chapels along the river. In the old days when the Nile inundation was at its highest, the pharaoh came with his nobles to celebrate the Nile Festival. The nobles built chapels with statues of themselves carved into the rock so that they could look out on the Nile forever. We watched a tourist boat drift past, but it was empty. No one takes a cruise these days because the boats have been shot at.

We spent the last days of our three weeks in the Sinai. No place in the world has been fought over like this land bridge between Asia and Africa, and signs of the latest war—barbed wire, the shells of tanks and guns left on the desert floor in 1967—are still visible. Perhaps it's the eternal mood of the Sinai: an armed security guard arrived at our hotel assigned to climb mountains with the khawagas, as Egyptians call the foreigner. According to some, the word, a leftover from British colonial days meaning "the man in a hat," is endearing. To others, it is an insult.

We headed for Wadi Sidri in search of the pharaohs' turquoise mines. Lost almost immediately, we were spotted by a young boy who jumped onto the running board of our Jeep and offered himself as guide. His name was Deuf Allah Hussen, eleven years old and barefoot as he led us single file up the thousand-foot ascent. At the summit he spread his arms like wings and flew at breakneck speed over the shale. He knew the name of every flower and bird, every hidden culvert and cave. He had staked this terrain as his childhood paradise. Before we left, he wrote me a letter to prove proudly that he could write: "Deuf Allah Hussen from mul El Nasb this Friday afternoon. Greetings."

The next morning I found myself alone on the beach of the sea the ancients called the Great Black. The sun ascended pink behind the black granite mountains on my left, and the full moon descended like a bright coin folded in a pocket of cloud on my right—in perfect balance. I know why the Egyptians believed in Ma'at. The sun and moon seemed more in Egypt, which might just be the absence of pollution in the Sinai. I am told the most beautiful compliment you can pay to a woman in Egypt is to say she is as beautiful as the fourteenth moon, the full moon.

There were many more riches to see: the salt flats stretching like snow at Pelusium, the nearby Roman fort, where we visited the baths and wandered in the theatre imagining the satires and plays that would have been performed there. The professor cried, "Oh! The earth to dig! Can't you feel it? What must be under our feet!"

We returned by ferry across the Suez to the lush delta, where blind-folded oxen still turned water wheels at the side of the road as they did in ancient days, and on to Tanis. As we wandered in the high wind through its ruins we noticed a squadron of soldiers fanning out and descending the hill. There were at least fifteen of them, and I thought, Oh god, we must be illegal trespassers. It turned out they had come as our personal guards. "So you've made it from Port Said," they said. The professor quoted Rudyard Kipling's favourite Egyptian tale as our escorts fell in behind us: "Ten men coming, ten men going, as I was ushered in to the King." In the adjacent museum I gazed at a tiny sculpted ear in one of the cases—it was the hearing ear placed in the god's sanctuary so that he would hear your prayer—and a soldier leaned over my shoulder. What must they make of us, I wondered, pursuing our obsession for archaeology in this tourist war zone.

We boarded our van. A small British Bedford army truck with eight soldiers in its bed took the lead and another with a half-dozen soldiers followed. We raced down the two-lane highway, sirens and lights blaring, terrified most of all by the narrow escapes from head-on collisions as we hopscotched the vehicles ahead. Our driver, Nasir, seemed to be enjoying himself, but even he was surprised as we roared through Zagazig, the soldiers on their feet poking bayonetted guns out of the truck. The traffic parted like the Red Sea. People gawked. We might have been the president himself.

Only as we slid into our hotel were we told what it was all about. A bomb had been deposited in a handbag on the Cairo train when it stopped in Asyut in Middle Egypt. There were injured tourists but no dead. We walked that night through the market stalls set mid-street, selling toys, balloons, and trinkets. We did not feel in danger. True, we were the only tourists in Mansoura, but people greeted us warmly. I thought of how casually we had taken all this. Perhaps we were versions of the intrepid Victorians. They knew travel was risky—cholera and banditry might await them—but they went anyway.

In the postmodern world tourism is risky. The tourist is an object now, a commodity like any other. To break an economy, you sabotage its wealth, and Egypt's greatest wealth is its tourism. It was a brilliant strategy on the part of al-Gama'a al-Islamiyya to threaten the tourist. Even if only a dozen among millions are really hurt, like a bird the tourist migrates elsewhere. In truth, we were never in more danger than a tourist in New York or Sicily. Our military escort was a staged performance to assure us that the government was on its toes—the next day they disappeared, and we never saw them again.

Modern tourists must know that they walk into whatever social unrest is brewing, whether in Miami or Cairo, and it was clear that what was going on in Egypt was much larger than fundamentalist attacks on unwitting tourists. Some said the terrorism here started with militant extremists filtering into the country after the Afghanistan war, when Egypt was picked for the next stage in the radical fundamentalist crusade. But the problem had become home-grown, with vendettas between the government and other groups. What can I, a tourist in Egypt for three weeks, know of this? I can only heed the warning that the situation is more complex than anything reported in the Western press. Just as we have failed to grasp ancient Egypt, filling our heads with the notion of a primitive civilization that made a fetish of death and was built on the backs of slave labour rather than the amazingly sophisticated and subtle culture I had glimpsed, so we have not begun to understand the complexities of modern Islamic culture.

My last day in Cairo I spent alone at the pyramids of Giza. The others had been too often to want to join me. I rode by camel through the back streets, among the houses with tin roofs held down by cartons of dung, up past the Muslim graveyard where the women gathered in their black mourning, out across the desert, galloping in the high wind behind my guide on horseback, moving with the camel's long strides. There were no tourist buses in the parking lot. I climbed up the interior cavern of Cheops's pyramid with its hundreds of steps to the great sarcophagus. For a moment I was alone inside with the full weight of its mystery on my head. I paid a guard to lead me down to the pyramid's belly among the dead. I visited the solar boat used only once to carry the pharaoh's corpse from Memphis to Giza and then buried in pieces with him 4,500 years ago, and I thought, How astonishing is human history. And I prayed that the modern world would not close down, that the miracles of our collective human past—not to mention all meetings of people across cultures—would remain accessible. It is easy to admire this country. If I had a statue of myself, I would leave it here to ensure that my ka, one day, comes back to Egypt.

CONVERSATIONS IN MEXICO WITH LEONORA CARRINGTON, 1996–2009

I first met Leonora Carrington in 1995. I was living in Mexico City for a month on a Canada–Mexico artists' exchange, staying at the Gran Hotel off the Zócalo in the historic heart of the city. My purpose in Mexico was to write an article about her.

Even in 1995 it was not easy to meet Leonora Carrington. She was already famous. As early as 1960, she'd had a retrospective of her work at the Museo de Arte Moderno. She'd been invited to work with shamans in Chiapas and had painted *El mundo mágico de los mayas* in 1962. The great Mexican poet Octavio Paz had asked her to create the set design for the first performance of his play *La hija de Rappaccini*, based on Nathaniel Hawthorne's gothic story. By 1995, her New York and Mexico galleries protected her privacy, and she kept a reclusive distance from the public.

But I had a name to drop: P.K. Page had told me how to reach Leonora. When I phoned and told her I was P.K.'s friend, Leonora immediately said, "I must see you."

P.K. Page arrived in Mexico City in 1960 as the wife of the Canadian ambassador, and it seems unlikely that the Canadian embassy had seen her kind of woman before. She was forty-four and already a successful writer, with a novel, several books of poetry, and a Governor General's

Award behind her. Her husband, Arthur, had just completed a four-year posting in Brazil. For P.K., Brazil had been a dazzling experience, a flamboyant world of Doric palms and flowering jungles, and she had turned for the first time to painting to fix the whirl of images. In Mexico, because of her, the ambassadorial residence on Monte Carpatos was suddenly filled with artists.

One evening after a dinner party, P.K. found herself recounting a strange experience from her childhood. She and her mother were standing looking from the living room window of their home and suddenly found themselves staring into the eyes of a completely terrifying creature who was watching them. "It looked," she said, "like current descriptions of aliens: round dark eyes like disks, pointed chin, narrow with languorous hair, soft like a baby's, as if it were under water almost." The creature was not threatening, but it frightened her. She turned to her mother, who had also seen it, and her mother quietly closed the blind. Little did she know who was in her audience as she recounted her story that night. Leonora Carrington approached and said, "It sounds totally true." Others would have dismissed the story as fantasy or eccentricity. For Leonora this was elementary stuff, but it had verisimilitude. They became immediate friends.

In 1960, P.K., Leonora, and Leonora's friend Remedios Varo became collaborators in art. They would race around Mexico in P.K.'s car, negotiating the glorietas where the traffic merged from eight different directions, hunting gold leaf and pigment. They shared many things, including physical beauty, but what bonded them most was the metaphysical impulse in their work, blended with an exquisite sense of humour and mischief.

I'd been to Mexico before — to visit its Mayan and Aztec temples, including Chichén Itzá and Teotihuacán, and had lain on its beaches and scuba-dived in its oceans, but I'd never really spent time in Mexico City.

It turned out my hotel was in the historic centre of the city, a great beast of a city with the ruins of the Templo Mayor and its wall of skulls at its excavated heart. It almost seemed ironic that the great cathedral to the Virgin dominating the square was slowly sinking into the Aztec ruins beneath it. The Gran Hotel had once been an elegant department store, built when art deco arrived in the capital city. On each floor a balcony circled the empty centre, and five floors above a magnificent stained-glass roof arched overhead like some monstrous exotic flower, so that one felt like an insect scrambling under its blossoms. Wrought-iron elevator cages climbed the floors. As you rose, you could look down into the lobby at two large cages with stained-glass ceilings where birds catapulted themselves at breakneck speeds among the artificial branches. It was surreal, one of the most exquisite hotels I've lived in, a perfect place from which to set out on a visit to Leonora Carrington.

When I entered Leonora's house in the Colonia Roma district of Mexico City, I was dumbfounded by its spartan rigour: a dark entrance, cement floor, interior patio with scraggly trees and plants. It seemed cold and austere, until I saw her sculptures. They filled every corner, were under the stairs beside the cat litter, behind the door, on the sideboard. Like bronze dreams: a sphinx figure with a human head held tenderly in its palms; a strange desolate god with a door that opened in his body; a Mary Magdalene riding backwards on something resembling a pig. I would later learn that this sparseness of furniture and decoration was calculated. Leonora would tell me that, apart from her books and art works, everything in her house was dispensable. Material things had no meaning. "I can pick up and leave at a moment's notice," she said.

All the warmth of the house was collected in the modest kitchen.

As we sat at the table with its checkered tablecloth, tea canister, and ketchup bottle, Leonora immediately put me at my ease by discussing the new "corset" she had just bought at Price Choppers in Florida to support her sore back—it was the kind train porters use for a weak back. She was thrilled with it.

And then she told me I was sitting in the seat where Aldous Huxley had sat. She had always admired him, but she liked him especially after he came to Mexico. Looking at one of her canvases, he immediately suggested that it be titled *Nobodaddy* after Blake's poem, to which she added *Nobomommy*. I was not surprised that Aldous Huxley, author of *The Doors of Perception*, should have sought out Leonora Carrington; all of her work, her way of being in the world, is about perception.

On my first visit, Leonora talked of her early days in Mexico, her friendships with Luis Buñuel, Benjamin Péret, and Remedios Varo.

"Mexico does something to everyone who comes here," she said. "The Mexicans have such love and respect for art, I don't know why—both male and female artists.... Which is surprising," she added, "since as a woman here you're blah!" She also talked of P.K. "Pat had a wonderful eye, a very textured verbal sense. She had exquisite taste. Once I invited a Hindu gentleman for dinner. He insisted on cooking and made this great pile of rice. It was awful. Pat said it was like congealed blood. Nothing more needed to be said."

...

When I returned to Mexico in 1997, I stayed at the Hotel Maria Cristina near the glorieta of El Ángel. I can still see Leonora visiting me there: wrapped in her belted, cream-coloured trench coat, her grey hair pulled back in a bun, scuttling anonymously through the lobby. And I thought, No patrons of this hotel know that one of Mexico's greatest artists has just graced their premises. Just the way Leonora wanted it.

Leonora was born in 1917 in a stately mansion in Lancashire called Crookhey Hall. It was large enough to accommodate a private chapel where the priest came to give her Irish mother mass and communion on Sundays. Though the family vacated the manor when Leonora was ten, its lush gardens, its gothic labyrinthine rooms, and its stables where she kept her Shetland pony, Black Bess, and her chestnut mare, Winkie, haunt her paintings and stories. Her father was a British industrialist, owner of Carrington Cotton until he sold it and became a principal shareholder in Imperial Chemical Industries. Her mother, Mairi Moorhead, was the daughter of an Irish country doctor.

Leonora told me she had a lovely childhood. Her mother, a remarkable beauty, loved nothing better than to read stories by her favourite Irish writers to Leonora and her three brothers. Her Irish nanny, Nanny Kavanagh, told them ghost stories. Her father was the disciplinarian who insisted on punctuality. Everyone had to dress for dinner. A gong sounded, and you went up to dress; another sounded to call you down. Her father's mother lived with them and loved to annoy her son by sounding the second gong too early; she thought the whole ritual silly.

Out of their father's sight, Leonora and her brothers ran wild. She remembers them wanting to play with a local girl. The girl agreed, but only if they helped her to kill her father. They would wait in the bushes with a pellet gun while he sat reading his newspaper. Much to Leonora's disappointment, the girl always missed. "How we loved to visit my grand-mother," Leonora says. Granny Moorhead, her maternal grandmother, lived in County Westmeath in an exquisite Victorian cottage. She loved rituals and believed in banshees, changelings, and animals who could transform themselves into humans. "I have always considered animals angels," Leonora tells me. "Why do they put up with us? They have beautiful minds."

In her grandmother's village there was only one local policeman, so he was the head of the jail, which was usually empty. He let them play at locking each other up. Leonora was sent to boarding school, which didn't go well. She tells me she was marked as unpopular and was eventually put in a special class — two girls who didn't speak English, a slightly retarded girl, and her. This began her pattern of flight. "I became very good at climbing out of windows," she says. After finishing school at Miss Penrose's Academy in Florence, she returned to England and was presented at the court of George V, with a debutante party at the Ritz. Somehow she then convinced her parents to send her to art school. At the age of nineteen, she attended the Ozenfant Academy of Fine Arts in London. It was through a school friend that she met the surrealist painter Max Ernst at a dinner party. The meeting was "un choc amoureux." They ran away to Paris together, where Leonora found herself embattled with Ernst's second wife, whose ten-year marriage with Ernst was floundering. Still, she was young, and caught up in "love madness."

Leonora doesn't much like to talk of the past, but in one of our con-versations she did say her time in Paris was marvellous.

In the spring of 1938, Leonora and Max Ernst moved permanently to Saint Martin d'Ardèche, where they covered their home with sculptures and shocked the neighbours, who peered through the hedges, by paint-ing outdoors — naked. Leonora began to write stories in French, the language she and Ernst spoke together. Soon she had a book: *La Dame Ovale*, with humorous erotic collages by Ernst. Ernst painted his mar-vellous *A Moment of Calm* that summer and, later, *Leonora in the Morning Light* in which Leonora stares out at the viewer from a landscape of minotaurs, unicorns, and skeletons, herself an exotic dream creature suspended from a phallic vine.

She told me how in early September of 1939, just days after France and England declared war on Germany, the French police ordered the arrest of all "enemy aliens." They knocked at her and Max's door in Saint Martin d'Ardèche, put Max in handcuffs, and took him away to a hastily improvised internment camp set up in an abandoned brick factory in the town of Les Milles, just outside Aix-en-Provence. Ernst had lived in France since 1922. It never occurred to him that he might be included in an enemy roundup. It took Leonora three months of cajoling bureaucracies before Ernst was released from Les Milles through the intercession of the poet Paul Éluard. In May Ernst was denounced by a neighbour as a spy, arrested again, and returned to the camp. For Leonora, the injustice of it still seared.

In June 1940, as the German army advanced on Paris, two friends pressured Leonora into joining them as they fled by car across the Pyrenees to Spain. There was no point in waiting for Max, they said. Who knew where he might be? But the terror of not knowing what had happened to Max was leading to disaster. In Spain, under the pressure of anxiety, Leonora began to spiral out of control. She was sure that if she could meet the Spanish dictator General Franco, she could stop the war. When she was found standing outside the British embassy in Madrid threatening to assassinate Hitler, the embassy interceded. She was committed to an asylum in Santander, where her multiple experiences of being shackled and given the drug Cardiazol to induce seizures were so horrendous that she came to call them "death practise."

She said that her father sent her nanny from Ireland by boat to collect her, with the intention of taking her to a mental hospital in South Africa. She managed to climb out a window and escape to the Mexican embassy, where she had a friend. Such was the painful route that brought her to Mexico.

"Why didn't you and Max try to get out of France before the invasion?" I asked her.

"We should have left after Max was released from the concentration camp the first time," she said, "but Max couldn't imagine a life outside Paris. Paris was freedom." Paris was the City of Light.

At the exhibition *Entartete Kunst* organized in Munich by Joseph Goebbels in 1937, Max Ernst had been labelled a degenerate artist. There is a picture of Hitler standing in front of Ernst's painting *The Beautiful Gardener*. Over the painting is a banner that reads "A Slur on German Womanhood." I asked Leonora why totalitarian minds are afraid of art. "Because it gets inside," she said. "It can terrify you or give you joy."

She told me: "The Nazis opened up a forbidden door in the soul. I suppose if you have to stake this little bit of ground that says you are a superior race and then defend it, something horrible always happens. When you claim certainty, when you say that you know."

At the encouragement of André Breton, Leonora wrote the story of her flight from France and her incarceration at Santander in her novel *Down Below*. When I asked her if the novel was autobiographical, she replied that it was completely autobiographical, and added, "At least when you go mad, you find out what you are made of."

Down Below is possibly one of the most lucidly hallucinatory accounts of madness ever written. With a precision that is astonishing, Leonora records her own breakdown, replicating the surreal logic of an anguished mind negotiating a world that has somehow to be brought under control. What makes this so powerful is the context: Spain itself, which was under the hypnotic spell of Franco's triumphant fascism, its somnambulistic citizens caught in a murderous vise of violence and denial. However mad Leonora may have been, she was saner than most of the world around her.

Leonora knew about the pain of madness. I remember P.K. speaking of Leonora's breakdown in 1964, just as P.K. and Arthur were leaving Mexico to return to Canada. For days, she said, Leonora had been looking astonishingly beautiful. She seemed to be engulfed in the scent of flowers, so powerful was the natural perfume she emitted. Then Leonora's husband, Tchiki Weisz, called P.K. to say that Leonora would not leave her room, refused to eat, and said the only one she would talk to was P.K. He begged her to come over. When P.K. arrived, she found Leonora scrunched in a corner of her room looking terrified. She was gluing together the pages of a book to prevent people from discovering its terrible secrets.

But in our conversations, it is always Leonora's humour that I remember. She was brilliantly adept at one-liners. Over the years I collected them.

Once she said, "Tchiki's doctor said we come back as energy. 'What?' I asked him. 'You mean as traffic lights?'"

She said she went to a Freudian analyst once, who said she was not adjusted. "To what?" she inquired.

And she ended a conversation with a Jesuit who'd asked her if she believed in God by asking, "Which one?"

I remember inquiring once about what she was reading. "A book on criminal profiling. That's the kind of book I enjoy these days." We laughed. "I love watching detective stories," she added.

"Why?" I asked.

"It appeals to the inner criminal, the killer in us all."

Leonora was ambidextrous and was something of a child prodigy as a pianist. She occasionally painted with both hands and amused herself with mirror writing. With astonishing speed, she wrote me a note, which I had to use a mirror to read: "Well Hello Rosemary! I hope you come back to Mexico soon." And then played a riff on the old nonsense song: "Do horses eat oats? Do mares eat oats? Do goats eat ripe oats?"

...

When I think of Leonora's work, both prose and painting, I think of humour, of rebellion, of an understanding of just how susceptible the human mind is to authoritarian control.

I rarely asked Leonora about the meaning of her work. She didn't like such questions, but I did ask her why the autobiographical Francis in her story "Little Francis" (written in 1937) is male. "Why not?" she replied. "I have out-of-body dreams to this day. But I don't know what sex I am. It seems irrelevant."

Of her writings undertaken in Mexico, the most impressive is *The Stone Door*, written in English in the 1940s but not published until 1977. I cannot attempt to summarize the narrative: there are stories within stories, quests within quests, but the inner story involves a character called Zacharias who must open the stone door that leads to the country of the dead. There is a female voice calling for release from behind the door, but when Zacharias finally opens it, he doesn't meet the person who owns the voice. Instead, a flock of white sheep pour through like a "deluge of curdled milk," and Zacharias is swept aside by the stampede. Puzzled by the story's ending, with some temerity I asked Leonora why Zacharias didn't meet the girl, the object of his quest.

"Because I think that's it. We still must meet the female. Buried under so much pain. There is the biological fact. The two genders. But never have I heard an adequate explanation of what the meeting of the two sexes would mean. The kind of explanation where you say, 'AH! Yes!'"

Leonora has sometimes been called a feminist, but no label sits easily on her. She would say, however, that "women's spirituality is grounded in everyday reality, which makes it sane. Men kick free to abstraction, metaphysics." This is dangerous. "The compartmentalization of the mind and the body is convenient for institutions to control us."

Once Leonora was the surrealists' Bride of the Wind to Max Ernst's Loplop, Father Superior of the Birds, but she came to dislike the heroic myth of male artistic genius, the grandiose gesture. "Painting," she said, "is like making strawberry jam—really carefully and well."

When André Breton asked Leonora to participate in an exhibition of eroticism in Mexico City in 1959, she described her intended contribution: "A Holy Ghost (albino pigeon) three meters high, real feathers (white chickens', for example), with: nine penises erect (luminous), thirty-nine testicles to the sound of little Christmas bells, pink paws....Let me know, Dear André, and I will send you an exact drawing." On one occasion she remarked, "If you have to, get on with your genital responsibilities, but I won't be the Lady of Shallot."

Leonora took me to meet her closest friend, the Canadian painter Alan Glass, who'd been living in Mexico for decades. Glass was raising the ceiling of the downstairs room where he had his studio. It was a wonderful space, stark white, ordered, full of light. I remember giant glass flowers in alcoves. He'd just had a flood, with the drains backing up in a sudden inundation. As we toured his studio, we talked about art and artists. We each remarked that we suffer from whatever that disease is that keeps you inside, immobilizes you from time to time. I told Leonora that I've twice had panic attacks. She said, "I don't think you can be an artist without having panic attacks. We are all driven by fear. We act to keep the fear under control."

Leonora wanted to see Glass's new "box." She had hoped to buy it, but he had already sold it to André Breton's daughter, Aube. The "box" was actually a standard-sized oblong Peek Freans box with a logo of a cookie at one end that served as a peephole. Glass had used mirrors to create a magic Alice in Wonderland world inside. When you looked through the peephole, you could see a pair of dice, a creature like a seahorse, and a string of names cut into a paper chain. "A soldier made the paper chain in the trenches in World War One," Glass said. "They are the names of the women he loved." Glass had found the delicate chain in a local flea market. In his art, he has a rule: all objects must be found. As we left, he gave me a small sesame bun with a little marzipan head sticking out of it. "From the bakery around the corner," he said. "Wonderful what the Mexicans do."

The next day we took a taxi to the local Sanborns, a popular department-store chain with restaurants serving typical Mexican fare. Leonora insisted we walk through the store to see what she called Mexican kitsch—a white truncated Christ in a glass case, ceramic pigs, and plastic flowers. "See the horrors people are capable of!" she scoffed. As we sat down, she directed my attention to a corner where a group of suited men sat. "The cops," she said. "Shall we go up to them and say, 'Hey murderers'?"

We began to talk about books, influences. "These days I'm interested in Fritjof Capra, the meeting of physics and consciousness," she said. "It's not who we are but what we are that's important. We have taken a wrong turn, refused magic and swapped the power of instinct for intelligence. The mysteries which were ourselves have been violated. Wisdom has been covered up. There is a lot of dogma turd to clean away. Our machine mentation is the problem—I am, I am, I am."

But then she corrected herself. "The problem is not ego. I spent a week in Canada living with Tibetans when I was on one of my investigations about ten years ago. I liked the Tibetans because they were so reasonable. As they said, the greatest sin is ignorance; one must proceed towards enlightenment. But I get bored.

"All this talk about ego and getting beyond it. I finally told the Tibetans, what are human beings without ego? If someone gets hit by a truck, what is it to me? If I know him I get upset. If it's a loved one, I'm devastated. That is where we begin. There is nothing wrong with ego.

"The problem is not ego, but the mannequins. I have one for the gallery, one for each of my sons, one for Tchiki, one for my cats. We must sometimes do things we don't like or are afraid to do to control the mannequins."

Our talk turned to C.G. Jung. I spoke of his book *The Visions Seminar*. Leonora said that she had worked for three years with a Jungian when she lived alone in New York. It had helped, but it was mostly because the Jungian provided companionable conversation.

"Still, Jung was absolutely right about one thing," Leonora said. "We are occupied by gods. The mistake is to identify with the god occupying you."

Our conversation continued. "I prefer the Jungians to the Freudians, and I prefer the shamans to the priests. When I worked with the shamans in Zinacantán I learned from them that the soul has thirteen parts and an animal-spirit companion. It is possible for a part of the soul to get lost because of fright and to leave. That seems to me eminently believable. It has happened to me.

"Entities do enter our lives," Leonora said. "One I experienced was malevolent. It has happened six or eight times since I was very young. It was a thing without shape or boundaries, amorphous. It comes as a sound. It was voracious, sucking, a sucking force, and inside this entity were millions of other entities, equally voracious, crying desperately, one of which was me. As in hell."

"Was this evil?" I asked.

"Yes, evil is an entity, a force with its own momentum. Like Hitler."

"What moves it?"

"An absence of attention. That is the only thing I can think of," she replied. "The Gnostics were right. A diabolical entity rules each planet. I can feel it. The only thing we can do about evil is pay attention."

I told her that I'd recently had the strangest dream. I had visited the Egyptian collection at the Metropolitan Museum in New York and been dazzled by the hieroglyphic image of the human eye on bird-like

Leonora Carrington,
Untitled Drawing, 1962
(collection of the author)

stick-legs. In my dream there were four eyes on legs staring from their corners into the centre at something that I could not see. In the dream I knew that if I could just see what they saw I would understand all the mysteries.

She didn't dismiss the dream. She simply said: "There are phases or layers to reality that we don't have the equipment to experience. But there are moments you see, and then you lose it." She told me that her paintings are not dreams or made-up symbols. They are hypnagogic visions, things she sees. "The human apparatus is limited by body and time," she added, "but it can open up more. The world is marvellous. It looks at you. You look at it."

As we walked back to her house through the labyrinthine streets, dodging the traffic, we passed a park with a statue of Juan Rulfo. "Do you know who he is?" she asked.

"Yes," I replied. "The author of *Pedro Páramo*, that marvellous conversation among the dead."

"He was a wonderful man. His favourite pub stood here before the earthquake," she said. "He died of drink. Most people who die of alcohol are good people. In that tavern, there"—she pointed across the street—"I wrote *The Hearing Trumpet.*"

When we reached her house, she called me a taxi. We kissed each other goodbye at her door. Such was a typical quiet afternoon with Leonora Carrington.

In 1989, P.K. presented me with a pencil sketch by Leonora, a gift she knew I would treasure. It is such a privilege to own it because it captures Leonora's spirit.

Two figures stare at each other with mutual knowledge and intimacy. Each holds the other in an erotic visual embrace. Who is the delicate spirit the human creature is speaking to? Each time I look at the sketch it changes, perhaps as I change. At the moment, I see the human as herself almost animal, with a carapace enveloping her body and raccoon eyes. The spirit is the other, what Leonora called "our animal spirit companion," superior, with a knowledge of and a capacity for at-tension (as P.K. used to call it) that most of us have allowed to dissipate. If you look long enough, the spirit creature pulls you back to your better self. That, of course, had always been Leonora Carrington's intention.

THE MAN WHO WAS BURIED
STANDING UP, 2000

For years, Juan and I had been going to Cuba for holidays, and I'd always intended to visit the Necropolis Cristóbal Colón (or Christopher Columbus, as we call him). To meet the remains of the man who had once planted his flag on a small island off Cuba and declared he had discovered India was beginning to feel like an obligation. So when I found myself alone in old Havana—Juan was with the musicians—I decided to spend the morning at the cemetery.

A taxi took me to Twelfth Street and Zapata. In the midst of shops selling flowers, fruit, and coffee, I found the north gate, an intimidating, triple-arched stone structure over sixty feet high. "I am the Door of Peace," it said. The gate is also a tomb. Though I didn't know it at the time, I was, appropriately, walking under somebody's ashes. To the right were the necropolis archives, where I was to meet José Octavio Pérez Cubillas, my guide for the morning. The archives house the books registering the more than one million people buried here since the mid-nineteenth century.

Short, rotund, and sexually ambiguous, Octavio was everything you could hope for in a necropolis archivist. Thick glasses covered the upper half of his pale face, and behind those lenses his eyes darted like flies. From the neck down, his body had melted. He had no edges. When he stood, he stood immobilized, with hands folded placidly behind his back, and when he moved, he moved stealthily in a slow shuffle. He had the voice of a tape recorder; information came in long, rehearsed swatches. The most impressive thing about Octavio was that he clearly loved his dead.

I asked to see Christopher Columbus. "Ah, yes," said Octavio, "but I must tell you of the Switch Conspiracy." He explained to me that Columbus was a sailor, and just because he died didn't mean he stopped sailing. His bones kept travelling for years after his death in 1506. They'd been on a pilgrimage from Valladolid to Seville to Santo Domingo, ending up back in Havana in the National Cathedral. By this time, it had to be admitted, no one was entirely confident that the remains were still actually Christopher Columbus. After Cuba gained its independence from Spain at the end of the nineteenth century, the Spanish vindictively wanted Columbus back. But wily Cuban conspirators dressed as priests entered the sacristy where the remains were kept and switched them. Someone else's bones sailed back to Spain.

I looked ahead at the magnificent congestion of mausoleums, crypts, and chapels bisected by alleys of towering royal palms, and thought, This may or may not be the final resting place of Columbus, but it is clearly one of the world's great cemeteries.

I soon discovered that once Octavio was on a roll, he was not to be interrupted. He explained that in 1806, the bishop of Havana, Don Juan José Diaz de Espada y Fernández de Landa (ah, the Spanish language!), inaugurated the first cemetery in Havana. But with the cholera epidemic of 1867, the old necropolis filled to bursting, and this new site was hurriedly opened. The first person buried here was a seventy-year-old Black slave. Her name went into the burial book for Blacks; there was a separate book for Whites and Chinese. (Octavio said this "ignominious racist practice" was discontinued in 1924.) On opening day, the ninth of November, 1868, eighteen people were interred.

Octavio continued his exposition. "In the beginning, the necropolis was divided into sections for the rich, the lower classes who could pay, the poor, and the slaves. But the Jesuits kept selling off bits of land, and nobody kept a record of which section was which. So democracy of a kind came to the dead. Pale death treats us all the same," he said mournfully.

I responded with my favourite Colombian proverb: "Who must die, must die in the dark, even though he sells candles."

Octavio smiled appreciatively and continued. "In Cuba, to thwart the tropical heat, burials happen within two days. The body is buried and then dug up two years later and the bones are put in a box. This must be done," he explained, "because there are so many of us."

We moved on.

Octavio was light-hearted, almost ebullient. We stood in front of the grave of Constantino Ribalaigua, a man he described as an eminent inventor. It turned out he invented cocktails. His great work was the whipped and iced daiquiri. Octavio elaborated: "The son of a poor Spanish fisherman, Constantino arrived in Havana in 1914, and with diligence and thrift, bought a tavern that became the famous Floridita where Ernest Hemingway drank." (Hemingway's ubiquitous ghost slips into everything in Cuba, so I was not surprised to find him in the cemetery.) According to Papa, the sensation of drinking Constantino's daiquiris was "like the skier who slides over the frozen peak of a mountain amid the dust of snow." Octavio smiled endearingly. Constantino was clearly one of his favourite dead.

But when we passed to the mausoleum of Catalina Lasa, I saw the fidelity of a lover in Octavio's misted eyes. "Catalina was married young to Luis Estévez, a rich Cuban patrician," he said, still bitter at the injustice of it. "Traumatized"—a favourite Octavio word—"by boredom, luckily she met the rich and famous Juan Pedro Baro at a cocktail party. Amor a primera vista! The lovers made little effort to disguise their passion. It was a great scandal." Octavio was in high gear: inexorably repudiated by polite society in 1920s Havana, Catalina and Juan Pedro ran off to Paris. On their return, they attended the theatre. When the other patrons realized who was in the audience, the theatre emptied. But the actors went on with the play. As the final curtain fell and the lights came on, Catalina stood up, took off all her jewels, and threw them onto the stage to thank the actors for their performance. Octavio gestured as if he were tossing jewels through the graveyard.

"How did Catalina die?" I asked.

"Wait, wait," said Octavio impatiently, "Catalina is not dead yet." I looked at the tomb over his shoulder and felt ashamed to have interrupted a man with such an exquisite sense of narrative.

"Don Pedro went to Italy to see the pope and demanded he annul Catalina's first marriage to Estévez. Once the annulment was granted, he married her and, in celebration, gave his wife a precious gift. But what do you give a woman who has everything?" Octavio asked as if he had mulled this question over for a lifetime. "He created a rose for her. The Catalina Lasa rose. It is yellow, her favourite colour.

"Don Pedro built this mausoleum after she died," he explained. (Since I didn't have the nerve to interrupt Octavio a second time, I never found out how or when.) "It's a fortress to protect her from the lecherous gaze of society. The Catalina Lasa rose is engraved on the skylight so that when the sun penetrates the glass and shines on the sarcophagus, she can see her rose." The look of benignity on Octavio's face was so undiluted, it was unnerving.

We moved to the grave of Amelia Goyri de la Hoz, also known as the Miraculous One. The gravesite was covered with bouquets of gladioli of every colour from pale yellow to bright red. An old woman was on her knees spreading the flowers into wreaths. Octavio told me that Amelia had died in childbirth in 1901 at the age of twenty-four. When she was buried her dead child was laid between her legs, as custom dictated. Her desolate husband, José Vicente, visited her grave every day. On his arrival he would hit the gravestone with his wedding ring to wake her up and would then talk to her for several hours. As he left, he would never turn his back on his wife. Several years later, when the grave was opened to accommodate José Vincente's father, Amelia's body was found perfectly preserved. "But the child had moved," Octavio said. It now lay in her arms.

Over the years, people began to leave flowers anonymously at the tomb. Soon it became traditional for pregnant women to visit Amelia. And indeed, as we watched, a beautiful young woman with a slightly protruding belly and an armful of flowers came through the small gate. She laid down the flowers, prayed a little, and then retreated, careful not to turn her back on the grave. I looked down at the hundreds of small rectangular tablets, like stone postcards, left as grateful testaments to Amelia's interventions.

Cuba is a small island and its necropolis reads like a book—the country's whole history can be divined here. For Octavio, it is a family story of love and miracles and of treachery and betrayal.

We visited the monument to the medical students executed on November 27, 1871, for desecrating the tomb of a Spanish journalist. The gate of the monument is sculpted with flying bats whose open wings signify death by treachery.

"To be executed for something so trivial? How is that possible?" I asked. "Was the journalist so important?"

"The students were Creole," Octavio replied, as if that explained everything. And of course, it did. Their deaths had nothing to do with what they did but were a consequence of who they were—they shared the blood of the Indigenous people of the island.

We stopped at the grave of Samuel A. Cohner, the man who died because of the colour of his tie. He was an American photographer who owned a studio in Havana in the tense days of 1869. Angry militiamen gunned him down in a local bar. He did not know that the blue of the tie around his neck was the same colour adopted by the independence movement.

I looked down an avenue of eucalyptuses and willow trees and noted the Carrara angels staring out from their crypts. Octavio explained that Cuban trade increased dramatically in 1914 with the onset of the world war and vast fortunes were made. The sugar barons and the soap barons and the makers of Bacardi rum and Crystál beer competed in the grandeur of their graves, importing marble from Italy, crystal from France, and stained glass from Germany.

Almost every decade brought its new dictator and its martyrs. There was the sad case of Eduardo Chibás, famous for his slogan "Shame Against Money." He shot himself on the radio in 1951 at the end of a speech, shouting, "People of Cuba, get up and walk! This is my last loud bang!" He believed he was about to be assassinated for exposing political corruption.

Octavio shuffled me on. We were soon standing at the grave of the great writer Alejo Carpentier. He's a writer I love. I can still enter the jungle he described in *The Lost Steps*. I learned that he began his first novel in prison in 1927 under the dictatorship of President Machado. He was then exiled to Europe, where he became a friend of Federico García Lorca. He was able to return permanently to Cuba in 1959 and worked as a publisher, dying on a diplomatic mission in Paris in 1980. He coined the phrase *lo real maravilloso*.

The extraordinary exists in the real, he claimed. There can be no more perfect expression of what he meant, I thought, than Necropolis Cristóbal Colón. Octavio trudged us off to the grave of the man who was buried standing up.

"There's Eugenio Casimiro Rodríguez Carta," said Octavio, pointing. "An excellent rogue." When he was chief of police in Cienfuegos, he assassinated the mayor over some local dispute. He was imprisoned and condemned to death in 1918. One day, while he was sweeping the prison yard, who should chance to pass but the daughter of the president of the republic. A furtive romance began between them. Her father soon pardoned him, and he entered politics. He had a very successful and prosperous life. Shortly before his death, he ordered a vertical niche built in the family grave. "A man who has fallen on his feet in life, must also fall on his feet in hell," he explained. He'd saved the bullet with which he'd killed the mayor and insisted it be buried with him.

At a short distance I could see the torso of a baseball player in uniform and cap rise from stone. "It's the Pantheon to the Ball Players," Octavio explained, "owned by the Christian Association of Players, Umpires, and Managers." Cubans are passionate fans. They've been playing the game here since 1865. Octavio smiled enigmatically. "Perhaps if you come to the necropolis at night, you will see the ghosts playing baseball."

"Before an audience of a million dead," I added. We grinned appreciatively at the thought.

The tropical sun was bearing down on our heads ever more relentlessly, and I could see that even Octavio was tiring. Doggedly, he turned our attention to the nearby grave of Victor Muñoz. A sports reporter in the 1920s, Muñoz secretly wrote a women's column under the pseudonym Margarita and became famous for successfully lobbying the government to celebrate Mother's Day.

I felt like some madcap spirit was loose in this necropolis. Death was casual here, lugubrious, but also playful. One tomb was literally a huge carved domino that had come up a double three. Octavio said that Juana Marín was a fervent domino player until the day she died. She suffered a heart attack when she could not place the double three on the board and died with the counter still in her hand. On the side of the tomb, her family had a domino board sculpted, reproducing the exact sequence of the game on that fatal day.

In the distance a chess piece, the white king, stood at least five feet high over the grave of José Raúl Capablanca, who won the World Chess Championship in 1921. There were airplanes on some graves. "Death by plane crash is heroic—like a phoenix consumed in flames," Octavio commented laconically. Even the maudlin was here in the tomb of Mrs. Ryder. The American woman lay recumbent on her sarcophagus covered in a blanket. At her feet was her faithful dog, which had refused to leave the corpse until it, too, had died.

But my favourite tomb was the Embroideress. Two bronze hands rose from the ground in the gesture of threading a needle. These were the almost life-size hands of the mother of the sculptor Fernando Boada. They had a dignity about them, a spiritual tranquility that cracked the heart. Such a tender epitaph for grief.

I realize that Octavio reminded me of something I'd forgotten: that I too once loved cemeteries. I have a childhood memory of a small grave-yard and of running through it in a state of high ecstasy, as if I were kicking free of gravity and the dead, immobilized in their graves, were cheering me on.

When did we start to exile the dead to a sanitized place in our minds so that they cease to be real?

Octavio, I would like to tell you that I want to end up in your necrop-olis where I will be family and have a story that survives me. I want you to keep talking to me long after I'm gone.

Le Palais Idéal of the Facteur Cheval in Hauterives, France (Émile Duchemin)

THE POSTMAN'S DREAM, 2001

My old friend Jeronimo Gonzales Martin had said, "If you're going to Dijon, there's something you must visit. It's called Le Palais Idéal du Facteur Cheval. It's north or south of there. Better than Gaudí's La Sagrada Familia in Barcelona. André Breton called it a work of genius." This wasn't much of a clue, but I filed it anyway in my mind.

For Juan and me, one of our favourite countries is France, and we visited as often as we could. After seeing friends in Dijon, we rented a car and headed south. We were driving near Lyon in a region called the Drôme, an undulating landscape of poplars and elms bisected by the Rhône and Isère rivers. The country road was lined with huge plane trees, and we were admiring the chiaroscuro play of light in the mysterious tunnel their branches made. Suddenly there was a sign: Le Palais Idéal du Facteur Cheval (The Ideal Palace of the Postman Cheval), Hauterives, 25 kilometres. We turned off just in time. I had no idea what to expect.

Hauterives had that withdrawn look of small French towns at noon when everyone's inside eating. There was no one to ask who or what the Facteur Cheval was. Finally we found an empty parking lot at the south end of town. It took us another fifteen minutes to locate the entrance to the site. But there it stood, the most extraordinary folly in France.

What is it? A structure? A sculpture? A dream? The inside of a man's mind? Impossible to categorize. The postman's palace is a pastiche of the world's myths, and yet it is totally original. It's like walking into the fantasy world of Henri Rousseau but in stone.

The palace is huge. It is about twenty-six metres long, fourteen metres wide, and twelve metres high, with north and south facades and a balcony with a stairwell on the east. It has an interior tunnel twenty metres long with grottoes covered with inscriptions.

The story of its creator, Ferdinand Cheval, is full of tantalizing absences. Born in 1836 in the tiny village of Charmes, he was the son of a peasant farmer. His mother died when he was eleven. He was literate, having attended the local primary school. At the age of twenty-one he fled to Hauterives and married. Then one day he walked out of his life. "Il prend le large" (he took the big), the French say, as if it were the most common thing in the world. Abandoning wife and son, he took to the open air for six years. No one knows what he did or where he spent those years, except that he worked briefly as a baker's boy. Legend has it that he walked to Algeria.

In 1870, he was back in Hauterives living with his wife (she would die within three years). His in-laws had found him a job as a postman, or facteur, delivering mail through the countryside of Drôme. He walked from dawn to dusk, thirty-two kilometres a day for twenty-five years, through landscapes almost empty except for the occasional town. What visions did he have on those solitary walks? He said he dreamed of a fabulous and immense city, studded with towers and strangely carved superstructures. It was animated, moving as if it were alive. He felt he was walking beneath its walls. He thought he was mad.

It was 1879, and he was forty-three years old. He had passed what he called the grand equinox of life. In *Le Facteur Cheval, piéton de Hauterives* (1988), Claude Boncompain quotes him: "My dream," he said, "appeared to me the result of a sick imagination and I didn't dare to talk about it to anyone. I was on the point of forgetting all about it when something happened to bring it all back. As I was walking one day my foot hit an obstacle that nearly made me fall over. I wanted to have a closer look at my stumbling block."

It was just an oddly shaped stone. But it seemed to him as if his dream had materialized, as if the stone had fallen from the walls of his ideal palace, and he decided then and there that he would submit to the appeal of the stone. He would build his dream. Until his death at eighty-nine he would remember the startling sensation, that epiphany when a stumbling block turned out to be the solution.

He had no training as a mason. He simply started collecting stones as he walked along. He would make hills of stones at various stations along his postal route, returning at night to retrieve them, which added another dozen kilometres to his daily walk and often kept him up until well past midnight. "I cannot tell you the misery I endured," he said. Over the next six years, he became a connoisseur of stones, collecting a mountain of every shape and size of stone until he was finally ready to make a copy of his dream.

He began by building a fountain in his garden. His neighbours thought him odd but harmless. His second wife, Claire, was irritated, but at least she knew where he was. Day by day, year by year, the palace grew, like a living organism. He was Noah building his ark in the face of disbelievers. For decades he kept faith with his project. When his palace was finally completed, he wrote inside its cavernous interior: "1879–1912; 10,000 days; 93,000 hours; 33 years of toil."

How impossibly compelling is total obsession! So exacting was his concentration on his dream that he did not seem to require any confirmation from without. His art was a pure act with no obligation to anyone. "Happy the free man brave and working. The dream of a peasant," he wrote on the east wall of his palace. He was convinced he was a genius and that his genius came from a source outside himself. He called his work the "pantheon of an obscure hero."

Anecdotal reports are that he was pretty useless when it came to ordinary living. He was absorbed in his visions. Claire is said to have been appalled when he suggested they both be buried inside his palace. She had long ago joined the chorus of derision. There are only a few photos of Cheval. In one, he is in his postal uniform, a man in his sixties. His face is taut and drawn, his mouth firmly clamped. His eyes stare intensely, not at the viewer but at something over the viewer's shoulder. But this pose is typical of the romantic portraiture of the time. More telling is a photograph of a simple peasant in an apron, wheeling a wheelbarrow through a garden, an artist quietly going about his work. To have asked him to live for anything other than his palace would have been a grave mistake.

What was this vision he was so compelled to communicate? He filled the dark interior of his palace with benevolent platitudes: "The simplicity of the body makes the spirit virtuous." "We are shadows that come from dust and return there." "Help yourself and the sky will help you." "What God writes on your forehead will happen." But the energy he found in stone is another matter. He made the stones flow, move like water, live.

As I walked around his monument, entered its innards, a line formed in my head: the pulse of life beneath the skin of a stone. The swirls of stone that he had pounded with his own hands reminded me of the swirling energy of a Van Gogh sky. It seemed a vision of the universe as a totally interconnected fluid form of living energy. Was that what his dream had told him?

There was something else as well. I realized that the Palais Idéal had no relationship to the objective world. It was composed entirely of symbols: his elongated giants of wisdom, tumbling fountains, rows of breasts, Adam and Eve, serpents, stone vegetation, beasts, temples, grottoes, crypts. A man had lifted the curtain to his own subconscious mind and stood there naked and exposed, embodied in his work. The undiluted chaos of the mind was revealed. The postman was totally uninhibited in offering it. That was the beauty of it. He was constrained by no filters, no censors of propriety or even of art. Nothing diluted his dream.

In his lifetime, Cheval had no hope of recognition or of financial reward. His work was dismissed as the "hideous insanities" boiling in the rustic brain of a peasant. Yet he never doubted that he would be applauded posthumously. When a soldier passing through Hauterives dismissed the idea that the palace could be the work of one man, Cheval was outraged and dictated his account of its construction to the mayor and others, demanding that they sign testimonials to his sole authorship.

Cheval completed his palace in 1912. His final gesture was to enclose his tools behind an iron grill on the south facade, and there he gave them voice: "I, the wheelbarrow, had the honor of having been his companion for 27 years of labour." "I am the faithful companion of an intelligent worker," says the pail. Over the arch to his crypt the tools speak in chorus: "Your Palace, born of a dream / We, your tools, companions / and witness of your labour / From century to century the work of one man."

Cheval died twelve years after completing his palace. It remained in its private garden, the only patrimony to his sons. Over time only a few people visited. For some reason I keep thinking of the palace sitting undisturbed, its benign vision of the unity of the conscious and subconscious mind unheeded, as two world wars wreaked destruction beyond its locked gates.

Just before his death, Cheval received recognition for his work from the Surrealist poet André Breton and even from Pablo Picasso. He would have been delighted to hear the debate that raged in 1969 at the Ministry of Culture in Paris on the subject of his palace. Affronting many skeptics, the novelist André Malraux, then minister of state for culture, had decided to declare the obscure Palais Idéal an invaluable historical monument, the only example of naive architecture in the world. Then, in 1986, the postman was given a tribute that would have met with his approval. The government of France minted a postage stamp in honour of the Facteur Cheval.

A TRIP TO TARQUINIA
WITH D.H. LAWRENCE, 2003

In the spring of 2006, accompanied by D.H. Lawrence, I travelled into the past. In fact, I travelled into death. I have always been drawn by cemeteries and tombs. It feels like one is walking into history.

Lawrence has been a passion of mine, although it is not popular to say that now. He is outdated, but his novels intrigue me with their strong, three-dimensional women (unusual for a male writer), and I love his poetry and his essays. He was so loquacious, so opinionated, so unafraid of being verbose.

As a university student in England in 1969, I and my then husband visited Lawrence's hometown of Eastwood, outside Nottingham. We walked the back lanes and peered into the yards of the appallingly ugly tenement row houses where he'd grown up. We met an old man who remembered Lawrence and his girlfriend, Jessie Chambers. I can still see that old man leaning confidently toward me, breathing into my ear: "Don't you think Lawrence was a sex maniac?"

When Juan and I were travelling through Tuscany on a pleasure trip thirty-four years later, I stumbled on a copy of Lawrence's *Etruscan Places* in a bookstore in Siena. The painting on the cover pulled me in: an Etruscan man in profile, his left hand touching his head, five fingers spread as if drawing out his own thoughts, and his right hand stretched in front of him in a gesture of either blessing or warning. He seemed to be in a kind of trance. With his unkempt red beard and fiercely gentle eyes, he resembled the author. So I bought the book, determined to follow Lawrence in his quest for the Etruscans.

I bought a guidebook as well, and the necessary maps. We drove along the coastal highway south from Grosseto. Factories and high-rise apartments edged onto the grey-black lava sand. The sea was flat and the coast forlorn, a shock after the beauties of Tuscany. We exited at Tuscania and found ourselves an agriturismo, one of those farms or vineyards refurbished to accommodate tourists. Through an olive grove and past a barnyard menagerie of lethargic pigs was our little bungalow with a plaster Virgin in the driveway. Our room was decorated with pink chintz, and the lamps had skirted ladies holding up naked light bulbs. The proprietress was very sweet, but she spoke no English. Whenever we wanted anything, we waited while she scurried across the courtyard to find a neighbour to translate.

The next morning when I hunted for my tourist paraphernalia, it had all disappeared. No guidebook, no map, no phrase book. These items had apparently fallen out of the car, or simply been sucked into the black hole of misplaced objects. We were travelling blind without language.

Our host brought out a hand-drawn mimeographed map that told us nothing. "Go," she commanded, as if she longed to see the backs of us. Our destination was the Palazzo Vitelleschi in the main square of Tarquinia, but I didn't want a museum experience. I wanted to visit the Etruscan tombs, to walk into them as Lawrence had. "Ah, then," said the museum attendant, "just follow the highway out of town and keep going."

I already knew a bit about the mysterious Etruscans. If they weren't autochthonous, as some anthropologists suggest, they probably came from the eastern Mediterranean, possibly Asia Minor, and established themselves on the Italian peninsula somewhere between the tenth and ninth century BCE. They were a sophisticated people, with an alphabet based on the Greek alphabet, a powerfully original artistic tradition, a religion based on anthropomorphic gods, and a complicated set of ritual sacrifices for divining the future. And — perhaps this is why I remember those old anthropology lessons — they treated men and women as equals.

As we drove north, I reread the first sentence of Lawrence's book: "The Etruscans, as everyone knows, were the people who occupied the middle of Italy in early Roman days and whom the Romans, in their usual neighbourly fashion, wiped out entirely to make room for Rome with a very big R." He was on a rant about the Romans—those militaristic, puritanical, life-hating exterminators, models of the rationalist system builders and ideologues he so hated. It didn't matter to me that he wasn't exactly accurate—it was the Greeks who first defeated the Etruscans, who were probably the aggressors, and the early Christians who destroyed what remained of their "heathen" literature. But I wasn't reading Lawrence for history. The Etruscans in his book were his own invention, a marvellous and mythic embodiment of what human beings might be if they lived a fully conscious, passionate life.

"Perhaps the tombs are on the other side of Tuscania," I said. Soon we found ourselves trapped in the labyrinthine medieval streets of the next town, Viterbo, and only because Juan has the instincts of a homing pigeon were we able to extricate ourselves. We tried a side road toward hills that surely would contain tombs. Very soon the road became a rutted dirt track, and we were driving blindly through a field of corn six feet high. We turned back. In town once again, we went the wrong way down a one-way street and were pulled over by a policewoman. As I stammered pathetically that I didn't speak Italian and was looking for the tombs, she threw up her hands with that exquisite contempt only beautiful Italian women have mastered and waved us on. Juan was getting impatient. "Why not quit now?" he asked. I replied desperately: "You don't understand. This isn't just tourism. I'm following Lawrence."

The next morning, we went back to the Palazzo Vitelleschi and this time looked around. It is a spectacular museum, filled, as Lawrence put it, "with things rifled from the tombs." Endless rooms with glass cases of amphorae decorated with boxing scenes and chariot races, bronze banquet vessels, gold jewellery, mirrors, even wood and bronze sandals —stacked like objects in an ancient shopping mall, too numerous to hold in the mind and eventually rather tedious to look at. But then on the top floor we found a precise reconstruction of one of the ancient tombs. It was breathtaking. I suddenly understood why Lawrence had been so excited when he visited them.

"No," the museum attendant said, "not north. Go west out of town."
We'd been going the wrong way. West we went, and finally we saw a
little cardboard sign with a crayoned arrow that read: The Etruscan
Tomb. We parked and set out on a hike down a hill through apartment
complexes to a park. Beyond a locked fence was a German beer hall and
the entrance to the Etruscan Tomb. Closed for the season. We got back
to the highway, but my disappointment was so palpable Juan softened.
"Let's just go west a few more kilometres," he said. And there, within a
stone's throw, were the telltale roadside kiosks selling Etruscan tchotch-
kes. Passing through a turnstile onto the site, we were handed a crude
map of the two dozen excavated tombs. Nothing could have been easier.
I felt sure Lawrence was making me pay the modern equivalent of the
effort it took him to get here seventy-five years ago.

In the necropolis of Monterozzi outside Tarquinia, the oldest tomb
dates back to the sixth century BCE and was excavated in 1827, but
archaeologists can say little of the people who were buried here, beyond
the fact that these were obviously the tombs of the elite. When Lawrence
visited in 1927, his journey to the Maremma Coast, as the area is known,
lasted a mere six days, but he had read everything there was to read
about the elusive Etruscans. The area was still a wasteland, and he was
one of the first tourists. With his American companion Earl Brewster,
he had taken the train from Rome and then the omnibus from the
station up through the gates into the walled city of Tarquinia. Only one
of two modern houses sat outside the ramparts. The Palazzo Vitelleschi
was, even then, a museum, though somewhat battered, and there was
only one inn, with most of the rooms occupied by the fascist blackshirts
Lawrence detested. Alberto, the twelve-year-old boy who ran the hotel
in the seeming absence of any adults, assured his guests that the walls
were so thin that they would feel neither lonely nor frightened at night.
In the morning, the two men found a guide with a dog and trekked out
to the tombs.

I wonder what it would have been like to walk with Lawrence across
those fields. In his system, things fitted—or they didn't. "I was thinking," he says, setting out, "this would be a sacred clearing with a little
temple to keep it alert. Myself, I like to think of the little temples of the
Etruscans; small, dainty, fragile, and evanescent as flowers. We have

reached the stage when we are weary of huge stone erections, and we begin to realize that it is better to keep life fluid and changing than to try to hold it fast with heavy monuments. Burdens on the face of the earth are man's ponderous erections.... Even Michelangelo becomes at last a lump and a burden and a bore. It is so hard to see past him." Lawrence's outrageousness is part of his genius.

It was not caves I should have been hunting for but mounds. They looked like giant molehills covering chambers that had been dug into the earth about twelve feet deep. There was the odour of dank cement as I climbed down the concrete steps and sat on the bottom one facing a small glass door. Above my head was a light switch, the kind that used to be found in the hallways of cheap hotels. They turned on the electricity just long enough for you to get your key into the lock before you were plunged back into darkness.

I pushed the button, and a tiny room about five feet wide and twelve feet long with a peaked roof emerged. The walls were covered with drawings and the ceiling with painted tiles. I had entered the Tomb of the Leopards, so called because of a frieze of two spotted leopards facing each other in the peaked tympanum on the back wall.

Men and women stretched out on couches in animated conversations, their gestures so natural that they seemed to be momentarily frozen in the glare of the light. The handsome men were naked to the waist, their skin a gorgeous brown. The women had complexions as pale as water, and the drapery of their almost transparent dresses looked so fresh they might have put them on that morning. Naked youths carried amphorae of wine to the tables. On side panels, musicians moved through shrubbery, one playing a double flute, the other a lute. Their knee-length robes of yellow and burnt sienna trimmed in cobalt blue seemed to float lightly on the breeze. I had never imagined such gaiety in a tomb.

I climbed down into a second tomb and sat entranced. It was the Tomb of Hunting and Fishing. Though damp and mould had destroyed the edges of the murals, the figures were still clear and the colours stunning. On the sea floated a small boat, from which three men fished while one stood naked, aiming his slingshot toward a sky filled with birds. Some of the birds were drawn in detail while others were just a

Wall fresco of dancer in the Tomb
of the Augurs, Etruscan Necropolis
of Tarquinia, Italy, 525 – 500 BCE
(photographer unknown)

suggestion of wings. They were a beautiful cerulean blue against a pale white sky, while the men were bright ochre. From just the suggestion of a cliff, a naked diver floated down vertically with such grace I caught my breath. In the tympanum above, the Etruscans banqueted.

In the third tomb, the Tomb of the Bulls, the central panel depicted a man on horseback. The horse was drawn with dazzling simplicity. Pure white with a black mane, it was so tall it dwarfed its naked rider. Its giant nostrils were drawing huge drafts of air into its cavernous chest. The legs were straight and delicate. It would have bounded like a deer had it moved.

Now I understood why, for Lawrence, the Etruscans embodied the Life Force. "For them," he wrote, "all was alive; the whole universe lived; and the business of man was to live amid it all. He had to draw life into himself, out of the wandering huge vitalities of the world. Every creature and tree and lake and mountain and stream was animate, had its own peculiar consciousness."

I followed a well-worn path down the side of the hill. Flowering clumps of yellow asphodel blanketed the ground, the thick perfume hanging like musk on the sea air. This next tomb had no steps, and I walked straight into it between high stone walls. On the front panel was the head of a girl in profile wearing a wreath of crown of leaves. The

Tomb of Orcus is the only tomb to carry the name of its occupant, and I was almost shocked to recall that these small exquisite chambers once contained corpses.

I spent all afternoon popping in and out of the ground. Sometimes, exhausted, I would sit reading Lawrence's book, imagining him here. He loved these drawings. And he loved the people who produced them, the fact that they preferred the charming to the monumental. "To face life with natural humour," he wrote, "is a task surely more worthy, and even more difficult in the long run, than conquering the world or sacrificing the self or saving the immortal soul." He loved the Etruscans because they were filled with the ripple of life—fluid, changing, spontaneous. He found great consolation among them.

And he needed consolation because, as Brewster wrote in letters to friends back home, Lawrence was dying. These walks over the hills surrounding Tuscania would be the last long walks he would take.

Which makes *Etruscan Places* a revelation of sorts. There is no faking here. Lawrence was rehearsing his own death with equanimity. Many of the tympana in the tombs contain a repetitive frieze of heraldic beasts facing each other across an altar, a tree, or a vase. The deer and the leopard, the goat and the lion, the dove and the cat. These, Lawrence remarked, represented the polarized activity of the cosmos in equilibrium: creation and destruction. "The fertile, gentle creatures, guardians of the treasures of life, were always in conflict with the tearers asunder of those that must depart from life." He was departing. But like the Etruscans, he insisted on celebrating the divine cosmos. So enamoured was he of life that he could forgive it his own death.

We made our way back to Tarquinia. With its crumbling walls and tacky shops, it now seemed more real than some of the manicured perfection of Tuscany. Near the ramparts we found a restaurant that looked out over a landscape of churches and wheat-covered fields as tranquil as any I remember. The swallows, turning their blue backs to us, skimmed over the air in dizzying circles, and the yellow light of evening spilled over the long flat grass only to climb up the stone quarry in the distance.

Guthrie family farmhouse near Smiths Falls, Ontario, ca. 1910.
Grandma Guthrie is on the left; her daughter Mary, with her siblings,
is on the right. (Sullivan family archive)

THE TRAIL THAT LED TO ME, 2006

One day in 2006, I got a phone call from Marty Gervais, whose press, Black Moss, had published three books of my poetry, as well as *Molito*, the kids' book Juan and I wrote together. He said that his Irish patrons were funding a lecture on Irish writers. Would I give it? I told him I loved Irish literature, but I was no expert. I joked that I could give a talk about growing up Irish. "That's perfect," he said. What follows is the meditation I wrote on ancestry and family, which I eventually expanded into my book *The Guthrie Road*.

...

For years I thought I knew what home was, but I've since discovered it is not a place at all, not even a landscape. It's the strangers I carry in my blood.

I learned this from my aunt Mary, a one-room schoolteacher from Picton, Ontario, who, one day in her seventies, with arthritic hands, decided to write the family history. Though she'd been there all along, I really only discovered Mary at the end of her life. In the early days of my childhood at the end of the 1950s, the nostalgic days of family values, we made one trip a year to visit family.

My father owned a car, always a second-hand car with a radiator that blew on long-distance journeys. Every year during his two-week vacation, we'd set out for Smiths Falls to visit my mother's mother, who, by then, had given up her farm. The trip to Grandma's was a full-day's journey on a narrow two-lane highway with a stop for a picnic lunch. Fast-food restaurants hadn't yet been invented.

They were scary to me, those relatives we visited. My grandmother was a matriarch; she seemed to me as tough as the barbed wire she'd once strung around the homestead she'd somehow managed to save after her husband died at the age of forty-five, leaving her with eleven children and pregnant. When the child was born, she called her Joy. My mother was only two when her father died, but she said her mother always spoke of him lovingly.

There were strict rules to be kept at my grandmother's, and my mother was always struggling to hold her wild daughters in check. Great Uncle Willie lived with Grandma, and we had to be quiet since he seemed always to be asleep in the front room in the leather armchair, his silver watch chain rising and falling over his paunch, his black vest stained with snuff. The best times were when we went to visit the home of Aunt Lizzy Bluett—how we loved that name—and she would spread a feast of fresh vegetables and pies over the huge harvest table. But to us children these people all seemed old and frail and like phantoms, surfacing in our lives for only two weeks every summer.

In my memory we went to visit my mother's older sister, Mary, just once in all those early years. She and her husband, Nellis, had a farm in Napanee. There would have been only three of us children then; two were not yet born. In a photo I have we're standing in bathing suits and caps in front of the farmhouse facing the lake, me with one arm stretched protectively around the shoulder of my older sister, Patricia, the other hand on my baby sister Sharon's head. I had already assumed the protective stance, since I was the one who knew the world was dangerous, but I was still confident I could beat it up if it came too close. We'd never seen a farm before and we went wild, jumping from the high rafters into the hayloft and pestering the horses. Mary called us hoodlums and said we'd scared the cows from their milk. My mother was highly insulted, and we never went back again.

I thought it was because nobody in the family approved of Nellis. He was eight years younger than Mary, and they said he'd never worked at a proper job. He kept the farm haphazardly, occasionally drove a taxi, played the fiddle, and hunted bears. Everyone felt sorry for Mary, who had to teach school and earn all the money. But all along Nellis had been haunting local auction sales and filling his barn with what the family referred to as "Nellis's junk." When he died suddenly of a heart attack, he left more than a hundred thousand dollars he'd squirrelled away from selling that junk. Two days before he died, he sold the old violins he'd collected, some dating back fifty years. We went to the funeral for Mary's sake, but the man in the coffin with the grey hair that still sat up in a cowlick was a stranger to the rest of us.

Every Christmas there were Mary's letters and Grandma Guthrie's frozen turkey with molasses cookies sent by express rail, but we so seldom saw those members of my family that my idea of family never stretched beyond my mother and father and, by now, the five of us children. Then, gradually, the world changed, and people travelled in fast cars on six-lane highways with restaurants, but by that time all these strangers were either dead or in old folks' homes.

I found Aunt Mary in Hay Bay Rest Home in 1985. When I asked my mother's advice about a present, she suggested I buy Mary a pair of soft-soled shoes. When I gave them to her, Mary said she hoped I hadn't paid a lot for them because she wouldn't have time to wear them out. Then she gave me the family history she'd written out in longhand in her perfect schoolmarm script, eighty pages illustrated with daguerreotypes and photos dating back to 1847, when the Irish Morrisons had fled the potato famine. And there they were, all the phantoms I had been afraid of in my childhood.

When I was in my early twenties searching out literary shrines—were those dead writers a kind of family?—I'd been to Sligo to visit Yeats's grave, not knowing at the time that my great-great-grandmother Mary Morrison had buried two children in the same cemetery before despair sent her in quest of a new and more just world. In her book, Mary imagined her great-grandfather Darby Morrison speaking to his wife: "They're saying in Sligo Bay we can go to Canada, Mary. The Flahertys, the O'Gradys, and the MacNamaras are leaving. The government pays the passage. They owe us. Two's enough to bury."

Mary Morrison was forty-five and pregnant with Bridget when she crossed the ocean. You can be that tough, I guess, with nothing left to lose. They used to say in the family that Bridget crossed the ocean but never saw the water. When the Morrisons arrived at the Port of Montréal they were met by a British government agent. Aunt Mary saved the deeds indicating they were awarded two hundred acres of uncleared land in Smiths Falls, Ontario, a cow, a pig, a plough, an axe, a shovel, and seed to sow in order to start life as pioneers in the new world. It was not a generous endowment. The limestone plain around Smiths Falls was sour land, as the locals called it. Almost impossible to scrape a living from it. But the Morrisons carved out a life among the rocks of Smiths Falls that laid a faint trail through the bush that eventually led to me.

It's curious to read a story and know it's your story. Not just written for you, but maybe even explaining you. As I read it, it is Mary who surfaces from its pages. She had gathered the family history from her father's mother, Catherine Morrison. When Mary was a child, they would go to her farm and sit with her in the evenings. Mary especially remembered the look of contentment on her father's face as he turned the wagon onto the side road that led to his mother's house. She said: "His heart was always at the old homestead." Clearly, she adored her father.

Trussed up in the kitchen rocker in front of the open stove, Great-Grandma Morrison would get out her basket of pictures and tell the stories of the people in them, and sometimes she would recount some of the old Irish tales. I can almost see them all sitting there before the open wood fire. Almost one hundred years later, when I finally went to Ireland and tracked down lost cousins, we sat before a similar kitchen stove with our Irish whiskey, and the neighbors came from miles around bringing gifts of white heather and more family stories.

Mary said she kept the stories for the edification of the younger generation. "Perhaps some of the stories may help some members of the family to make a right decision which will bring happiness and contentment," she wrote in her preface. For her, it seems life was a matter of right decisions.

To Mary, every life was a story. Her great-grandmother Mary Morrison and her husband, Darby, had ten children, including Annie, Saul, Bridget, Jeremiah, Sara, and Catherine; the youngest was born in 1855, when Mary Morrison was fifty-three. My aunt tells each of their stories, and I discover her great-uncles, the ones who went off to the American lumber camps or became volunteers in the Boer War. She tells about Great-Uncle Saul's soldier's uniform that was kept for years up on a kitchen shelf at the old farm until one day her mother cut it up to make a pair of red boots for my aunt Kay, who was then a toddler, and everyone superstitiously expected the sky to fall down because it seemed a sacrilege to turn a soldier's uniform into baby boots. It was Saul who bequeathed his two hundred acres on Georgian Bay to my grandfather, who traded them to the Massey-Harris dealers for a grain binder and ever after said his binder cost a farm.

Aunt Mary was too honest to leave out the black sheep. There was the story of Great-Aunt Annie whose husband, William Blake, drank too much. On a drunken binge he came home and killed Annie and her daughter and hanged himself the next morning. The son, Willie, somehow managed to escape the slaughter. He made a life as a cook on the boats that travelled the Rideau River, often living at the Guthrie farm to help out when he wasn't on the river. He was a good cook and a fastidious housekeeper. Mary and her siblings didn't like him because he was always making them "put things up," and once they snuck into his room and cut up his fancy ties. And got a birching for it. Her father hid Willie's whisky in the potato bin next to the hive of bees in the cellar where he knew Willie, afraid of all insects, would never look for it, but he would produce the bottle when Willie got "restless." There was Annie's brother Jeremiah, who, in his teens, got the hiccups and couldn't stop and died within the week. Annie's sister Sara began to "fail" in her early teens and "faded away and died." It must have been TB, but the stoic tenderness of that ghostly fading lingered in my aunt Mary's mind.

My favourite is Mary Morrison's daughter Bridget, the pretty one, who always worked in the fields in her bare feet. (She's in my blood somewhere; I too can't stand shoes.) When she was twenty-one she went with her mother to a vaudeville show in Smiths Falls. One of the "showmen" fell in love with her, and, though she gave him "no encouragement," he stuck like glue. Her father said no showman was going to call on his daughter, but the man persuaded Brid to go with him to the fair in Perth. In the tearoom of the local hotel, he proposed. When she refused, he spiked her tea with poison, vowing if she didn't marry him, she would never marry anyone. With Brid unconscious on the floor, he saw his "work accomplished." He was never heard of again.

Mary said the showman had used too much poison, and Brid had vomited it up. This saved her. The family eventually tracked her down and brought her home, but she was always referred to as "simple Aunt Brid" after that, and she would spend days at a time sitting and staring into space. Of course, I wonder if Mary couldn't resist a good story, and if so, what moral she intended for me. At least I've never been seduced by a circus man.

Catherine, Mary and Darby Morrison's last daughter, is the one I find most fascinating. Beautiful in the Irish way, with straight black hair that reached below her waist and "flashing" black eyes, she was her father's favourite. She hated domestic work and could be found out in the fields ploughing with the men. According to Mary she was high-spirited, outspoken, and vain. She regarded men as a sort of "legal prey," and when Gentleman Guthrie came along, he didn't stand a chance. Her sister Brid would tease her: "Watch for Gentleman Guthrie to come a-calling with his prancing black horses and fine carriage and his silk top hat and gold-headed cane."

Douglas Guthrie, then forty-five and widowed, was a stone mason. The marriage wasn't a happy one. Catherine used to say she couldn't walk, talk, dress, or do anything to suit her husband, nor his many children who were her own age. After two years and the birth of her son, my grandfather Jeremiah, she headed back to the farm. When she decided to return to town, she found the stone mason's house was locked up; he'd gone out West. He'd bought her a small house and, through a lawyer, had left her a small annuity. She never saw him again.

Her child became her project. She would educate Jeremiah — education provided "the wings to get away." She worked as a cook at the Arlington Hotel in Smiths Falls and, later, on the tourist boats travelling through the Thousand Islands and plotted her son's escape from that narrow life. She bought him a bicycle so that, if his father ever returned to reclaim him, he could cycle away. In his teens my grandfather became national cycling champion for Canada. But in his twenties, Jeremiah thwarted her desires — he upped and married a Protestant wife. Despite her independence, Catherine remained a staunch Irish Catholic and never accepted her daughter-in-law nor ever forgave her son.

I find some of Catherine's stubbornness amusing. In 1905 her wealthy American cousin Daniel Grady invited her to join him in Providence, Rhode Island. Having made his money in cement, he was by then widowed and looking for another wife. Renting herself some fine jewellery on a six-month trial—why buy when the future was uncertain?—Catherine headed south. But she soon found the rich life smothering. She couldn't stand how the day was laid out in dresses: in the morning she was expected to have a bath, then put on a special gown to comb her hair, then a breakfast gown, a street dress to go to market, an afternoon shopping dress, and then a fancy dress for dinner. Every day was planned for her! Catherine headed home.

I think Catherine's independence, finding no outlet, turned sour. She disinherited her son for marrying the Protestant and willed the small property she had left to his child, her grandson.

The more I read the family stories, the more real my ancestors become, and even though I have only met them through Mary's eyes, I am now very fond of them. This poem was written for Mary in 1987. It's rather gothic, but that was my mood then. I guess I was talking about the mystery of identity. How much of who we are is a product of our own choices? How much is determined by genetic makeup? How much am I the creation of all those strangers in Mary's story, whose lives wove the complex web in which my own life began?

I once asked Mary if she would consider publishing her book, but she said, "The problem with books, Rosemary, is that people can read them the way they want to." The book was written for the family. Strangers might misread it. But I admire my ancestors, their toughness, their humour, their sheer will for survival. And I am no longer fearful of them. In fact, I hope to spend more time unearthing these phantoms I hear calling in my blood.

WORDS
Aunt Mary used to warn me about words.
They never stay where you put them.
They're loose.
Any no-good can use them.

Like a woman, she tried
To keep them safe in the family.

Family was her story that added down to me
— always fenced with a lesson:
Words break loose if you let them.

She stored the family photos in a basket.
Trussed up in her rocker, warty as any gourd,
each night her hands plunged the corridors of blood.
I knew she was hooked on danger.

She could go all the way back to wind,
how it falls and picks itself up in a field.
Or fog empties a valley til all you see
is your hands where the world was.

From her I learned there were others
pacing inside me.
She said they had made me up.
I was meant to love them.

But it terrified me to think I was lived in
by strangers I had never met
or knew only by name.
They made me alien fiction.

In my bones
an old woman dies over and over,
I dare not look
in the room with the blooded axe
nor speak to the men who walked out.
Their tracks in my blood. Their lust
for edges.

I could spend
a lifetime digging graves
in my head.

—

I have a photograph of my grandmother, Lottie Guthrie, surrounded by her ten children. It must be about 1925. It is summer. They are standing in the orchard. She is not smiling, but I have never seen a photograph of my grandmother smiling. She is simply there, as rooted as a tree, a hub holding her children together like spokes on a wheel. They are a handsome bunch, the boys in shirts and neckties, the girls in dresses. They look happy, even prosperous. It took discipline to pull this off; it took fortitude; it took love.

After her husband died, my grandmother continued to work the farm with the help of her two bachelor sons until the late 1940s. Her eight daughters left to become secretaries, nurses, or teachers. Aunt Mary, who had no children of her own, kept up a voluminous correspondence with her siblings. I remember that when we phoned her at the old folks home to tell her that her younger brother Malcolm had died unexpectedly, after a routine operation, she cut us off before we had a chance to say anything: "I know why you've called," she said. "I know Malcolm is dead. He was just here." I believed her.

As I was writing these family stories, I had the strangest dream. I was walking in a forest. There were others with me, though I didn't know precisely who they were. As we moved through the dark, we came upon a clearing in the centre of which were two circles of light. They looked like fluorescent tubes, about ninety centimeters in diameter, glowing with a green light. As soon as I saw them, I had a euphoric sense of well-being. That was all. I woke up.

Whatever those circles were, they had to do with family. As I think of them now, I imagine that all families are closed circles, completely knowable only to those who live within them. And yet, however inaccessible they are to those who follow after, they are the source from which we take our being. We turn to them hoping to solve the mystery that is ourselves.

MARSEILLE AND THE VILLA AIR-BEL, 2007

To find the book you are destined to write is a slow process. A book moves in on you and occupies you. After having written eleven books, I can almost say a book finds you.

By serendipity, I read *A Quiet American* (1999), Andy Marino's excellent biography of a man called Varian Fry. A friend had passed the book to me saying it was a good read. A photograph reprinted in it immediately caught my attention.

In the photograph a man and a woman perch precariously in the branches of a plane tree. The caption reads: "Varian Fry and Consuelo de Saint-Exupéry at Villa Air-Bel, 1940 or 1941." Consuelo was the wife of Antoine de Saint-Exupéry, the dashing pilot and author of *The Little Prince*. She and Fry were hanging paintings in the branches of the tree. What intrigued me was the frivolity of this activity in the midst of danger. Outside the photo's frame, the Vichy police and even the German Kundt Commission were arresting people.

The Villa Air-Bel, located in the suburbs of Marseille, was an imposing three-storey house with a stone terrace running its length, and extensive gardens. During the war it provided refuge to artists waiting for exit visas out of France and for emergency rescue visas to any country willing to accept them. The villa was also the residence of Fry and a number of young people from the Emergency Rescue Committee who were working to save the artists.

I had been struggling over how to write about Varian Fry and his rescue committee in a way that would be new (there was already a biography), and it suddenly occurred to me that the Villa Air-Bel was the core of my story. The villa could become almost a character. I had to visit it.

In 2004 I travelled to Marseille in search of the villa. In the taxi on the way to the suburb where the villa was located, the driver warned me that I was visiting a banlieue chaude, a hot, dangerous neighbourhood. Muslim immigrants from North Africa had moved into the area, which was now clustered with tenements. The villa itself had been torn down and replaced with a nursing home. All that was left where the villa had once stood in the 1940s were three plane trees.

But the adjacent building, called the Castellan, the groundskeeper's house, was still there. The main floor was a tiny, improvised museum of sorts with imitation Calder mobiles dangling from the ceiling and photographs of Max Ernst on the walls. On the second floor local Muslim students had installed a small radio station. When I told them I wanted to write a book about the Villa Air-Bel, they were thrilled and insisted on interviewing me. I thought how very pleased Varian Fry, who had dedicated his life to saving refugees, would have been to see these young Muslim students honouring his legacy.

I walked the streets of Marseille in the company of shadows. I sought out the office Fry had set up in the rundown rue Grignan, now lined with fashionable shops. I sat in sidewalk cafés in the Vieux-Port, though the old ones where Fry and his group had met had changed their names or disappeared. I walked through the squares where the roundups and arrests took place. I sat in the Bouches-du-Rhône Archives reading police reports. In one a policeman reported how a young Jew had locked himself in his room; when they broke down the door, they discovered he had slit his throat. They carried him to the hospital to repair him so that he could be sent to a concentration camp in the east.

As I got down to work on the book, the questions accumulated. Who were the artists at the Villa Air-Bel, and how did they get caught in the deadly web of war? How did they not see the war coming and escape in time? Did they refuse to believe war could happen, or did they believe that, if it did come, it could only touch others? Nameless, abstract others.

And who were the young rescuers at the villa? What convinces young people to risk their lives saving others? Is it a matter of temperament, or does this transformation happen gradually, by a series of spontaneous decisions, until there is no other choice, until the risk has already been taken?

Wars build slowly, cumulatively, often years before the history books date their beginnings. In Europe, long before the bombs fell and soldiers and civilians died, long before extermination camps did their work of horror, there was the war of nerves, the propaganda war fought for people's minds. Despite the stories that are told in retrospect, where everything is clear and predictable, it is never easy to decipher where the real enemy is or who will be the victim. In France, the illusion of normalcy was sustained for years. And then, in a matter of weeks, the world collapsed like a burnt husk. Millions of people were blindsided. Despite the ominous signs, they could not believe a world war could happen. Not a second time.

In France in 1940, people soon learned how quickly everything could change. Suddenly destinies ceased to be a matter of personal control. The life and death of any individual became merely something to be haggled over in bureaucratic ministries: who was an alien, who should be imprisoned as an enemy alien, who should be deported to certain death? Not chance, not contingency, but someone else, a stranger, arbitrarily decided who lived and who died.

I wanted to ask what it feels like to move from freedom to occupation: to feel threatened, administered, restrained? Suddenly bits of bureaucratic paper control one's life and death. The words *forbidden, investigated, imprisoned* enter one's vocabulary and everything is uncertain — life, home, children, lovers. All can be taken away or left behind.

The story of World War II has been told thousands of times. It is one of our core stories. How could I make my version new and immediate? I decided to begin the book with a dinner party. In the fall of 1940 twelve people sit around the dinner table at Villa Air-Bel — the artists and the young rescuers who are attempting to save them. These people would provide the thread of my narrative.

But I needed to go much further back in order to examine how wars happen. I began the narrative in 1932, when one of the young Americans who eventually worked with Fry arrived in France. Then I followed two stories: the web of connections that brought these people together at the dinner party, and the story of how war creeps up slowly, inexorably. Even if you see it coming, you are paralyzed. You cannot imagine what can be done to stop it. Even as you sense the danger, war remains a phantom threat. Until it happens.

As I wrote *Villa Air-Bel: World War II, Escape, and a House in Marseille,* I discovered how much of my own experience informed its subtext. I had lived in Dijon and Bordeaux in 1972–74 and was fascinated by the legacy of World War II and, in particular, by the French Resistance. My ninety-year-old neighbour in the adjacent échoppe — I called her Notre Dame des Fleurs after Jean Genet — had been a clandestine radio operator during the war. We often talked about her "work."

But my mind also flew back to Chile in 1985, when we visited the home of the young students in Talca and they'd shown us their subversive, treasured books. I remembered their sudden terror when they asked Juan to tell them how the dictatorship started and he'd replied, "Who do you think I am?" That moment, when the world turned from amicable comfort to nightmare, permanently grafted itself onto my mind. That was the feeling I wanted to reproduce in *Villa Air-Bel.*

To know who this man Varian Fry was, I travelled to New York to read the enormous correspondence and official documents in the Varian Fry collection at Columbia University. Only then did I have a sense of his extraordinary stamina and stubbornness. I read his letters home to his wife and parents; his indignant correspondence with officials; his letters back to France after the Vichy government expelled him. I saw how he continued to work tirelessly for certain refugees, even after all hope was lost. The man emerged as a real person to me, someone I seemed to know.

I remember my excitement when I received copies of correspondence by André Breton, Benjamin Péret, Max Ernst, Peggy Guggenheim, and others sent in manila envelopes from the SUNY Albany library, the Houghton Library, Yale's Irving S. Gilmore Music Library, or the Getty Research Institute, each containing voices out of the past. But the most extraordinary experience was receiving the correspondence of Victor Serge, whose papers are housed at Manuscripts and Archives, Yale University Library.

Serge was one of the people who sat at the dinner table at Villa Air-Bel. His efforts to escape France were the most desperate. I had read his *Memoirs of a Revolutionary* and knew his story. He was born in Belgium and travelled to Russia as a young man to fight in the Russian Revolution. But it did not take him long to see that, under Stalin, Russia had turned into "the most terrifying State machine conceivable." Serge was probably the first to call the Soviet Union a totalitarian state. For his dedication to truth, he spent years in exile in Siberia before he was finally released and fled to France. Trapped in Marseille in 1940, he waited for Fry to secure emergency rescue visas for him and his family. But he never received them. This fiercest of anti-communists was never allowed into the United States on the grounds that he had once been a Communist.

I had written to Yale requesting copies of the correspondence between Serge and his American supporters Nancy and Dwight Macdonald between 1938 and 1942. One day two huge padded envelopes arrived in the mail. They contained about eight hundred pages, so many letters that I had to seek the help of a friend in translating Serge's side of the correspondence. I read avidly. Through these letters I felt more deeply than from any other source the desperation, fear, and hunger that was the life of a refugee in Marseille — not second-hand through books but from Serge's own candid words to his friends.

Under the Freedom of Information Act, I had earlier applied to the FBI for the file on Victor Serge that I knew must exist. I had to wait a year, but again a large manila envelope arrived at my door. The 331 pages of material it contained were shocking. There were copies of some of the private letters between Serge and the Macdonalds that I had just read. There were also surveillance reports by agents and copies of interviews they had done with Serge. The FBI hounded the man from the moment his first letters to the Macdonalds brought him to the Bureau's attention until the day he died in Mexico in 1947. I felt a terrible sadness for the sufferings of this extraordinary man.

I sought out Serge's son, Vlady, who had been twenty when he resided with his father at the Villa Air-Bel. He was now one of Mexico's most colourful artists. Apart from André Breton's daughter, Aube, who was a young child at the time, Vlady was the last witness of daily life at the villa. We corresponded and had several amusing phone conversations in Spanish and French.

I made arrangements for Juan and me to visit him at his home in Cuernavaca. The very night we arrived and phoned Vlady's residence, I was informed that he'd just suffered a stroke and had been rushed to hospital in Mexico City. We left Mexico shortly thereafter. I did not want to disturb the family's grief. Vlady died within the week.

I knew I needed to spend more time in France, and so I applied to the Camargo Foundation for a residency in the fishing village of Cassis, just outside of Marseille. Jerome Hill, an American filmmaker and artist and the son of a railway magnate, had bought the property and turned it into a foundation. The main building had once housed Napoleon's troops, and adjacent buildings were scattered about the property. I had asked for an apartment for Juan and me. When I arrived, the director greeted me in a thick French accent: "Ah, Madame Sullivan. Everyone will hate you. You have the best apartment."

And indeed, we did. Our building abutted the sea, and sometimes the waves of the Mediterranean lapped against its bricks. Our bedroom had a terrace overlooking the water, a living room with a fireplace, a stately ground-level entrance onto a foyer, and a desk in an alcove where I could work on my book.

Juan had just completed a sound engineering and film course at Trebas Institute in Toronto. He was intrigued by the story of the villa.

"Why don't we make a film?" he asked.

"Why not?" I replied.

His film opened in Marseille in front of the city's infamous carousel, and the soundtrack was carousel music. I was narrating. At the Villa Air-Bel I sat under the three plane trees and contemplated Fry's story. We visited many sites: the Camps des Milles, where the artist Max Ernst was interned in 1939 and again in 1940, along with other German refugees in flight from the Nazis; the home of Max Ernst and Leonora Carrington when they were lovers in Saint Martin d'Ardèche and had covered the external walls of their house with exotic sculptures. I quickly sent Leonora photos of the house.

We drove to Oppède-le-Vieux where Consuelo de Saint-Exupéry had hidden out after she'd left Air-Bel. Then we followed the secret escape route set up by Hans and Lisa Fittko from Banyuls-sur-Mer across the Pyrenees to Portbou in Spain. Fry had sent many desperate refugees to the Fittkos to guide by foot over this precipitous mountain pass. We stayed at the rundown Hôtel de la Loge in Perpignan, where Fry had spent five days while he awaited his forced deportation from France in early September 1941. On this pilgrimage, it always struck me how thinly the skin of the present lay over the frightening past.

On the one hand it was a wonderful adventure: I driving as Juan leaned out of the car window with his camera. He called himself Jean Luc Picante, and I was his assistant, Philippe Raton. But it was also heartbreaking. We ended the trip (and the film) at the grave of Walter Benjamin. When he'd been stopped by the Spanish border guards and threatened with deportation back to France, Benjamin had committed suicide. On his grave is written: "There is no document of civilization that is not at the same time a document of barbarism." A steep shaft of covered stairs leads down the cliff face to the water and ends in a glass wall through which you look out to the oblivion of the Mediterranean. It is one of the most powerful monuments to Europe's refugees that I have seen.

Back in Toronto, Juan finished his film, a fifteen-minute masterpiece that exactly caught the feeling of the time. I always aired it at my book launches and readings.

...

When a writer sends his or her published book out into the silence, it is impossible to predict the impact it will have. You wait for the reviews, of course, but more meaningful are the personal letters that come like missives out of the darkness, making the years of work worthwhile.

In the early 1940s, the Mexican government had been generous in accepting refugees. In the course of my research I visited Mexico several times. This was how I met Walter Gruen. Gruen had been the husband of the Catalan painter Remedios Varo, who had spent time at the Villa Air-Bel in 1940 before fleeing to Mexico, where she befriended the painter Leonora Carrington. Varo died tragically in 1962. On one of my visits, Walter and his second wife, Alexandra, invited me to dinner at an Argentinean restaurant in downtown Mexico City. As we emerged from the restaurant, we encountered a man with his dog, a Rottweiler: black, broad-shouldered, with brutal teeth. The dog was straining fiercely at its leash, as if about to pounce. Alexandra and Walter froze, and Walter said, "Alexandra doesn't like those dogs. They used them in the camps." The simplicity of his remark moved me deeply. *The Pianist* was playing in the local cinema. I asked him, "Can you see films like this?" With a catch in his breath, he said, "No."

Later I learned Walter Gruen's story. As a stateless refugee, he had been imprisoned in an internment camp but was released in 1939, one year after the Anschluss. The Swiss Red Cross visited the camp and was authorized to release some prisoners. "I never knew why they let me out," he said. He remembered two brothers in the camp. "One brother was released, one brother saved," he said. "I mean that exactly. When I left the camp only one brother was freed. My God, that was a parting."

Walter made his way to Switzerland and then worked as a gardener in a vineyard in the south of France. Eventually he obtained an emergency rescue visa for America. The day he went to the consulate in Marseille to collect his visa was the very day the Japanese bombed Pearl Harbor. The consulate was closed. He went into hiding.

I sent him a copy of *Villa Air-Bel*, and here is a part of his reply: "Dear Rosemary. Your book left us trembling thinking about the outcome of this terrific war. The work of Varian Fry and his collaborators was really extraordinary.... Reading this book, the nerves of the reader arrive to a breaking point.... your book keeps us astonished at what people were able to endure."

I received another letter that touched me. It was from Madeleine Masson, a friend of Mary Jayne Gold. Gold's was one of the numerous stories I recounted in *Villa Air-Bel*. Mary Jayne had lived at the villa from 1940 to 1941. A young American heiress, she had given a great deal of money to help support Fry's rescue mission. After the war, she bought a villa in the south of France and, out of respect and nostalgia, named it Air-bel [sic]. Masson and Gold did not meet until they were middle-aged. Masson had read Mary Jayne's memoir *Crossroads Marseilles, 1940*. They shared the same story. She too had spent her youth in Paris and, in June 1940, had joined the terrifying flight from the city, an experience she writes about in her own compelling memoir, *I Never Kissed Paris Goodbye*. The two women had much in common: they were both writers and loved reading, adventure, poodles, and people. Masson often visited Air-bel. Her fondest memory was of Mary Jayne swimming. Because she was allergic to the sun, Mary Jayne always swam fully clothed. She would plunge into the sea wearing a wide-brimmed hat and shoes and stockings and holding a parasol. When Mary Jayne was dying of cancer, she sent for Masson, and they spent a precious last weekend together. Mary Jayne was still rollickingly funny. She died three days after Masson's visit.

Mary Jayne once commented that she wrote in order not to disappear. Even if Air-Bel, the house that was the symbol of her past, was destroyed shortly after her death, she survives in the pages of her own memoir. Madeleine Masson invited me to visit her in England so that, together, over a glass of good French wine, we could toast the memory of Mary Jayne.

After reading *Villa Air-Bel*, a man named Alfred Amant wrote to me with an inquiry. As a Jewish orphan hiding among a group of French orphans, he had lived at a villa outside Marseille from June 1942 until November 1942, at which point German soldiers occupied the villa, mounting machine guns on its terraces. Could that villa have been the Villa Air-Bel? It will take further research at the Bouches-du-Rhône Archives to know for sure, but it might well have been. The French representatives of the Emergency Rescue Committee had been forced to vacate the villa at precisely that time.

Alfred wrote me his story. In the early days of the German invasion in 1940 he had been separated from his parents, who were eventually killed in the camps, and from his younger brother, Hans. Hans, who was ten years old at the time, had been shipped off to a children's home while Alfred was sent to a home for teenagers. Eventually, with the assistance of the French Resistance, who provided forged identity papers, Alfred was transported to the French-Swiss border in a convoy of about thirty children. When the coast was clear they ran to the border, scaled a ten-foot-high fence, and fell onto the free soil of neutral Switzerland.

Only later did Alfred learn the fate of his brother. Hans had been living in a farmhouse in Izieu, a remote village in the Rhône River valley. The farmhouse was registered as a "Settlement for Refugee Children from the Hérault." The locals protected its disguise, including two Vichy officials who helped the director, Sabine Zlatin, by providing the children with ration cards and false identification papers. The farmhouse had an alarm system. Children were to ring bells if any suspicious vehicles approached, at which point everyone would run to the woods. But April 6, 1944, was a holiday, and vigilance was low. That morning the Gestapo raided the farm. At 8:10 p.m. that night, SS First Lieutenant Klaus Barbie, commander of the Gestapo in Léon, sent a telegram to his superiors in Paris: "This morning a Jewish children's home…in Izieu was cleaned out. In total 41 children, aged 3 to 13, were captured. In addition the arrest of the entire Jewish staff, or 10 individuals, including five women, has taken place…. Transport to Drancy will take place on April 7, 1944." One week later the children and their minders were deported to Auschwitz. None of the children, and only one adult, survived.

...

When you are writing about the recent past, you always have in the back of your mind what biographers call "the survivors," the family and friends of the people you are writing about. Will you have stepped, however inadvertently, into private spaces that still bring them pain? Varian Fry is a central figure in my book. It was he, after all, who organized the rescue mission for the refugees and gathered together the young people who saved them. Fry was a man of enormous courage and complexity who worked in appalling conditions, under pressures both from the refugees and from the police who hunted them. Did I bring him into focus in a compellingly human and accurate way? With trepidation I sent my finished book to Fry's widow, Annette Riley Fry. She wrote back that the book is "the most complete and most readable account I have ever read about that amazing group of people who were welcomed at the Villa Air-Bel."

Writing *Villa Air-Bel*, I lived in the past for years. But it did not feel like the past. It felt as real as anything gets. After my book was published, I felt those postpartum blues writers talk about. In my mind all these people had become living people, and now I had lost them. They stepped back into the pages of my book, but I learned from them. I doubt that I will ever be tested as they were, but if I am, I hope I can emulate their courage.

THE THREE SUITCASES AND ROBERT CAPA'S MYSTERIOUS *FALLING SOLDIER,* 2008

Perhaps there is no such thing as a true story, just echoes between the different versions, and the desire to know, that keeps us speaking, and listening, at all.
— Janice Kulyk Keefer

In January of 2008, three suitcases were delivered by hand to the International Center for Photography (ICP) in New York. The battered cardboard valises had travelled from Paris, via Marseille to Mexico and then to New York, a journey that started in 1940 and had taken almost seventy years to complete. In those suitcases was what the ICP considered an incalculable treasure—thousands of negatives of photographs taken by Robert Capa, the "pioneer of modern war photography," during the Spanish Civil War. Cornell Capa, who had founded the ICP, was overwhelmed. Already ill and just eight months shy of his own death, he had lasted long enough to see the evidence that would exonerate his brother and solve the mystery that had tarnished Robert Capa's most famous photograph: *The Falling Soldier.*

Detractors and slanderers had for years been suggesting the photograph was faked. Here at last were the negatives that would place the photograph in its context and prove that it had been taken during a real battle in the small town of Cerro Muriano on September 5, 1936.

Cynthia Young, curator of the collection, invited me to New York for the exhibition of the suitcases. They intended to publish every roll of film in the Mexican Suitcases and asked if I would contribute an article for the catalogue. It would focus on the photographer Fred Stein and his friendship with Robert Capa.

When I arrived at the ICP, the sight of the three battered suitcases displayed in a glass case, mute and yet so resonant with history, shook me with that poignant feeling created by objects that survive us. Where had the suitcases travelled in seventy years? What mysteries did they hide?

I wrote the article for the catalogue, but I wasn't satisfied. My interest in Capa's famous photograph had been piqued. I decided to travel to Spain to see things for myself. When I got to Cerro Muriano, I discovered that little had changed since Capa photographed the area. I recognized the same barren landscape and the small country train station where he'd photographed terrified women running down the railway tracks with their children in their arms.

The journey of the Mexican suitcases had been dramatic enough. Anticipating war, in 1939 Robert Capa had abandoned Paris for New York, leaving his darkroom in the hands of his associate Tchiki Weisz. As the German army marched on Paris in June 1940, Weisz packed the most valuable of the studio's negatives into three cardboard valises and fled to Marseille. A Hungarian refugee, he was soon arrested as an undocumented enemy alien and sent to an internment camp in Algeria. The suitcases were confiscated. Weisz (who would later become the husband of Leonora Carrington) eventually made it to Mexico, but, as far as he knew, the suitcases were permanently lost. They entered the lexicon of lost treasures, like Walter Benjamin's manuscript in a suitcase, which disappeared in Port Bou, Spain, in 1940 when Benjamin was arrested and committed suicide rather than be returned to a concentration camp in Germany.

In the late 1930s the government of Mexico, which was one of the few countries to openly support the Republican government of Spain during the Spanish Civil War, had stationed its diplomat General Francisco Aguilar Gonzales in Marseille to help anti-fascist refugees immigrate to Mexico. General Aguilar, it turns out, was a very complicated man. There are suggestions he had pro-Nazi sympathies and was involved in smuggling. The valises somehow came into his possession and he kept them, taking them with him to Mexico and hiding them for decades in the family vault. To the family they were probably grandfather's old battered suitcases from the war. When Aguilar died in 1967, his daughter inherited them. She gave them to her nephew, a Mexican filmmaker, who was probably the only one to understand their value. He finally decided to return them to the Capa family and, after discussions that lasted almost a decade, donated them to the ICP in New York, where they are being processed.

Up until now there have been three possible versions of how Robert Capa took his most famous photograph. Each version teaches us that how we read objective reality is a product of who we are and what we need to know.

Version One

It is September 5, 1936. The Spanish Civil War is just seven weeks old. On July 17, a faction of the Spanish military, under the direction of General Francisco Franco, staged a coup d'état from Morocco against the democratically elected Republican government of Spain. In the village of Cerro Muriano, the northern wing of the Republican army is preparing to mount an attack to take back the city of Córdoba, which had fallen to Franco's Insurgents in the early days of the coup. War correspondents of the foreign press are already arriving in the village, hungry for footage of the war.

Just outside Cerro Muriano is a low wooded ridge. The trees are burning from a bombing raid by Franco's forces that morning, and the occasional volley of machine-gun fire from that direction rattles the village houses, though the fighting is not heavy. It is 3:30 p.m., the end of the siesta, which had begun at one and which, so far, is respected by both sides and always marks a lull in the fighting. The bombing by Franco's Insurgents has now resumed. But, astonishingly, the antique bombs are completely ineffective. The holes they make are only a few inches deep. It takes a direct hit to kill someone. Though the village has suffered little damage and no buildings are burning, the terror the bombardment creates, mostly from the nerve-shattering sound of the bombs and the feeling of exposure, is devastating. The whole village is in flight. Men, women, and children, hauling whatever possessions they can carry, are streaming out of their houses and along the dirt roads. The occasional Republican deserter runs with them. They are trying to commandeer the cars and lorries of the Republican army that is stationed at a slight distance outside the village. Anything to escape.

A young man is on his belly in the mud with a Leica camera in his hands. He has positioned himself so that he can take a photo of the Republican troops as they come over the hill. His name is Robert Capa.

This is really his first war assignment. He is twenty-three years old and a refugee. What this means is both simple and complex. He has been stateless for three years, forced to leave Berlin when Hitler was named chancellor and began the systematic persecution of all political opposition, including artists and intellectuals, sending thousands into exile. Capa, whose real name is Endre Friedmann, is a Jew and a dissident. Making his base in Paris, where most of his fellow Hungarian dissidents have fetched up, he has taken up photography because that is what you do when you don't have the language to be the journalist you intended to be back home. But being a refugee means an odd kind of freedom. Because you are at the edge of survival, you are willing to invent yourself in whatever way is necessary. Capa has learned to use his enormous charm to create a fiction of himself. He first called himself André to hide his Jewishness from the editors of the *Berliner Illustrirte*, and then Capa, after the celebrated filmmaker Frank Capra. He chose Robert because it was so malleable a name that it could easily cross borders. In Spain he is Roberto Capa. He has been desperate to get to Spain because he believes here is where the fascism that destroyed his youth and is engulfing Europe can and must be stopped. He also hopes to make his reputation as a photographer. Before he left for Spain, he had written to his mother that conditions in Paris were dreadful, especially for undesirable aliens like him.

He waits as the young Republican troops career over the hill and down the exposed hillside. Just as he lifts his camera, he hears the bullet and sees the soldier on the crest of the hill, only thirty feet from him, being hit in the head. As he clicks the shutter, the man falls back into the empty air. His rifle falls from his hand. He is dead before he hits the ground.

Capa keeps shooting, and the enemy keeps shooting. He is not thinking about why the verbs are the same. He is in the midst of the action. He does not know he has taken one of the most famous war photographs of the twentieth century; the iconic photo of the Spanish Civil War.

Later that afternoon he will take numerous shots of the frightened refugees running along the road out of the village of Cerro Muriano. This will always be his gift as a war correspondent. His portraits of ordinary people achieve a level of empathy as if he, as much as they, understands the terror of their flight from war. Here he aims at the peasant woman out of breath and running with an infant in her arms and shoots a photograph of the mother cradling her son in a blanket on the back of a donkey. At the end of the afternoon he collects his gear. By dusk, when the bombardment ends, they are gathering the bodies. It seems there are twenty wounded among the soldiers but only three or four dead.

Two weeks later Capa returns to Paris. He turns over his film to his developer Tchiki Weisz at his atelier at 37 rue Froidevaux, across the street from Montparnasse Cemetery. That, he feels, is the end of his duty. He will not think about what happens to it. He has sold his Cerro Muriano photos to the magazine *Vu*.

On September 23, the photo of the dead man falling, titled *Death of a Republican Soldier*, appears in *Vu* with the caption: "With lively step. Breasting the wind, clenching their rifles, they ran down the slope covered with thick stubble. Suddenly their soaring was interrupted, a bullet whistled—a fratricidal bullet—and their blood was drunk by their native soil."

Vu is a leftist, strongly anti-fascist magazine. The comrades who work there have only one purpose: to counter fascist propaganda and to win over international opinion in support of the Republican government that is under assault. Capa's photograph is perfect for their purpose. It is like an execution. In its accidental composition, the image of the man falling backwards from the force of the bullet, his arms spread behind him, posed against a backdrop of open fields and a setting sun, has all the drama of the central figure in Goya's painting of Napoleon's soldiers executing the defenders of Madrid.

The photo has an immediate impact in galvanizing public support for the Republican cause.

Almost a year later, in the July 12, 1937, issue of newly created *Life* magazine, Capa's photograph, which now carries the title, *The Falling Soldier*, appears as the lead photo in a collection of stills from a film called *The Spanish Earth*. The caption reads: "ROBERT CAPA'S CAMERA CATCHES A SPANISH SOLDIER THE INSTANT HE IS DROPPED BY A BULLET THROUGH THE HEAD IN FRONT OF CORDOBA."

There are two things odd about this caption. First, the majority of photographs in news magazines are published without attribution. But here Capa is identified. This is because, in the year since he took this photograph, and precisely because of it, Capa has become the "Most Famous War Photographer in the World" (*British Picture Post*, December 1938). The second thing that is odd about the caption is that there is no indication which side the falling soldier is fighting on and dying for.

It is impossible to recover the impact that the photograph had on American readers seeing it for the first time in 1937. What is it, after all? An anonymous man falling in the air.

In fact, what is most shocking and what made the photograph famous is the new technology it represented. Up until now, the standard camera, even for war photography, has been the medium-sized Speed Graphic that used plates and a bellows, making action shots difficult and dangerous. The new camera, the 35mm Leica, invented only three years earlier, is portable, giving the photographer mobility and enabling him to take multiple exposures; it has made it possible to stop time. This is the first photograph of a soldier as he is dying. It's all in the participle. Time has been frozen at the second that death itself penetrates a body. This is the most intimate moment of the violence of war yet captured on film.

Version Two

Robert Capa is a young photographer anxious to make his reputation. Two weeks after the outbreak of the Spanish Civil War on July 17, 1936, Lucien Vogel, owner of the magazine *Vu*, has invited Capa and his girlfriend, Gerda Taro, to fly with him and a group of journalists to Barcelona. Vogel's magazine is currently the best French photographic magazine, famous for its strong reportage, and Vogel wants to do a special issue on the Spanish war. Plagued with mechanical problems, the plane crash-lands in a field a good distance outside Barcelona. Capa and Taro walk away unhurt, but Vogel and one of his reporters suffer broken arms.

Capa and Taro, who has learned photography and become a pretty good photographer in her own right, set out to look for the front line of the war. In the photographs they send back to *Vu*, they have taken scenes of Republican troop trains pulling out of the station in Barcelona.

The soldiers raise fists in enthusiastic salutes as they go off to fight the fascists. Capa photographs the anarchist militiamen, Spanish workers who have refused to wear uniforms or accept military hierarchy and who are ill-equipped with ancient weapons but are enthusiastic enemies of fascism. Taro photographs members of the women's militia. It is news that women have been allowed to take up arms and fight with the men. One of her most famous photographs is of a woman soldier in skirt and high heels kneeling on a beach taking pistol training. There is still a lot of resistance to women soldiers wearing trousers.

Capa and Taro drive to the Aragón front, but the fighting between Republicans and Insurgents is at a stalemate, reduced to the occasional skirmish and these mostly at night—no good for filming. The photographers find the same problem at Huesca and Zaragoza, in Madrid, and on the Guadarrama and Toledo fronts. Apart from soldiers on manoeuvres, guarding barricades, digging trenches, or even participating in the harvest, there is nothing to photograph.

The deadly assaults will not begin in Madrid until November, when the city will come under bombardment from German planes and the front line of fighting from building to building will be at the university.

In this new warfare where civilians will be targets, the defending Republican soldiers will take the public tram to the battlefront.

Finally Capa and Taro hear that the Madrid government has begun an offensive to retake Córdoba, but at the so-called battle-front at the village of Cerro Muriano, nothing is happening. Capa complains to the commanders of the CNT (the Confederación Nacional del Trabajo, or anarcho-syndicalist trade unions). The commander decides that the only solution is for the militia to stage some manoeuvres for Capa to photograph.

Capa gathers the soldiers of the CNT brigade. They are fresh, optimistic, sure they will win this war.

He takes some shots of the soldiers carousing, then a shot of them in a line leaping over a gulley. From the photos, it seems clear that Capa is running beside them. Suddenly they fall on their bellies, taking aim. Next they charge down an exposed hillside. Taro too takes some shots of the soldiers running, hunched over in attack mode, up and across the open fields.

Capa asks one soldier to make as if he is hit. He shakes the camera ever so slightly to blur the image, to give the impression that the photo has been taken under the duress of battle. Photography is an improvisation and you can never be sure of the shot, so Capa poses another falling soldier just in case.

In 1974, almost forty years after Capa took his photograph, the journalist Phillip Knightley was writing *The First Casualty: From the Crimea to Vietnam: The War Correspondent as Hero, Propagandist, and Mythmaker* (1975). In the course of his research, Knightley came across a sensational piece of information. The world-renowned Robert Capa, the greatest war photographer in the world, had faked his famous photograph, *The Falling Soldier*. The falling soldier's death was entirely staged.

Knightley based this claim on an interview he did with a South African journalist named O.D. Gallagher, who had served as a correspondent for the London *Daily Express* during the Spanish Civil War. Gallagher claimed he had shared a hotel room with Capa in 1936 when Capa took the famous photo. The image was one of a series of action shots faking an attack. Gallagher later told another journalist, Jorge

Lewinski, that the soldier Capa was photographing was an Insurgent, one of Franco's Nationalist soldiers.

Gallagher provided no proof, and his claims seemed hardly credible. Capa was travelling with Gerda Taro when the famous shot was taken, and he never photographed any of Franco's Nationalists. However, Gallagher had sown the seeds of doubt that called into question the authenticity of Capa's most famous photograph.

Capa was not able to counter the charges. While covering the French Indochina war in 1954, Capa had stepped on a landmine and died immediately. He was only forty years old.

But slowly, evidence surfaced that it was indeed possible that Capa had staged *The Falling Soldier*.

The most telling evidence, which had been there all along but which nobody had thought to examine, is a series of Capa's photographs taken at Cerro Muriano in which we see young CNT militia cavorting in triumph, waving their rifles in the air. Among the photos are not just one but two shots of falling soldiers, both of whom appear in the earlier image very much alive. It looks as if these shots have been staged.

The question is: does it matter if Capa staged the shot? Does it matter if the soldier is faking or dying? Yes and no.

Those who feel that a deception has been perpetrated say that Capa has violated the contract between photographer and viewer, which, oddly, puts such people in the ironic position of insisting that the event of this individual man's death should really have taken place.

But what is the contract between photographer and public regarding photographs taken in war? There was nothing out of the ordinary about staging photographic events. Henry Luce himself—founder of *Fortune, Life, Sports Illustrated*, Time Inc., and known as Father Time and Il Luce—ordered "fakery in allegiance with the truth." In Civil War Spain, "Faking was the order of the day." Both sides were doing it. Photography, it was understood, was not about what happens; it was all about reception. Photographs were a kind of weapon in the fight. They were explicitly taken and used for their propaganda value for the people back home, to convince of the justness and rightness of the cause.

In a fascinating book called *War and Photography*, Caroline Brothers offers a study of photographs of the Spanish Civil War published in the British and French press by newspapers controlled by the right-wing and left-wing parties. Of course, the war is a different war, depending on the politics of the newspapers reporting it. Brothers examines Capa's photograph, in her mind clearly staged, suggesting that it:

> bears the traces of something broader, of the desired belief of a particular historical era.... What this image argued was that death was heroic, and tragic, and that the individual counted and that his death mattered.... Moreover, it was aesthetic. Clean, rapid, and taking place in a natural world where mountains and a lake and the open sky were visible from where he fell, the circumstances implied that death had its own particular beauty.

We in the twenty-first century understand the aestheticizing of war and its multiple euphemisms — *war games, the theatre of war, anti-personnel devices, friendly fire*—as well as the management of war's reception. Yet for all our postmodern cynicism, we still accept the rhetoric of the heroic soldier.

I think what is fascinating about the man who took the photograph of the falling soldier and about the Spanish Civil War itself is the astonishing arc they both experienced—from the highest idealism to the deepest disillusionment and cynicism. This is the lesson of *The Falling Soldier.*

Capa began by believing he was testifying to the need for truth to be told. And speaking urgently about the human cost of this most brutal war. He made it clear whose side he was on. He was a committed partisan. As he said to the writer Martha Gellhorn, companion of Ernest Hemingway: "In a war you must hate somebody or love somebody, you must have a position or you cannot stand what goes on."

For him, as for Taro, both refugees from Hitler's Reich, Spain was the country where international fascism must be defeated. Capa could see his photograph as one more weapon in the fight.

Ernest Hemingway, who travelled to Spain in March 1937 to undertake the filming of *The Spanish Earth*, a film subsidized by US writers John Dos Passos and Archibald MacLeish and intended as propaganda to raise money to buy ambulances for the Republican side, wrote a story called "Night Before Battle" about filming the war. It was published in *Esquire* in February 1939.

> [At] eight hundred to a thousand yards the tanks looked
> like small mud-colored beetles bustling in the trees and
> spitting tiny flashes and the men behind them were toy men
> who lay flat, then crouched and ran, and then dropped to
> run again, or to stay where they lay. Spotting the hillside
> as the tanks moved on. Still we hoped to get the shaped
> of the battle.... But we were kidding ourselves plenty that
> it was not too far.... [I said:] "We got some good tank shots
> [at Pingarrón]." "The tanks were no good there," Al said.
> "I know," I said, "but they photographed very well."

As he swaggered through the trenches, borrowing rifles to take pot shots at the enemy, Hemingway was adored by the Spanish Republican soldiers. He was the Republican side's best propaganda weapon. But for all his macho posing, he saw things clearly. The sarcasm of the comment that the Russian-built tanks were a disaster but that they photographed well says it all. For the photographer the battle is an aesthetic and technical problem; real dying is a secondary consideration. Hemingway's story is about a commander of the Lincoln Brigade who knows, because his troops are so poorly armed and so badly led, that he will surely die the next day. There is a difference between photographing and fighting; getting a good picture and dying. The fiction writer falls into the same chasm of bad conscience as the photographer. How do you make your work count? Capa once wrote: "It is not always easy to stand aside and be unable to do anything except record the sufferings around one." Hemingway too wanted to make a difference. When they met in Spain, Capa and Hemingway, both knowing themselves ironic tourists to the war, became good friends.

And yet, for all Capa's conviction, if he staged *The Falling Soldier,* he participated in a deception.

Do we have a tolerance level for deception? In human experience, there is all manner of petty lies, duplicity, deceit. As long as they remain at a human level, social order can absorb them. But is there a point when the deceptions and lies, too-long tolerated, spill over and run rampant, become the very structure of reality? The paranoia, the violation of law, the justification of murder in the name of security that characterized life in Civil War Spain were astonishing.

Is Capa's *Falling Soldier* a fake death, poised at the beginning of this slippery slide into total duplicity? Is then participating in the fakery tantamount to accepting it?

It is perhaps the nature of war that it must be built on lies. An appeal has to be made to people's heroism, and the death machine glossed over. I wonder how many men (and women) who go to war actually anticipate the fact of their own death. But the Spanish Civil War was brutal to a degree unimagined before because it was an ideological war, played out over the heads of most of the soldiers fighting it, and atrocities were committed on both sides.

In his book *The "Red Terror" and the Spanish Civil War*, the Spanish historian Julius Ruiz concluded that "although the figures remain disputed, a minimum of 37,843 executions were carried out in the Republican zone in what was called the Red Terror and a maximum of 150,000 executions (including 50,000 after the war) [were carried out] by Franco's insurgents" in what was called the White Terror.

But it was the involvement of the international community that determined the war's outcome. The Spanish Civil War soon became a prequel, a kind of proxy war, the dress rehearsal for the Second World War. The real battle in Spain would be between the German and Italian allies of Franco and the Soviet allies of the Republic.

The Germans saw the war as a chance to test the saturation-bombing technique that was part of their new theory of blitzkrieg (the lightning strike), with which Hitler and his generals expected to win the Big War. German pilots of the Condor Legion, under the direction of Lieutenant Colonel Wolfram von Richthofen of the Luftwaffe, carried out bombing raids against civilian targets. The total destruction of Guernica was only the most infamous, perhaps in part because Pablo Picasso's outraged and terrifying painting commemorated the tragedy. Franco denied any German involvement in the bombing and claimed the city was burned by the fleeing Reds.

Stalin used the Spanish Civil War as a chance to continue the paranoid work of purging all political opposition, a process he had begun with his show trials in Moscow in August 1936. He had secret agents operating in Spain, using the same tactics of assassination and slander as they were using back home to purge dissidents. The Spanish Communists targeted for liquidation the thousands of Spanish anarchists and anti-Stalinists fighting against Franco. They also targeted oppositional elements among the International Brigades.

It took a long time for the brigadistas to believe that their own side was killing them. As the horrible atmosphere of political suspicion and hatred swelled among the pro-Stalinist members of the Communist Party, not just Spaniards but foreigners in the International Brigades were hunted down and imprisoned or disappeared.

Capa wrote his brother Cornell, who was now in the United States, that he couldn't understand what was happening in Spain. It was grounds for despair. Many of the writers who went to Spain out of motives of moral commitment of the most disinterested kind came back disillusioned and bitter, wracked by guilt and self-recrimination.

W.H. Auden, who had written his eloquent poem "Spain" in 1937, would refuse to allow it to be published again, calling it a "dishonest poem." The German novelist Gustav Regler, who had served as a Communist commissar, took until several years into his exile in Mexico to believe the deception perpetrated by the Communist Party in Spain. Hemingway wrote *For Whom the Bell Tolls*, the best novel about the war, which had an astute portrait of the murderous French Communist leader André Marty, but the novel has always been read as a heroic love story.

It was George Orwell who told the undiluted truth. In *Homage to Catalonia*, he wrote:

> I suppose there is no one who spent more than a few weeks
> in Spain without being in some degree disillusioned. My
> mind went back to the newspaper correspondent whom
> I had met my first day in Barcelona, and who said to me:
> "This war is a racket the same as any other." The remark
> had shocked me deeply... [but] the fact is that every war

suffers a kind of progressive degradation with every month that it continues, because such things as individual liberty and a truthful press are simply not compatible with military efficiency.

When he got back to England, Orwell was shocked that the reports in English newspapers about Spain were not merely inaccurate. They were complete inventions. His notions of Newspeak and Big Brother were hatched out of his experiences in Spain.

Version Three

It is approaching the end of siesta in Cerro Muriano, about 3:30 p.m. With the assistance of the commander of the CNT brigade, Capa sets the stage for his photograph. He lines the men up and takes a propaganda shot of them raising their rifles dramatically in the air and shaking them in a battle roar of victory. He wants to film a mock attack, with the men leaping the gulley, diving for cover, creeping up the shadowed hill to storm an Insurgent position. They follow his orders enthusiastically. He then tells them to run down the exposed hill as if they were charging the enemy. As he is framing the lens on a single soldier, he hears a shot whistle from out of nowhere. It may have come from the stand of trees that had been burning earlier in the afternoon and where Insurgent snipers have been sighted.

Capa feels a sudden nausea. His hand shakes. The image will be slightly blurred. He has had the sudden realization that his posing of the soldiers running down the hill has exposed them to the enemy. His desire for the right photographic shot has killed a man.

Still, Capa is a professional. He poses his camera to take a shot of a second falling soldier.

The context of the famous photograph of the falling soldier may have been a stage-managed assault, but the death of the soldier himself was as real as any death gets.

Is this a likely scenario?

When asked in 1937 how he came to take the photograph, Capa replied: "No tricks are necessary to take pictures in Spain. You don't have to pose your camera [or your subject]. The pictures are there, and you take them. The truth is the best picture, the best propaganda."

But the version he gave to an interviewer from the *New York World-Telegram* on September 4, 1937, one year after the photo was taken, is uncanny. He said he was stranded in a trench with the soldier. The soldier was impatient and wanted to get back to the Loyalist lines. Finally, the soldier "clambered out of the trench" and was hit. Capa said he automatically snapped the soldier's picture. Two hours later when darkness fell, he crept out of the trench to safety. But this is unlikely—the photographs from Capa's contact sheets show there were always dozens of soldiers around, and Capa seemed never to be alone.

Perhaps most convincing is Capa's account to a female friend, Hansel Mieth, who said that, clearly still visibly upset, Capa once told her "the soldiers were fooling around. We were all fooling around and knipsing." When she asked him if he'd staged the attack, he said, "Hell no. We were all happy. A little crazy maybe. And then suddenly it was the real thing. I didn't hear the firing—not at first."

"Where were you?" she asked.

"Out there, a little ahead and to the side of them." Beyond that, Capa told Mieth only that the episode haunted him badly.

If he did feel implicated in the soldier's death, this is the closest he comes to telling the truth of the experience behind the photo.

This, of course, is the most ironic and most painful interpretation of all. We can coat over the shameful thing, convincing ourselves we are not entirely responsible, but it surfaces. Robert Capa left behind some seventy thousand negative frames that he exposed during his lifetime. But was the photograph that became synonymous with his name and for which he was congratulated over and over again a staged death that became a real death in which he felt implicated?

Robert Capa's biographer Richard Whelan was frustrated by the enigma of the photograph. He insisted *The Falling Soldier* was a haunting symbol of all the Loyalist soldiers who died. To obsess over its veracity was "morbid and trivializing."

But not to the man who died. And after all, isn't this the only measure that is authentic? Capa had never sought to find out the name of
the falling soldier. But perhaps this was a moment like any other in war,
a death like any other. Capa did not know he would be haunted for a
lifetime by this image.

On September 1, 1996, Rita Grosvenor, a British journalist based in
Spain, published an article in the *Observer* reporting that a man named
Mario Brotóns Jordá had identified the falling soldier. Brotóns had been
a member of the Republican militia at Cerro Muriano on September 5,
1936, and had been wounded that day. He had never "focused his attention" on the Capa photograph, but when asked to do so by a Spanish
historian, Ricard Bañó, he recognized the man as Federico Borrell
García. Nicknamed Taino, the falling soldier was a twenty-four-year-
old textile worker from the city of Alcoy. The widow of Taino's younger
brother, Everisto, confirmed that her brother-in-law was indeed the man
in Capa's photograph. Finally the soldier has a name. His dying was a
real death.

Capa was caught on the knife-edge of a dilemma. War, the experience that appalled him, also made him famous. For the rest of his life
he would have to keep his stories up to the inflated reputation of Robert
Capa.

But Capa was changed by the Spanish Civil War.

His lover, Gerda Taro, died in Spain. She had stayed behind after
Capa returned to France. Capa had always been careful not to align
himself with any political group. But Taro had moved into the Alianza
de Intelectuales Antifascistas Españolas, run by the poet Rafael Alberti
and his wife, María Teresa León. She was having an affair with a young
Canadian named Ted Allan, the political commissar of Dr. Norman
Bethune's blood-transfusion unit. She was with Allan on July 25, taking
photos in Brunete, when the Republicans came under unprecedent-
edly brutal bombardment. In his novel *This Time a Better Earth*, based
on the battle, Allan describes Taro's courage and recklessness — at
one moment she jumped out of the trenches, exposing herself to the
strafing of Franco's planes in order to exhort soldiers not to retreat. By
late afternoon, she and Allan had made it off the battlefield and were
able to hitch a ride on the running board of a retreating touring car,

carrying the wounded. Then a Republican tank lost control and came careening in their direction. Taro was crushed. She died the next day. The irony that she was killed by poorly trained friendlies operating the archaic Russian tanks was not lost on Capa. The virtually unknown Taro's funeral in Paris, organized by the Communist Party, was attended by tens of thousands.

She was a modern Joan of Arc, the first woman photographer killed in action. Her fame grew. A card devoted to Taro's death was among the packaged set of 240 bubble-gum cards issued by a company in Philadelphia illustrating true stories of modern warfare. Her tomb in Père Lachaise Cemetery was designed by Alberto Giacometti. The inscription read: "Photojournalist, killed July 25, 1937, on the Brunete front, Spain, in the line of duty." In 1942, during the Nazi occupation of France, when history was being rewritten with an amazing attention to detail, Taro's tomb was replaced by a concrete black slab with only her name, incorrect year of birth, and the year of her death.

Beginning in January 1939, four hundred thousand Republican soldiers and civilian refugees fled over the Pyrenees, pursued by Franco's victorious army. Capa was among them, recording the tragedy. Capa's editors thought he was either dead or captured, but he turned up in Paris, where he had a nervous breakdown. He wrote to his mother a few months later: "I do not know how I have changed so much but without work I can hardly breathe. It is true that after Spain...for four weeks I walked around like an idiot." In fact, he had been almost comatose with grief. For Spain, for Gerda Taro, for Europe, which was moving inexorably toward war.

The young man who shot the Spanish Civil War would go on to photograph many others. He came to know what war was. When a bullet grazed him during the Arab-Israeli war in 1947, he commented: "They went too far — or rather — got too close this time. I am not going to continue to photograph for posterity the men who play this little game." Then he muttered: "That would be the final irony — to be killed by the Jews."

There are many Capas. All more or less true. The debonair romantic who was Ingrid Bergman's lover, the courageous photographer who got the best shots of the Omaha Beach landing on D-Day. And the broken man, described by his friend Irwin Shaw, who staggered out of bed in the morning, his face grey, his eyes haunted by "peering at so much death and so much evil…regretful, not stylish, undebonair who shakes himself, experimentally tries on his afternoon smile, and discovers that it works."

Or there is the laconic, unheroic Capa who said: "The best fate for a war photographer would be to be out of work."

It turns out that the three suitcases—expected to be the "Holy Grail" of Capa's work, and containing wonderful material such as original portraits of Ernest Hemingway and Federico Garcia Lorca—do not solve the mystery of *The Falling Soldier* at all. The negatives in the three cracked and dust-covered suitcases are of photographs taken later in the war.

The truth is we will never really know about the authenticity of *The Falling Soldier.* There are arguments to support and to refute each version. In the end we will read reality dependent on our own version. The photograph of *The Falling Soldier* illuminates. It tells us that we do not read history; history reads us.

THE PASSIONATE HISTORIAN, 2010

When you travel, you enter a fictional universe. It is impossible, even with a trusty guidebook at the ready, not to make up the world you see. Onto the ordinary day-to-day life, you will inevitably overlay an imagined, intensified, and partial reality. As long as you recognize this, it may be part of the very reason to travel. Whether rooting about among archaeological ruins or tasting exotic treats in foreign cafés, your imagination is at work absorbing what you see, always refracted through your own subjective expectations. So it is with a warning that I tell you of one of my encounters during my recent visit to Crete. I have no way now, except by instinct, to verify what I heard. But the encounter intrigues and amuses me because it speaks to the slippery nature of history.

In the summer of 2009, our friend Androulla, who lives on the island of Crete, invited us to visit for a month; she'd found us accommodations in a friend's house. While Juan was off working with some Cretan musicians, I decided to visit the Archaeological Museum in Heraklion. We'd toured the beautiful Minoan palace outside Heraklion, and I wanted to know more about Minoan culture. I was able to meet one of the curators of the museum, Dr. Eleni Sirigakis, who gave me a deeply informative, personal, after-hours tour of their stunning Minoan collection. Discovering my fascination with things historical, she said she wanted to take me to visit a friend called Kostas who is a passionate, not to say obsessed, amateur historian.

Two days before Juan and I were set to return to Toronto, I walked with Eleni through the back alleyways of Heraklion, negotiating the lovely shadows of early twilight, to reach a modern apartment building just opposite the harbour. We stopped to buy ice cream. Kostas had just moved into the new building and, in Crete, you always bring a small token as a housewarming present.

A handsome man in his fifties answered the door. I could already see that he was wired with a compelling intensity. He led us down a short hallway, past the kitchen and bathroom, and we entered a room that felt like a miniature Victorian museum. He told us he had salvaged the room from the chaos of his collection. It was impeccably tidy, the walls covered with photographs. There were two display cases that Kostas explained he had built himself. When I asked about the large photographs on the wall, he said they were portraits of his great-grandfathers. They were dressed in traditional Cretan costumes: loose pant-skirts, chains of bullets hanging diagonally across their chests, and carrying swords. Were they soldiers? I asked. No, they were a shepherd, a village mayor, and merchants.

We looked at the display cases. Kostas explained that everything in the cases came from his family. He had started collecting at the age of six. The family was astonished that Kostas bothered to collect these old things. The cases held an eighteenth-century rifle, several blunder-busses, a Smith & Wesson gun, bullets, ornate medallion-shaped boxes to store grease for the guns, pouches for gunpowder. On the floor, next to the couch where I sat, was the top part of a metal diving suit that seemed to have come out of a Jules Verne novel.

A consummate host, Kostas served me raki and Greek coffee. Eleni had tea. We had brought along a third visitor, a young archaeologist researching sites of the Battle of Crete in 1941. He also had tea.

Kostas said he had another room that was filled to the ceiling with boxes of archives. "And what is in this collection?" I asked. He explained that he had files of years of personal correspondence with men who served as British spies in Crete during and after the Battle of Crete. He had tracked them down in the history books and set out to meet them. He brought out carefully organized file folders. In one, the correspondent recalls the disappearance of five Americans who had infiltrated

Greece without informing the British. Reading between the lines, Kostas wonders if the five were accidentally killed by the British themselves. He said he has learned that history is usually to be found between the lines.

The Second World War had become Kostas's youthful obsession. Wanting to know the German side of the story, he travelled to Germany. To picture him as a young man going to Germany to visit Nazis, he told me, I had to imagine "a man whose stomach was churning with disgust." But it had to be done. He met Leni Riefenstahl, Hitler's favourite filmmaker. He said he had copies of films taken by Hitler's mistress Eva Braun of their parties at the Führer's Alpine retreat. The Americans confiscated the originals after the war.

"What were Hitler and Eva Braun's conversations about?" I asked Kostas.

"Their conversations were all about pride," he told me. "They believed what they were doing was right, even when it was murder."

Kostas continued his private researches, visiting East Berlin in 1986 where he stayed in a house in which the family on the first floor was pro-Nazi and the family on the second floor was anti-Nazi. In East Berlin, he met an SS officer. "There were so many of them," he says. "The Allies gave up hunting them and just let them fade back into society." He explained that the East Germans kept extensive archives on the Nazis because they thought one day the Nazis might come back, and they weren't sure who would win. "If the Germans had really read *Mein Kampf*," Kostas added, "they would never have followed Hitler, but instead they put the book on their shelves, unread."

"What did you learn about Hitler?" I asked him.

"What we must learn is never to humiliate people. This is what united the Germans and turned them maniacal."

I told him I was interested in the Spanish Civil War. He said he had letters from Stalin directing the execution of Communists in Spain. He said it with glee. He was a collector.

The conversation turned to Kostas's family stories. He brought out a folder in which he had filed a magazine article about a recent Greek film called *Brides*, made in 2004. He found the article by chance. It profiled the novelist Ioanna Karystiani and her writing of the screenplay for the film. The film's story is set in 1922 and is based on historical research. Seven hundred mail-order brides are travelling aboard the SS *King Alexander*, bound for America. The Greco-Turkish war, called the Asia Minor Catastrophe, has decimated the male population, and the women have been forced to accept arranged marriages with Greek men who have emigrated. They are all heading to strangers. The brides-to-be have only a name and a photograph of the men they will marry. The plot concerns a love affair between a Greek bride and an American photographer.

In the article, Ioanna Karystiani explains that one of her inspirations for the story was a photograph she had found of three people leaning over the corpse of a young woman in her coffin, who seems to be dressed as a bride. Kostas said that he was astonished when he saw the photograph Karystiani was referring to. It was a photograph of his great-grandfather. He produced the original photograph from his album and told us a story as compelling, if not more so, than the one the screenwriter recounted.

In the early 1900s, his great-grandfather had been working in Athens, where he had a love affair. A female child was born. He returned to his native Crete, married, and started a family that produced three children. At one point, Kostas's great-grandfather went on a trip to the eastern Peloponnese and decided to stop in Athens. He brought gifts for the daughter he had never seen, who by now was seventeen and had lived most of her life with his brother. The day he arrived was the day they buried her. This was the photo that had inspired the novelist's film script: Kostas's great-grandfather, with two other relatives, lean over the corpse of the beautiful young woman in a wedding dress. Traditionally, unmarried men, women, and young mothers were buried as for marriage, with a wedding crown on the head and a gold band on the ring finger of the right hand. In those days, it was a standard practice to hire a professional photographer to take pictures of a funeral. The photograph Karystiani had seen had obviously come from a studio.

Kostas continued the story. His great-grandfather left his brother to continue the trip and returned to Crete. During his absence, his young son had mysteriously died. He'd simply collapsed one day in the village, perhaps of a sudden heart attack. As Kostas's great-grandfather approached his village, he was met by a group of local women who berated him for travelling up and down the country when they had just buried his child. "But I have just buried my child," the old man replied.

"You have to remember," Kostas explained, "life was hard, life was cruel in those days."

As we were leaving the apartment, we stopped to admire a portrait of a fierce young man in tall leather boots leaning against a tree with his arm outstretched. He was handsome and looked out from the photograph with an insouciance that was challenging. Kostas said this was a portrait of his uncle. He told us his story.

Kostas's uncle was fighting with the partisans in the Second World War. During the Battle of Crete, they came across five Germans who had jumped from planes. This was the first aerial assault by an army using parachutes. The Germans were dangling from trees in which their parachutes were tangled. The other partisans killed four Germans, and Kostas's uncle was assigned to kill the fifth. He went up to the soldier and examined him carefully. Instead of killing him, Kostas's uncle cut several of the parachute strings, stabbed the knife into a block of wood, and gave it to the German.

In 1947, during the brutal civil war between the Nationalists and Communists, five men came to kill the brother of Kostas's uncle. When Kostas's uncle learned of his brother's murder, he snuck into the village at night, killed the five men responsible, and dragged their bodies to the spot where they had murdered his brother. He covered their bodies with branches, leaving them for animals to eat, which was an act of desecration, and then waited to be arrested. He was charged with six life sentences—five for the men he'd killed and one for the act of desecration. He was imprisoned in Chania.

One day a stranger came to his village. The villagers didn't distinguish between foreigners. They called all strangers Americans. The mother of Kostas's uncle asked the "American" to take a bag of tobacco to her son. She wrapped it in a wet cloth to keep it fresh and wrote her son's name and the name of the prison on it. She expected the stranger to fly over the prison and drop the tobacco. He was, it seems, the German parachutist.

In jail one morning soon after, the guards told Kostas's uncle to shave his beard and clean himself up. He thought this meant he was to be executed. He refused. He was dragged into the corridor. He was now certain he was to be executed, but as he approached the guardroom, he saw the mayor was there, the chief of police, and a number of dignitaries. As he entered the room he also recognized the German parachutist he had not killed. It turned out he was a first cousin of Queen Frederica, born in Blankenburg, Germany, who had ascended the throne in 1947 as queen consort of Greece. Within a few months Kostas's uncle was released from prison, supposedly for good behaviour.

Years later, when Kostas asked his uncle why he'd spared the German soldier's life, his uncle said it was not out of pity or compassion. "You have to remember my uncle was a simple villager where life was brutally basic," Kostas said. When he approached the German parachutist hanging from the tree, Kostas's uncle saw that the man was wearing a pressed shirt; he had a gold chain around his neck and smelled sweet, like perfume. Kostas's uncle had never seen such a man, and so he decided to spare him.

How much of Kostas's stories was true? How much of what is called history is distorted by anecdotal detail? Do I care? Not really. I hold these stories as a record of passionate obsession. Kostas is one of the strangest men I have met. Isolated in his small apartment in Heraklion, he has devoted himself to saving documents as a bulwark against the modern plague of collective amnesia. He seems to me to be archetypically Cretan: a passionate individualist for whom the stories we tell each other are essential to the fabric of our being.

FRED STEIN: THE GEOGRAPHY OF EXILE, 2013

We were staying at the Warwick at the corner of Sixth Avenue and Fifty-Fourth, a charming old New York hotel built in 1926 by William Randolph Hearst for his Hollywood friends, whose photos now line the stairwells and hallways. I had arranged to meet Peter Stein and his wife, Dawn Freer, for lunch. Stein is a cinematographer. He has shot over fifty films, TV movies, and documentaries and teaches at the Graduate Film School of NYU. His wife is an editor and scriptwriter. But we weren't getting together to talk about film. We were meeting to talk about Peter's father, Fred Stein.

Peter had contacted me by email to say he had read my book *Villa Air-Bel: World War II, Escape and a House in Marseille.* The book filled in the holes in his father's life, a story that they had never really talked much about before his father's death in 1967 at the age of fifty-eight. Peter said he now understood what his father had gone through as he escaped from Nazi-occupied Europe in 1941. If only I had written the book when his father was alive. But I hadn't come across Fred Stein in my research. Varian Fry's Emergency Rescue Committee eventually used codes to disguise the names of the refugees they helped, knowing the Nazis could raid their offices at any time. But Fred Stein's story deserves to be told because it is full of uncanny parallels to our current climate.

Born in Dresden in 1909, Stein was a law student, first in his class, and working as an apprentice at the Court of Justice when Hitler came to power on January 30, 1933. Stein was dismissed at the end of June. He was then called before the Nazi commissar of the Ortskrankenkasse and asked: "Are you the same Stein who was just dismissed from government service because of race and national unreliability?" That was the end of his university career.

When the SS began making inquiries about him, Stein realized it was imperative to leave Germany. He married his fiancée, Lilo, in August and, claiming to be on their honeymoon, the couple left for Paris. "The ocean of swastikas on the last day," Fred Stein told friends, "made an otherwise difficult departure easier." Like most refugees, they viewed their exile as temporary.

Before fleeing Germany, the Steins had bought themselves a Leica camera as a joint wedding present. With the audacity of the displaced, they opened the Stein Studio in their Paris apartment. To attract business, they scoured newspaper ads for festive events and club meetings and donated their services free. Only the small trickle of money they received from family back in Germany kept them going.

Initially foreign refugees were well received in Paris, but as their numbers increased, the right-wing newspaper *Action Française* began to refer to them as German invaders who were taking bread out of the mouths of Frenchmen. Rumours spread that Jewish refugees would seek Hitler's pardon by spying for him. The last straw was when the refugees began monopolizing the cafés of Montparnasse. The nationalist press began a xenophobic campaign to demonize foreigners: they were responsible for the economic and social ills of France and a threat to public order. They should be interned.

On September 5, 1939, two days after England and France declared war on Germany, a French government decree called for the arrest of all German nationals. Whether they had lived in France for decades or were refugees who had recently arrived seeking asylum from the new Germany, thousands suddenly found themselves branded enemy aliens.

Having been granted asylum, the German exiles assumed they were being commandeered as prestataires—work soldiers. Fred Stein was among those required to report to the Stade Colombes, where posters still announced the last football games and tennis matches. Before he surrendered himself, he arranged Lilo's evacuation from Paris to Évreux in the northwest of France. With her she took their infant daughter, Marion, who had been born the previous year.

Over several days, it is estimated that between fourteen and eighteen thousand ressortissants de nations ennemis were rounded up and isolated in Paris sports arenas and other centres. People ordered to the collection centres were told to bring forks and knives and two days' worth of food. The criblage, or screening, of pro-Nazi sympathizers, who might prove to be enemy spies, and of anti-Nazi exiles, who had the right of asylum, would be worked out afterwards.

Refugees' accounts of being rounded up contained the same details. Many were arrested without a chance to get in touch with friends; they were not allowed to bring extra clothes with them; they were herded into a sports coliseum or some such civic building where they slept on the ground.

They were then transported to detention camps. Fred Stein was one of fifty men herded onto a "sightseeing" bus. He remembered the trip through Paris with passersby waving their encouragement from the sidewalks; they thought the men in the bus were new recruits. Stein was taken to a camp in Blois in the Loire valley, joining 650 men in a circus tent commandeered for their use. They slept on the grass. When rain drenched the tent, they were moved to the village of Villerbon.

In the Villerbon detention camp, corruption was rampant. Conditions eased somewhat for prisoners who had managed to bring a bit of money with them. With a few francs, a prisoner could bribe the guards, or even the local peasants, to get decent food or smuggle a wife into camp. Everything had a price: heat, light, dishes, even the spot where one slept. But Stein had used all his money to get Lilo and his daughter out of Paris.

It's astonishing how quickly human ingenuity reasserts itself, even in the midst of disaster. Solidarity in the camp was strong. Stein managed the "library" (with books donated by locals) and the "Sorbonne." Prisoners, many of them intellectuals and artists, taught courses, though the classes were often interrupted when the commanding lieutenant ordered forced marches. Prisoners were supposed to work in the woods for pay, producing charcoal; the guards invariably stole their money. Stein asked to work as a photographer. A friend who was allowed to visit his pregnant wife in Paris brought him back his Leica, and Stein began to take photographs.

For the first two months of his internment, Stein heard nothing from his wife. He presumed she was safe in Évreux. But when her letters finally reached him at his camp, he learned that her experience was, if anything, more horrific than his. When she arrived in Évreux, she found she was considered an enemy alien and was told she would be imprisoned if she did not leave within hours.

Lilo was sent to a hospital run by nuns in Saint-Brieuc in Bretagne, where she was told not to speak German and was expected to work. Her one-year-old daughter was placed among the hospital's orphans. But Lilo's work permit was soon rescinded, and she was confined to the hospital grounds, permitted to leave only twice a month to go to the local gendarmerie to validate her papers. In the unsanitary conditions of the hospital, her daughter, Marion, became seriously ill. Lilo was allowed to see her only one hour per day.

Tormented by Lilo's suffering and terrified by his daughter's illness, Stein pulled every string he could to get a "furlough" from his camp. Amazingly, he was granted two days' leave in Paris to "get his papers in order." Once in the city, he called on every influential friend he could think of to get his wife and daughter the necessary travel papers to return to Paris. He succeeded but had to return to camp before he could be reunited with his wife. In February Lilo finally managed an illegal visit to Villerbon; she was smuggled into Fred's camp at night and, after a few days, smuggled out at dawn. She brought him photographs of his daughter, whom he did not recognize. They wept together. Fred Stein would not see his daughter for another year.

When the Germans invaded Holland on May 10, 1940, Stein and his fellow internees in Villerbon immediately found themselves designated prisoners of war. They were relocated to a camp in Marolles and then handed over to the British Expeditionary Force in Saint-Nazaire. The British confiscated all cameras, and Stein's Leica and photographs disappeared. He hoped to be allowed to participate in the fight against the Nazis, but internees were set to building roads and unloading ships.

Through May and into June, the Nazis advanced ever closer. Stein and his fellow internees saw the roads fill with fleeing refugees—one day a hearse jammed with Belgians passed the camp. When Paris surrendered on June 10 and the German Wehrmacht goose-stepped into the city in long dark columns, Stein panicked. He had no idea what his family might be going through.

The French Army and the British Expeditionary Force entirely collapsed before the German onslaught, and Saint-Nazaire, like Dunkirk, became an evacuation point for British soldiers to get back to England. German internees were barred from getting on the ships. They were told, "England leaves nobody in the lurch." The French would be evacuating them south by boat. But Stein was not taken in by the lie: "We were absolutely like animals in a cage who know that they will be surrendered to the butcher," he said. From June 17 to 19, the prisoners waited with their bundles ready. Their camp was now guarded by bayonet-wielding French soldiers, mainly men too old to fight who were drinking themselves into oblivion on the prisoners' wine rations. German planes flew over the camp, marking it with smoke signals. Stein expected to be handed over to the Germans at any moment.

On the nineteenth, a French lieutenant came tearing into the camp, shouting: "Messieurs! Les Allemands son la—débrouillez-vous en vitesse, mettez des vêtements civil (Gentlemen, the Germans are here: escape quickly, wear civilian clothing)!" The port that the British had just evacuated was even then being turned into a base of operations for the Kriegsmarine, the German navy.

Prisoners poured out of the camp in all directions like a human flood. With three friends, Stein headed south, making it onto the last ferryboat to cross the Loire estuary. In 1946, wanting to reconnect with old friends among his fellow German refugees, at least those who had survived, Stein wrote a collective letter in which he described his escape:

> We were free—in no-man's land. Children played in
> the streets in the summer sunshine, on the anti-aircraft
> cannons which stood in the open fields. With us went
> Poles, Czechs, Canadians. We slept in the woods, begged
> for food and drinks and finally hid near a village. We

heard rumors that the Nazis had already gone in motorized
columns from Nantes to the coast—more to the South—
so that it would be too late to get to Spain. In order to find
out, I was sent to the village to hear the radio etc. I spoke
French well—but we had military documents in which
our nationality was said to be "German"—so we preferred
not to meet French authorities, who either would think
we were 5th column, or because collaborators themselves
would denounce us as anti-Nazis. I confided to an intelligent businesswoman—after I had touched her heart with
Marion's picture—and she told us the whereabouts of a
hidden hamlet (which had been her home). There we four
were accepted by the old peasants (the young ones had been
drafted), were fed splendidly—in the whole neighborhood,
peasants knew about us and brought butter, rabbits, and
other things for our provisions. We helped with the harvest
work, hid our things in the woods and slept in the barn.
In the meantime, the Nazis were all over. I saw them when
I rode on a borrowed bicycle to the village (those peasants
did not even have a radio).

Stein and his friends were not alone on the route south. It is estimated that, beginning in mid-May 1940, between six and eight million
people abandoned their homes and fled west and south to Toulouse and
Marseille. The highways and fields were filled with the fleeing French
army, with Parisians, with refugees from Alsace, Lorraine, Belgium,
Holland, and scores of other places. This mass migration would be
called La Pagaille (the *Great Turmoil*). Entire towns became ghost towns
overnight. The fields were littered with cars abandoned when they ran
out of gas or broke down. They lay like skeletal remains, some burned
hulks, others overturned, their wheels spinning. The Germans were
bombing the roads to prevent the advance of the French soldiers and
to terrorize civilians. Overhead, German planes drew circles of vapour
in the sky to mark the spots on which to drop the next bomb load.
Other planes followed in a leisurely fashion, strafing roads and fields
with machine-gun fire to kill any survivors.

Amidst this infernal chaos, Premier Paul Reynaud fled with his government to Bordeaux, where he offered his resignation. It was accepted. On June 17 the octogenarian general Marshal Pétain was voted in as head of the new government and immediately shut down the French Parliament. Stein and his friends heard the rumours that Pétain intended to sign a ceasefire with the Germans. They waited.

On June 22, five days later, Hitler accepted the surrender of France. The country was divided into occupied and unoccupied zones, and Pétain committed his government to "surrender on demand" all German nationals requested for extradition by the Third Reich.

Stein and his party decided to split up. Two of the men headed back to Paris to say goodbye to their girlfriends. Having no idea where Lilo might be, Stein decided to flee with his third friend to the unoccupied zone. To the men's enduring gratitude, they discovered the peasants had taken up a collection for them, which meant they had a little money. They traded their decent clothing for bleus (a kind of coverall), carrying their utensils in one pocket and a full bottle of wine in the other. The two men tried hitchhiking, but when they discovered that a truck they had tried to flag down on the highway turned out to be a German truck, they decided to keep to the fields. Many of the villages were still occupied by French soldiers, whom they viewed as being as much a danger to them as the Germans. They searched for isolated farmhouses, where they always received food and drink, and took to travelling across the fields at night. Soon they decided it was best to travel separately.

Fred Stein was not much safer in the free zone. His name and address, his political affiliations, and his activities with the anti-fascist German kulturkartell were, as he put it, "nicely written down in the Paris police prefect's office, so the Nazis did not even have to ask me." In his letter, he describes his journey:

> It took me nearly three weeks to go a very short distance
> because I was in "Free" France. When I—sitting on a horse
> drawn vehicle—(my feet hurt very much) drove closer and
> closer to a French flag—the first in quite a long time—
> I felt insecure and got out of the way instinctively. I still
> had to do that very often during the following months,

because the flags of Mr. Petain now were hung in the
detention camps of Vichy—which I escaped with much
luck and effort (he even extradited his own citizens to the
German camps). During the flight in the occupied zone,
I sent two cards to Lilo in Paris—on June 22 on Lilo's
birthday, and on mine—July 3rd—in case she was there or
that somebody could send her the mail. I didn't know what
had happened to her. After I arrived in Southern France I
wrote to post offices of unoccupied France, of North Africa,
to England, to the USA—asking the relatives there about
Lilo and the child. It is said that many friends found each
other in this way. There were no newspapers, or if there
were—then only from one side. I had gone to Graulhet in
Tarn because I knew that years ago a family from Dresden
(Lonker) had moved there. I took a chance to see if they
were still there. In my last card to Lilo (of course with a
wrong sender in case the Gestapo was already interested)
I hinted that I would "appear" at those people and that
Lilo—if possible—should get in touch with them. On
July 8 this card came into the possession of Lilo.

By the time Lilo received his postcard, Fred Stein had moved on to
Toulouse. The city was a disaster zone. It had been designated a centre
for Belgian and Polish refugees, and the population had quadrupled
in a fortnight to about a million. Hotels were so full that people were
sleeping on billiard tables, under dining tables, and in lobby chairs or
outside in automobiles and on the grass in public parks. Everyone was
looking for someone. Advertisements appeared in newspapers searching
for lost husbands, wives, and children. "Mother seeks baby daughter,
age two, lost on the road between Tours and Poitiers in the retreat" or
"Generous reward for information leading to the recovery of my son,
Jacques, age ten, last seen at Bordeaux, June 17th." Messages were left
on city hall billboards until there were so many they fluttered in the
wind like tiny white flags. Stein found shelter with the socialist mayor of
Toulouse. He was given quarters in the chicken coop.

For some time Lilo had been trying desperately to get out of Paris. To evacuate by train or highway with a baby was too dangerous because the Germans were targeting both. When a friend suggested an acquaintance would take them through the interior canals on his yacht, Lilo jumped at the chance, but they had only gone a few miles when the French personnel abandoned ship. She returned to Paris only to witness the Nazis march into the city the next day. It was, of course, the Gestapo she most feared.

When Fred's postcard arrived, it was her first lifeline, but passage into the unoccupied zone was as controlled as at any international check-point, and to be found crossing the line illegally could be fatal. With a courage one can only imagine, she presented herself to the German Kommandantur.

Proficient in French, she posed as a French national who wished to join her demobilized husband in Toulouse. Astonishingly, her perform-ance was so good that the German official didn't even check her papers, which would have revealed her to be a refugee provenant d'Allemagne. She fled the Kommandantur with her safe-conduct pass clutched in trembling fingers. By mid-June she and her daughter arrived safely in Toulouse. She had managed to bring with her a backpack full of Fred Stein's negatives and prints. They were too valuable to leave behind.

Now that the Steins were reunited as a family, the question was how to get out of France. The French borders were closed. Anyone wishing to leave needed an exit permit from the French government at Vichy.

The only hope left was to make it to Marseille, the single major port in the Unoccupied Zone. But Marseille itself was in chaos. All that summer, thousands of refugees had poured down the Boulevard d'Athènes following the lure of the sea and the illusion of freedom car-ried on the wind. They settled into the obscure little hotels tucked away in the city's back alleys and waited.

Then, at the beginning of September, the city of Marseille passed an ordinance authorizing prefects to intern, without trial, individuals deemed a danger to public safety. On July 8 it was declared that no resident alien was allowed to travel or move from his actual domicile. Soon another ordinance was passed preventing refugees from living in a hotel for more than five days. Many took to renting rooms in bordellos because there the police could be bribed to look the other way. The Unoccupied Zone had effectively become a police state.

One hundred and ninety thousand refugees needed to apply to the prefecture for permis de séjour (temporary residence permits) to stay in the city legally. But to get the permits, they needed to prove that they had every intention of leaving; they needed to obtain international visas to another destination. Without these, they could be sent to internment camps. As often as they dared, they took the trolley to a château in Montredon on the outskirts of Marseille where the visa office of the US consulate was housed. They might have saved themselves the trip. The signs posted outside the visa office—Applications from Central Europe Closed; Quota Transfers from Paris Discontinued—made it clear that the embassy was issuing few American visas.

Only the port of Lisbon remained open to shipping, but the paper-work required to get there had multiplied exponentially. One needed a valid passport, a safe-conduct pass to the French border, a French exit permit, a Spanish entrada, Portuguese and Spanish transit visas, and an international overseas visa.

Everyone understood that it would take no time before any of these documents could be bought on the black market—Vichy officials would soon be conducting a brisk trade in exit permits, and even stateless refugees could always buy a forged passport.

But who, except the privileged few, had enough money?

It seemed there was one man who could help. The refugee grapevine carried the news that an American named Varian Fry had set up the Centre américain de secours (the Emergency Rescue Committee), which could get the required documents. More importantly, for refugees who were too well known to travel legally, Fry was organizing a secret escape route over the Pyrenees to smuggle them out.

The news reached Fred Stein in Toulouse. Leaving Lilo with the baby in the chicken shed, he boarded the train for Marseille to see if there were any truth to the rumours. French inspectors always patrolled the trains to check identity papers, and he was terrified of arrest—what would happen to Lilo and the baby? He hid out during most of the trip in the bathroom, only vacating it when other passengers demanded to use the facilities.

In addition to his anti-Nazi associations and activities in Dresden, Stein had been an officer of the Anti-Nazi Journalists' Association in Paris. He had reason to hope his name might be on Fry's endangered list. He made his way to CAS's office at 60 rue Grignan and joined the line of hundreds of men, women, and children waiting patiently on the stairwell. In the room at the top of the stairs, Fred Stein would have found five or six haggard employees engaged in interviewing refugees. The jarring sounds of multiple languages and the smell of shabbily clad people jammed together in an airless space would have been daunting.

But Varian Fry took the Steins under his wing. Since both Steins were prohibited from working, their money had run out. Fry's committee gave them a meagre stipend, a mixed blessing in that it meant their names were kept on a list in the office files.

When the police raided the rue Grignan office, some of those whose names were on the committee's lists ended up in Camp des Milles, an internment camp near Aix-en-Provence. The committee took to using code. "With luck and much effort," as Stein himself put it, he managed to avoid the detention camps. It took over eight gruelling months of terrified waiting until Fry obtained the Stein family's international emergency rescue visas to the United States.

On May 6, 1941, they sailed from Marseille on board the *Winnipeg*. After the rigours of incarceration, the long trek, and the food shortages in Toulouse, Fred Stein weighed only 125 pounds. On the way to Martinique, the *Winnipeg* was stopped on the high seas when a boat fired a shot over its bow. All the passengers thought it was a German war vessel, but thankfully, it turned out to be the Dutch navy. The boat was rerouted to Trinidad in the British West Indies. The Steins were again incarcerated in a British detention camp, where the men were separated from the women and children—Lilo and Fred were allowed to meet once a day across barbed wire. But in comparison to the *Winnipeg*, the food in the camp was "heavenly" and the conditions hygienic. Finally, through the intercession of the Jewish Labor Committee and Fry's Emergency Rescue Committee, the Steins were permitted to continue to the United States aboard the SS *Evangeline*.

The *Winnipeg* had already been well-used as a refugee evacuation ship. In September 1939, the poet Pablo Neruda, then special consul for immigration in Paris, had hired the *Winnipeg* to transport 2,200 Spanish refugees to Chile. The Spaniards had been languishing in French internment camps in the south of France since they had fled over the Pyrenees with Franco's victorious army hot on their heels. Neruda reported that this was "the noblest mission I have ever undertaken." According to Peter Stein, the accolade of "nobility" also belongs to Varian Fry. Varian Fry saved his father, mother, and sister from what would have been certain deportation and death had they been trapped in France.

The Steins carried little with them as they crossed the ocean, but they managed to save the bulk of Fred Stein's photographs and negatives. There were a few photographs they considered too dangerous to take with them, such as the images of the political rallies; these they sent to an archive in Holland for safekeeping. The archive was later bombed, and the pictures were permanently lost.

When they arrived in New York, the Steins were poor. Lilo Stein first worked in a curtain factory, then as a seamstress on a power machine, a homeworker putting labels on handkerchiefs, and finally as a photo finisher in various plants. Fred Stein struggled to find commissions and contacts as a photographer. Still, New York was freedom; it offered the oxygen of personal choice. Not to be controlled by fascist rules.

Stein turned to portraiture. Soon he was photographing the famous, including fellow exiles such as Albert Einstein, Thomas Mann, Hannah Arendt, Marc Chagall, and Salvador Dalí. Notable Americans such as Frank Lloyd Wright, Georgia O'Keeffe, and Norman Mailer came to him for portraits.

Stein's photograph of Einstein is iconic. Through his refugee connections, he had wangled a ten-minute interview with the great man that turned into a two-hour conversation. Perhaps they talked about the loneliness of exile, which Einstein captured perfectly in his diaries: "Well, then, a bird of passage for the rest of life. Seagulls accompany our ship, constantly in flight. They will come with us to the Azores. They are my new colleagues, although God knows they are happier than I. How dependent man is on external matters, compared with the mere animal....I am learning English, but it doesn't want to stay in my old brain."

In New York, Stein documented street life. His photograph called *Italy Surrenders* (1943) is emblematic. It is not a militaristic photo of a victory parade but a portrait of a family sitting in front of their shop reading the newspaper. This is where history impacts, where history hurts. The newspaper headline facing the viewer reads in huge bold type: ITALY SURRENDERS. The mother's smile, half obscured by the paper, speaks of joy and relief. The Allies are winning. An infant in his carriage sucking on his bottle, oblivious to this moment in history, is the central focus in the forefront of the image. He is the future.

Fred Stein, *Italy Surrenders*, 1943 (© Fred Stein Archive)

IN SEARCH OF STALIN'S DAUGHTER, 2016

When you think about it, biography is often a question of travel. To write someone's biography you must find the witnesses to that life. The mystery of a life is revealed through conversations with family, friends, and colleagues; through the intimate letters they have left behind that offer mostly uncensored access to the immediacy of a life in lived moments; and through unpublished manuscripts and diaries.

When my American editor Claire Wachtel phoned to inquire about my next book, it was shortly after the death of Stalin's daughter, Svetlana Alliluyeva, which was announced in a moving obituary in the *New York Times*. She was quoted as saying, "No matter where I go, to Australia or an island, I will always be a political prisoner of my father's name." Imagine being the daughter of such a father, and always being labelled as such. She could never escape him. What a fate! I was totally captivated.

Claire and I talked about the obituary, and suddenly she was saying, "Yes, you can write that." She gave me ten days to put together a proposal for a biography of Svetlana Alliluyeva, warning that others would want to write that book and the proposal had to be done quickly. A biography of Stalin's daughter was a daunting prospect. The canvas would be so large. But I thought, Why not? I had already written four biographies and knew the genre's mysteries.

It would be the story of a woman who had spent half of her life, until the age of forty-one, in the Soviet Union, and the last part of her life, until her death at age eighty-five, in the United States. What would it mean to live constantly in the shadow of one of the world's most brutal dictators? To be the prisoner of your father's name? The resonance of "Stalin's daughter" was so disturbing that she could never have been free of it. What had caused her to defect in 1967 when defectors paid such a high price? *STALIN'S DAUGHTER FLEES THE USSR*. It was outrageous. What had her government done to cause her to defy them so passionately? And what had happened to her in America that, after living there for seventeen years, she had precipitously re-defected to the USSR in 1984, as her obituaries noted? And then returned in 1986, only to end her life, seemingly quietly, in a small hamlet in Wisconsin. It was a huge life, spanning histories. The geography would be vast: Russia, Georgia, London, the United States.

Among the more than forty people I interviewed, the initial and most important interview was with Svetlana's daughter, whose permission I needed to quote from unpublished letters and manuscripts. In writing a writer's life, you always start with the literary executor. I located her address and sent her copies of two of my books, saying I would like to write her mother's biography.

I wonder if she was as anxious as I was about this encounter. I have to confess that on the plane to the West Coast, I was thinking that I was about to meet Stalin's granddaughter, doing to her what had always been done to her mother. I was projecting onto her the shadow of her grandfather's name. When I met her at her workplace, the forty-two-year-old woman who stood before me was a dramatic, statuesque, funky American, as far from her grandfather as it was possible to be. She was everything I valued in the best Americans: open, intelligent, witty, freewheeling with her opinions, and generous. Who would have thought this was the person Stalin's granddaughter would turn out to be? Though Svetlana had told her daughter all the family stories, she had brought her up an American.

We met over dinner, and I must have put her at ease since she invited me to her home the next morning. Over three days she narrated her own and her mother's story. She loved her mother deeply and understood her peripatetic life, a life in flight, a life in search of refuge. The woman she described was a complex mixture of enormous strength, which she used to protect her daughter, and extreme vulnerability. Among the many stories I carried home with me was one particular moment. Svetlana's daughter sat on the sofa in my motel room. Shadows were gathering as the sun descended in the window behind her. She told me:

> Sometimes my mother would fall into the night terrors of a child, alone and lost. It would be like a cloud passing over. It was as if her brain started with a thought and ran with it to the point that she no longer had any control over the thought or where it was going. Sometimes it happened when she was writing, but sometimes there seemed to be nothing that provoked it, or it would be a trivial moment, the milk boiling over. She would be inconsolable. Something triggered a volcano of thoughts, memories, pain, anguish, fear about something coming up, surfacing to overwhelm her.

If this was her daughter, who was the mysterious Svetlana? On the one hand, she was a deeply read, cultured woman of intelligence who spoke four languages and whose longing was to live as a writer. She was the best of the Russians. Yet, she was still Stalin's daughter, with a tragic history darker than I could imagine.

Svetlana's mother, Nadezhda Alliluyeva, committed suicide when her daughter was only six and a half. As a child, Svetlana lived through the Stalinist purges of her favourite uncle and aunt, Alexander and Maria Svanidze in the 1930s, too young to understand their disappearances. When she was sixteen, her father exiled the man who had the audacity to fall in love with her to the Gulag for ten years, leaving her reeling in guilt and bitterness. The Nazis killed her beloved half-brother, Yakov, in a prisoner-of-war camp. Her aunts disappeared in waves of arrests in the late 1940s. After Stalin died in 1953, the tragedies continued. Her elder brother, Vasili, died of alcoholism at the age of forty-one. Literary friends were arrested in the mid-1960s and sent to mental institutions or internment camps. When she finally found peace in a loving relationship with the Indian Brajesh Singh, the Politburo refused to sanction her marriage—it was inappropriate for Stalin's daughter to marry a foreigner. After Singh died, she was given permission to carry his ashes to India. The Politburo's motives were political: the Soviets were selling arms to India.

In Delhi, Svetlana's fuses had blown. She felt like she was state property. At the end of her trip, instead of returning to the Soviet Union, she walked into the American embassy and demanded asylum. Almost her first words were: "You may not believe this, but I'm Stalin's daughter." The American consul had looked at her nonplussed and said, "You mean *the* Stalin?" It took the embassy a few hours to determine whether she was crazy, a counteragent, or the real thing. But she was carrying a manuscript called *Twenty Letters to a Friend.* It was the story of growing up in the Kremlin. No one but Stalin's daughter could have written it. They decided to believe her and flew her out of India in the company of the second secretary, Robert Rayle, who, it turned out, was actually an undercover CIA agent.

Only in mid-air did the State Department telex arrive from Washington saying: "Kick her out. Have nothing to do with her." When Svetlana defected, a consular convention with the Soviets was being discussed in the Senate and there was talk of a spy swap. The State Department thought Svetlana's defection might derail a possible détente.

She was parked in Switzerland where American lawyers sold her memoir, which had been circulating as samizdat in Moscow and Leningrad, for $1.5 million. Svetlana was a Soviet and did not understand money. She mistook greed for love and was soon fleeced of her newfound wealth.

Writing biography, you learn that people want to tell their stories. I contacted the ex-CIA agent Robert Rayle, who invited me to visit him in Virginia. Juan and I flew to Washington. I was recovering from knee surgery and needed his help for the drive to Virginia. In Washington we stayed at the surreal Tabard Inn, recommended by my National Archives and Records Administration researcher Sim Smiley. You'd think Andy Warhol had decorated the hotel. On the way to our room, we passed a naked mannequin perched in a bathtub. Outside our door hung a print of the Mona Lisa holding a codfish, with the title *The Da Vinci Cod.*

A trio was playing in the lounge the night we arrived. I overheard the violinist speaking with a Russian accent and struck up a conversation with him at the bar. I told him I was writing a biography of Stalin's daughter. "Ah, Svetlana Alliluyeva," he said, savouring the name. "Her father must have loved her. Otherwise, he would have killed her."

The next morning, I phoned the Rayles. Apparently, Bob had had a bad night, but he still wanted us to visit. It took an hour to reach the small retirement community in nearby Virginia. As we approached the house, Bob's wife, Ramona, came out to say Bob wasn't well; he'd collapsed in the bathroom. But she said, "Come in. Maybe he wants to say hi." She retreated behind a door and, looking in, I could see a man's legs stretched out against the tiles. A neighbour was sitting on the floor, holding his head in her lap.

"Maybe not," Ramona said and handed me a large batch of files containing decades of Svetlana's letters to Bob, along with newspaper clippings that she and her husband had organized for me to look at. "Mail them back when you're done with them," she said. The ambulance arrived as I exited the front door.

I held that image of Bob on the floor in my mind. Would he be all right? This reminded me that my search was not fictional. These were real lives I was engaging, all backlit with their own complex stories. I phoned the next morning and discovered Bob was already out of hospital. He'd had an attack of pneumonia. We were due to fly out at 5:00 p.m. "I will come back," I said, gambling that his recovery would continue. I did not want to intrude on a sick man. "I will return the files in person," I said. I knew I would have more questions after I'd read them.

At midday I went to the International Spy Museum in the centre of Washington. As I entered the building, I was blasted with the sound of "Goldfinger"; James Bond's car sat in the middle of a display. There were cabinets of Cold War covert spy weapons — secret cameras, coded messages, hidden microphones. It was all very kitsch. But I was invited to proceed upstairs — escorted — into the real world of the spooks. Bob's friend Peter Ernst, a former CIA officer, ran the museum. On the upper floors, serious archiving was being done. I talked with Ernst about Svetlana and asked about the potential spy swap in 1967. He was forthcoming. The head of archives was sent to do a quick search for the Soviet counteragents I was looking for. They were professional and helpful.

Several months later I returned to Washington, and the Rayles invited me to stay over for two days. We had compelling conversations about India, about the world behind the Iron Curtain in the 1950s and 1960s, and about Svetlana. I knew from her letters that she'd deeply valued Rayle's humour and camaraderie in those dark and frightening days of her defection. She believed he'd saved her. And he'd continue to come to her aid on a number of occasions. Bob was loyal to Svetlana despite her Russian temper, which led her to turn on many people. They stayed friends.

Perhaps what is most compelling about writing biography is this encounter with strangers. You must earn people's trust by showing you know your subject, but then you enter their past with a phenomenal intimacy. Of course, at each encounter you must judge what is being edited, elided, obfuscated, but this you determine by measuring whatever you hear against the multiple other versions that you collect of any incident. Only instinct gets you through. The reader is left with the biographer's judgments and must ask: do the stories cohere?

My next priority was to visit Svetlana's surviving family in Russia. Having been warned not to go to Moscow alone, I had Juan with me and my two Russian Canadian researchers, Anastasia and Elena. We rented an apartment on the internet. The district was good and the furnishings in the apartment seemed traditionally Russian — antimacassars on the couches, glass baubles on the side tables, books by Lenin on the bookshelf. It was supposed to be two bedrooms, but when we arrived at dawn on the overnight train from St. Petersburg and entered the apartment, we soon realized there was only one bedroom — the master bed had been photographed with two different bedspreads. The landlord remained nonplussed. When he took us through the apartment he remarked enthusiastically, "You're so lucky. You have a brand-new bed."

Our fourth night in the apartment we got a phone call at midnight. The landlord said the police wanted to enter our apartment. "Why?" we asked. To bring the suspect and videotape her re-enactment of the murder that had been committed there three months before. "Murder!"

we exclaimed. "Well, yes," the landlord explained. An American businessman from Miami had picked up a woman in the trendy Arbat district, and when they got back to the apartment, she'd spiked his drink and stolen the $30 in his wallet. "He'd had a bad reaction," as the landlord put it. He was found dead the next morning. That was why we had a brand-new bed.

The cops had said that if we weren't there to let them in, they'd have to kick down the door. Spooked by sitting in the kitchen, we waited outside in the cold with the landlord. When we asked the landlord for details about the murder in our apartment, he said he didn't want to talk about it.

At 2:30 a.m. an unmarked car pulled into the parking lot, and six men and two women piled out. Lead detective Lermontov approached and extended his hand. I shook it tentatively. He introduced himself, apologizing profusely for the lateness of the hour. The cops behind him were laughing. I asked Elena what they were saying. "Cop humour," she said. I asked more firmly. They were saying, "In the old days we didn't need to apologize." Another replied, "Yes, in the old days, it was arrest without right of correspondence" — the Soviet euphemism for execution. I was sure the ghost of Svetlana was smiling; she'd managed to push me back into the sinister atmosphere of her past.

When I interviewed Svetlana's cousins in Moscow and told them about the murder, they were solicitous. "When we heard you'd rented an apartment," they said, "we were worried, but we didn't want to say anything." No one seemed surprised at the murder. It was just a Moscow thing.

After spending a month in the city we knew what they meant. An article appeared in the *Moscow Times* about the arrest of a cat in the northern republic of Komi. Beside it was a photograph of the suspect suspended by the scruff of its neck. The cat had been caught sneaking into a prison with two cell phones taped to its back. It had happened before. In January a cat had been apprehended slipping through the prison gates with a saw and drill taped to its body.

As we sat drinking coffee at the Hotel Sovietsky, a man was surrounded and escorted out by security guards. He'd tried to pay for his vodka with counterfeit bills. Elena was stopped and searched at the grocery store. When she objected she was told her purse was suspiciously large. "One in five people shoplift in Moscow," the store detective said.

But the best was the flower lady. I liked to sit in the window box of our kitchen and watch the world below. One afternoon the police stopped a woman selling flowers from a bucket. It was obvious the charge was selling without a licence. She and the cops milled around the police car for at least fifteen minutes in heated discussion, opening the car doors, lifting the hood of the trunk. Eventually one of the cops poured the water from the bucket of flowers and placed it in the backseat. The woman walked away fuming in disgust. They had arrested the flowers.

By the time we left Moscow, a murder in our rented apartment didn't seem so strange, at least as long as we weren't in it.

Meantime, my visits in Moscow accumulated: the Kremlin, Svetlana's Model School 25 where she'd studied as a child, Moscow University where she got her advanced degrees, the Gorky Institute where she worked, the apartment complex called the House on the Embankment where she lived with her children (formerly nicknamed the House of Detention because so many of the elite who lived there were arrested and sent to camps), her dacha outside Moscow, the government archives where her adolescent letters to her papa were housed (we weren't allowed to photocopy them, so Anastasia surreptitiously read them into my tape recorder for translation that evening). We visited the Memorial Archives dedicated to the victims of the Gulag, Svetlana's friends among them. We spent time in the Novodevichy Cemetery where Svetlana's mother is buried. An elegant life-size statue of her, wreathed in fresh flowers, marked her grave.

And then there were the multiple interviews with colleagues, family, and friends. To enter a family dynamic is to enter a minefield. Each person has his or her version, and hidden histories dictate responses. No one is disinterested, but who to believe? You have to read the interpretation of the biographical subject through the history of the one telling the anecdotes, as much as you can grasp it. Perhaps my vision of Svetlana was coloured most by her nephew, Sasha Burdonsky, the son of Svetlana's alcoholic brother, Vasili. Burdonsky had reason to hate both his grandfather and his own father, who had taken him from his mother and placed him in the hands of an abusive stepmother. Burdonsky was now a well-known theatre director in Moscow. He was also the most eloquent. He told me:

> I admired Svetlana as a woman and as a human being.
> I cannot say that of all my relatives. I loved her very much.
> Of course she was difficult. She was a personality, with
> charisma....I have compassion for her and it seems, at
> times, that I understand her very well. Each one of her
> actions, seemingly unexpected and spontaneous—to
> me they are understandable. I hold her in my heart.
> I am always on her side.

In Burdonsky's opinion, it is necessary to remember that Stalin was a "kind of sinkhole, a myth, a sort of gutter where everything is drained. Legends attached to his name." This, he said, evoked rage in Svetlana. In comparison to others, not to mention in comparison to those writing about him, she knew her father intimately, but no one really wanted to hear. She understood how power had drained her father of all human feeling. In her book *Only One Year* (1969) she wrote: "[My father] knew what he was doing. He was neither insane nor misled. With cold calculation he cemented his power, afraid of losing it more than anything else in the world."

But she wanted it acknowledged that Stalin did not act alone. Thousands had colluded in her father's crimes. She was not exonerating her father but insisted that the rot went deeply into the system, and the demonization of Stalin clouded this. Russia, she complained, had never faced its past and would be doomed to repeat it: "That wonderful past that sends out its deadly whiffs, like an opened grave." In 2000, when it looked like a former KGB officer named Putin would become president, she warned the West to be wary. The past was returning.

When I said to Burdonsky that I thought his father, Vasili, was the cliché of the dictator's son, while Svetlana seemed not to be Stalin's daughter, he replied that I was wrong. Vasili was not Stalin's son. He was "a product of the people, the freeloaders and leeches, who surrounded him." But Svetlana was her father's daughter. She had his "organized intelligence," his "unbelievable will." But she did not have his evil. He added:

Her fate is so interesting...just on its own it is so interesting—her whole path, her whole search for some spiritual
shelter, which she could never find...I understood that she
would never find it, even though she thought she would. She
is one of the most tragic figures that I know—tragic figures.
And fate treated her very cruelly. And unjustly.

I travelled to Georgia to visited Tbilisi, where Svetlana and her
daughter had waited a year and a half before they could return to the
United States in 1986. I visited Gori, with its humongous museum to the
great man and the two-room shelter he was born in, now enshrined with
stone awning held up by Greek pillars. Apparently one million visitors
came each year to honour Stalin.

Next, I stopped in London, where I had set up numerous interviews with people who knew Svetlana over the years when she had
lived there—from 1982 to 1984 and then again from 1989 to 1996. In
England, Svetlana's circle was tiny. Among others, I visited several lords
and ladies, a dowager, and a stately sixteenth-century home in the Lake
District. People I talked to were protective of Svetlana. Perhaps the Brits
are more worldly and more politically disinterested. They wanted me to
give Stalin's daughter a fair shake. They had liked her; some had even
loved her. The writer Rosamond Richardson's take on Svetlana moved
me:

> I read her as a deeply wounded person who was extremely
> bright. Her intellect was phenomenal, and she was also a
> great soul. She had such optimism and incredible energy,
> which of course could get channelled down the wrong
> alleyway for her and into a lot of anger. To me that's part
> of the whole story of her personality. She is both this and
> that. She had so many interpretations laid upon her....
> If you bear Stalin's name or if you're Alliluyeva and you've
> written bestselling books, everybody knows who you are.
> Nobody is ever going to see you as you really are...and
> I'm not sure she could ever see herself as she really was
> too, because we all reflected back to her at some level

that fact that she was Stalin's daughter. So a really kind of uncontaminated self-knowledge was perhaps not possible for her.

This was the woman I had to write about. A shapeshifter, a Proteus on the beach. I had to struggle to get her to hold still for a moment and tell her story. Often it was a frightening, rootless story. And yet, as her nephew Sasha Burdonsky put it, she was not running from; she was always running towards something, a version of life that would free her. Stalin had produced a daughter whose outsized will took on the world with an optimism and a life-affirmation that stood against his crimes.

What a fate. She lived her adult years as a kind of shuttlecock, batted between the two sides in the high-stakes game that was the Cold War. She was a woman in whose life the private domestic world and the world of global politics collided in spectacular ways. The KGB and the CIA were never far from the story. And yet she kept her footing. Who would have expected it?

THE GREAT BEAR RAINFOREST, 2021

We left at dawn in the first week of September. The sun was lifting slowly from the surface of the sea, turning the sky a dramatic red. We drove in silence through the moss-muffled forest, heading for the ferry to take us from Salt Spring Island to Vancouver Island.

My sister Sharon had organized this trip to the Great Bear Rainforest aboard the *Passing Cloud*—I loved the name; a boat passing through, leaving no trace.

On other trips to Vancouver Island, I'd always had to slow my mind down to meet the island rhythms of the West Coast, but not this time. It was toward the end of the COVID restrictions, and I'd been in lockdown in a city slowly unravelling, everyone in shock at how the world had flattened, and there seemed nowhere to put our rage.

Mid-afternoon a few days before I left Toronto, there was a cacophony of voices outside my window. I got up to look, thinking there was a fight in the high-rise next door. People were standing around on the pavement looking up. One man shouted: "Man, don't do it! It's not worth it!" I looked up and saw a man perched on the railing of the seventeenth-floor balcony. The height was incalculable. People on the adjacent balcony were wailing. The standoff lasted half an hour until, finally, they persuaded him down.

There was something loose in the air. Drivers in cars raged and leaned on their horns. On the streets the mentally ill shouted crude curses. People in masks avoided each other. The weight of anxiety had frozen the city.

This trip was not like the previous ones I'd taken. I wasn't researching a book, chasing down a writer, or trying to reinvent myself. I was struggling to come to terms with a new world. Eighteen months in lockdown had changed us. We'd come to the realization that the world we lived in wasn't as durable as all of us had thought. Was the human experiment failing? I was grateful to get away.

Standing on the bridge of the ferry looking out over the surrounding sea, buffeted by wind, I could feel it beginning—that elation as one loses oneself in the beauty of it all.

We had a five-hour drive through heavy rain to reach Port Hardy on the northeast end of Vancouver Island, from where we were to take a float plane to Bella Bella on the BC coast. We were travelling with Outer Shores Expeditions, a tour group that had won a Green Tourism gold medal. Six people on a seventy-foot schooner: my sisters Sharon and Colleen; Sharon's husband, Hans; Sharon's two friends whom I'd yet to meet; and me.

We'd booked a small hotel on the edge of the harbour. That night, Colleen and I bunked together. Waking before dawn, we watched the sun break free from the far shore. The dense salinity of the ocean air had penetrated our room. We were mesmerized, as if we'd entered another time. Then, abruptly, the sky darkened. Beyond the window, sheet lightning flashed above the Sitka spruce. The rain came down hard, pummelling the landscape.

By 11:00 a.m. the rain lifted. We sat with the others in the local airport parking lot under a huge totem pole crested with a raven while ravens cawed and screeched over our heads. We'd been told our small Grumman Goose float plane was grounded in Bella Bella, but suddenly it broke through the clouds and landed on the tarmac. Leon from New Zealand was flying it! The thirty-year-old sky cowboy said he'd found a hole in the clouds. Maybe it would still be open for us to get back through. "Let's give it a try," he said. "What have we got to lose?" Our lives, I thought, but why turn back now?

We headed out, fragile as paper in the shuddering air currents with Leon shifting mechanical levers that sounded like they'd been salvaged from a vintage Second World War plane. We were flying about six hundred feet above the sea, thick black clouds like a ceiling over our heads. The sea below was so clear we could see a pod of whales fishing. Leon gave a whoop: he'd found the hole through the clouds. We wouldn't be turning back.

We landed mid-afternoon at Shearwater near Old Bella Bella, territory of the Heiltsuk Nation. A huge carved grizzly stood on its hind legs on a rock at the edge of the harbour, welcoming people with a wave. It seemed everything here was a story, depicted visually with sculptures and carvings.

A wonderful painting of the sea floor with salmon and sea urchins hung on the door of the hardware store. Near the wharf was a warriors' pole depicting a raven. The inscription explained that Raven was the hero of the Heiltsuk origin stories; he stole the sun, moon, and stars to bring light to the people. The human faces sheltered inside the wings of Raven represented First Nation veterans who'd lost their lives in the First and Second World Wars.

The Zodiac was waiting at the dock to take us to where the *Passing Cloud* was anchored. I'd seen pictures of the boat, but in the flesh, it was beautiful. The helm in the wheelhouse shone with polished brass. Below deck, the salon had a massive skylight and woodwork of varnished old-growth Douglas fir. At seventy feet, the *Cloud* accommodated six passengers and three crew.

I met my fellow passengers: Mary, a woman who, at the age of sixty-four, cycled across Canada with thirty other women, and Leslie, who'd worked as an NGO in project developments in Africa. And the three-man crew: our twenty-eight-year-old captain, Matt, who told me he preferred water to land. On the water you can feel autonomous. Nothing controls you; you answer only to your passengers, your crew, and the sea.

The chef, Mathieu, was from Quebec. He came to the West Coast via Thailand, where he'd gone for a year and stayed ten. He knew books, food, the ocean's edibles. Mike, the first mate, studied biology in university but left the research lab to follow adventures on the open sea.

Our delayed flight had cut short our first day. After a dinner of local crab, we sailed out the Seaforth Channel, round Dowager Island, and up the Mathieson Channel to Rescue Cove, where we anchored over-night. When we woke the next morning, fog had encircled the ship. There's a strange seductive silence to fog, as if the world has suddenly disappeared. When the fog lifted, we sailed through Jackson Narrows and put down anchor. Mike brought round the Zodiac, and the six of us climbed in.

The air was soft in the bay. Bonaparte's gulls circled and dipped over our heads. The water was so still its surface was like satin. It was low tide, and the visibility was absolute. We saw a magical riot of sea creatures clinging to the rocks: red, green, and purple sea urchins; purple, magenta, and burgundy anemones. Impossible for anyone but a biologist to decipher. But we had our biologist on board to tell us what we were looking at. Mike spoke of blood stars, bat stars, sunflower stars, and six-rayed sea stars; helmet crabs, black-clawed crabs, and decorator crabs; sea spiders; ghost shrimp; acorn and gooseneck barnacles. There were forests of brown and green bull kelp floating vertically in the water, expanding and contracting like lungs. The density of living creatures was overwhelming.

Most amazing were the jellies: fried egg jellies, moon jellies, and the red-eyed medusa jellies — pale pink, almost transparent umbrella-shaped bells trailing tentacles that propel them through the water. Mike said they're Precambrian and were around a billion years ago. Most of the BC jellies (there are seventy-five varieties) don't sting much, but he told us the lion's mane can deliver a wallop that'll leave you moaning for hours. We withdrew our hands from the water.

Mornings and afternoons we went out in the Zodiac. Our days were full of sightings. In Mussel Inlet, we entered the estuary and saw a mother grizzly bear with her cub feeding in the shallows. At a farther distance a male was turning over rocks looking for crabs. A bald eagle eyed us from atop a spruce, but then ignored us; we were not prey.

We sailed along Sheep Passage into another estuary. Shades of fish swarmed beneath our boat. In Carter Bay, we watched the pink salmon and chinook leaping into the air with wild grace, as if dancing. That night we anchored in Horsefly Cove — I'd come to love the names.

I spent hours alone on the deck where the anchor was stowed. It felt good to absorb the surroundings and not to talk. I especially liked the sea in the late afternoons when the birds navigated over the water's surface, homing, and the sun stretched out long across the water. Bats skimmed over my head as the evening sky purpled. The world seemed wide and silent, our presence a mere ripple.

One afternoon on the west side of Gil Island we sighted a pod of nine humpback whales. Some were breaching, leaping completely out of the water, and falling back on their sides, sending the seawater surging in all directions. Others lifted their flukes vertically before disappearing into the depths. Then suddenly the nine humpbacks dove together. Mike said they were bubble fishing.

It's a co-operative technique. On the sea floor, one humpback blows bubbles from his blowhole and, swimming in a circle, creates a bubble net that traps the prey—this could be crustaceans, krill, or a school of herring. Then the whole pod of humpbacks surges upwards to the surface, mouths open, to scoop up the catch. Nine whales breaching at the same time was a dazzling sight. If we could have heard their signals to each other, we would have understood the level of coordination needed to pull this off.

Behind the captain's table in the ship's hold were shelves of books of natural history, marine science, and maritime biology. To rest, or to get out of the rain which came intermittently, I would occasionally find myself in the captain's chair, usually with one or two fellow passengers, reading about the sea.

It turns out the sea is a very noisy place with creatures singing in infrasonic tones below our auditory threshold, creating an avalanche of sound we cannot hear or, if we could, would not be able to stand.

I wanted to know about whales and picked up *The Great Bear Sea* by Ian McAllister and Nicholas Read. I learned that each humpback whale can produce a series of varied sounds and phrases for a period of seven to twenty minutes and then repeat the same series with considerable precision. Sound travels through water five times faster than through air. A whale's "song" can travel a distance of nine thousand kilometres (almost twice the width of Canada). Humpback whales have large brains (proportionally larger than ours) and live between sixty and seventy years, unless hunted by humans.

On our fourth day, Matt announced that he'd made radio contact with Janie Wray at the the Fin Island Whale Research Station, built in 2017 with the support and permission of the Gitga'at First Nation. We sailed up Squally Channel to the station's wharf. Because of the legacy of COVID we couldn't visit the small clapboard cabin up on the rocky outcrop. Instead, Janie, her two PhD research students, and Cohen, her golden retriever, came down to the dock to meet us. So far, they'd been in residence in this lonely outpost for three months. It must change you, I thought.

Their work of salvage is incredibly important. With visual hourly surveys, they are estimating the abundance of whales and their routes in the area. They want to assess the risk of ships striking the humpback whales, fin whales, and orcas who use the Squally Channel. And the problem isn't just deadly collisions or entrapment in nets. The whales negotiate the undersea by sound (their ears are located behind their eyes), and the sounds of container ships and oil exploration interfere with their capacity to find food.

The Fin Island Station monitors four hydrophones placed in a rectangular formation on the sea floor, creating an acoustic database to assess the impact of ambient noise on the whales. Could science convince industry to save the species? This is their hope.

By examining the whales' vocalizations, their songs and clicks, could scientists understand their language and one day speak to the whales?

Janie had stories, like the time a humpback whale noticed the three women watching from the rocks. It dove and "spy-hopped," coming up a few feet in front of them, and looked them straight in the eye. (Spyhopping is when humpbacks hold the top third of their bodies out of the water like a periscope.) "That look was unforgettable," Janie said.

On our trip, we got to watch porpoises racing each other in the boat's wake as if out on a romp, a sea otter floating on its back near Swindle Island, and three orcas carving the sea with their black fins. But our most precious experience was our excursion to Gribbell Island, home to the legendary spirit bear. (A recessive gene caused a genetic mutation in the black bear, turning the bear white.)

We left the Zodiac in the estuary and clambered over rocks slippery with barnacles and kelp. Our guide, Joleen, a member of the Gitga'at

First Nation, met us at Kwaa Creek. We were not on the side of the island where viewer platforms have been built and where the climb up is on a logging road. No, we were struggling up a narrow trail made by the local bears with an incline of sixty degrees. Joleen warned us that bears smell fear in other bears and in humans. If a bear came by, we were to clump together and make no noise.

We moved through impossible scruff, over spruce stumps slippery with mud and hanging moss, to a level stretch of land on the side of a seething stream up which pink salmon were struggling.

I'd read that salmon live in the ocean for four years and then return to the exact stream where they were first spawned. The current theory is that each river has its own distinct smell which a salmon can identify. (The mind of nature is stunningly precise!)

We observed the painful drive of the salmon as they mounted the shallow stream. Many had pieces hacked from their bodies and still they climbed. I watched one salmon make ten attempts to mount a small ledge of rock. On the tenth climb he made it.

We hiked up to the next level where a log stretched to the water as a kind of viewing platform. A splendid waterfall roared down this part of the stream. And there across from us on the opposite bank sat an eighteen-year-old black bear. Joleen knew him.

With intense concentration, he was shifting his gaze slowly from side to side, like a pendulum, searching the water for salmon. He had such power, such patience, such control that it was almost unnerving. Suddenly he leapt into the water, grabbed a salmon with astonishing dexterity, and climbed back to his post. Then he looked at us. It was not an animal watching a human; it was two creatures exchanging gazes in a still space. I almost felt him occupy me.

Joleen just smiled. She'd seen my reaction in others. She invited us to hold hands and speak to the forest. To my embarrassment I found myself crying. I felt such sorrow over our human arrogance that leads us to violate this world.

A man suddenly appeared from among the trees as if he were part of the forest. It was Joleen's uncle Marven Robinson. He'd grown up in the Gitga'at village of Hartley Bay and is now a local guardian.

We asked him about the legendary spirit bear. He said the Gitga'at name is Moksgm'ol. Locals call it the ghost bear. Its origin myth is about the wisdom of nature:

> When the land was green, the Raven decided to give the
> people a reminder of when the world was covered in ice
> and snow. He asked the black bear to create a white cub.
> This spirit cub would have special powers—to lead the
> people to special places, to find fish deep in the ocean.

Marven has been in this old-growth forest on Gribbell Island for twenty-five years, tracking bears. He said there are ten white bears on the island and probably fifty black bears. His favourite ghost bear is called Boss. Boss loves magic mushrooms, and when he gets high Marven said he can actually go up and touch him.

When he was a kid, the Gitga'at kept the existence of the ghost bears secret—they didn't want outsiders to know about them because people are not to be trusted. But as industry on the coast grew, they decided to speak of the ghost bears and use tourism to protect them, believing people won't harm bears that bring in money.

But sadly, it seems they are wrong. In the ship's library, I found the BC Conservation Service statistics for 2018. The conservation officers relocated nineteen grizzlies. They destroyed ninety-nine. They killed 1,691 black bears and 233 cougars. Supposedly the animals were threatening human habitats. But the truth is bears mostly eat plants and salmon and avoid humans. There are other versions of bears. Marc Bekoff, professor of ecology at the University of Colorado, writes that "bears are intelligent, social, gentle animals. They feel empathy and embarrassment. They judge. They get bored. They grieve."

I read Tom Mustill's *How to Speak Whale* and was thrown by the truth of what he said: "To be alive and explore nature now is to read by the light of a library as it burns."

We are living in a time of climate catastrophe, losing the planet as we know it. Any rational person should feel grief. With climate catastrophe comes extinctions. I read that under the heat dome phenomenon on the West Coast in June 2021, "one billion sea creatures in the Pacific Northwest were cooked to death as if trapped in a convection oven."

Approximately 40 per cent of insects are in decline worldwide, and a third are in danger. Seventy per cent of frogs, toads, and other amphibians are in decline, dying in large numbers from an aquatic fungus called *Batrachochytrium dendrobatidis*. The origin of this fungus is unknown, but scientists suspect that humans are helping to spread it.

The problem may be that we have always thought of ourselves as exceptional and separate from the rest of the planet, which we exploit as a resource. We have tied our world to the accumulation of objects and the battle for power. We still live the old hierarchy: humans above animals, men above women. But what if we are not the pinnacle of evolution but simply one of nature's experiments—and that experiment has gone wrong?

As the pandemic has proven, we are nature, and we still have so much to learn.

To despair is pointless. It's time to act. Early in the pandemic, when no one was travelling, the crew of the *Passing Cloud* acted. They helped to create the Marine Debris Removal Initiative (MDRI). This involved two twenty-one-day expeditions, a fleet of 9 ships and 17 skiffs, 111 small-ship tour operators, and 69 First Nation community members. Collectively they removed 127 tons of marine debris from 401 sites and 540.5 kilometres of shoreline on BC's Central Coast. The removal of this debris (much of it abandoned fishing gear, plastic beverage bottles, and Styrofoam flotation devices) will at least reduce the risk of costal seabirds and marine mammals ingesting or getting entangled in it.

On the *Passing Cloud* the last afternoon, Colleen and Mathieu, the chef, climbed to the bowsprit and launched themselves twenty-five feet into the frigid ocean. It was a celebration of the joy of being here. I didn't jump, but watching, I felt the drama of departure. We'd glimpsed the exacting order and infinite improvisation of Nature and its exquisite beauty. We were leaving the Great Bear Rainforest feeling renewed, but also overwhelmed by grief at the thought of what could be lost.

A Note on Sources

In "The Three Suitcases and Robert Capa's Mysterious *Falling Soldier,* 2008," the two-volume catalogue for the Capa exhibit to which I contributed an article is *The Mexican Suitcases: The Rediscovered Spanish Civil War Negatives of Capa, Chim, and Taro,* edited by Cynthia Young (New York: International Center of Photography/Steidl, 2010). Robert Capa's quotes are taken from Richard Whelan's *Robert Capa: A Biography* (Lincoln: University of Nebraska, 1994). Alex Kershaw's *Blood and Champagne: The Life and Times of Robert Capa* (New York: Thomas Dunne Books, 2003) was also useful in the preparation of this essay.

All direct comments by Fred Stein are taken from an unpublished letter written by him in 1946 for friends and family and held in the Fred Stein Archive, New York. Quoted by permission of Peter Stein and Dawn Freer.

Versions of some of these essays were previously published in: *Brick Books, Border Crossings, Descant, Exile, Harper's, Island* (Australia), *Literal* (Mexico), *Meanjin* (Australia), *Nimrod* (Oklahoma), *Pagina/12* (Argentina), *Rampike, Revista da Abecam* (Brazil), *Salmagundi* (New York), *Malahat Review, This Magazine, Writing Home: A PEN Anthology,* and *Memory-Making: Selected Essays.*

A Note on Sources

Acknowledgements

Where the World Was spans forty-five years of writing. As I look back, there are many people to thank. I would like to acknowledge P.K. Page who had an enormous impact on my early writing career, the remarkable South African/Canadian poet Jeni Couzyn who affirmed my work, and the great painter Leonora Carrington who invited me into her visionary world. Josef Škvorecký was instrumental in my organizing the international congress The Writer and Human Rights in Aid of Amnesty International. Professor Donald Redford, world specialist on the Pharoah Akhenaten, initiated me into the mysteries of the Egyptian imagination. Annette Fry was so very generous during the writing and publishing of my book about her husband Varian Fry; Peter Stein and Dawn Freer recounted the dramatic escape of Peter's father Fred Stein from Vichy France, enriching my story of Villa Air-Bel. Olga Peters, Svetlana Alliluyeva's daughter, was deeply supportive during the long process of writing *Stalin's Daughter.* Robert and Ramona Rayle invited me to their home and gave me Svetlana's original letters to copy; Sim Smiley undertook original research at NARA and found deeply important files for me at Stanford University; Anastasia Kostrioukova accompanied me to Russia and Georgia as my research assistant. Without her I could not have completed this project.

From University of Toronto Libraries, I would like to thank Natalya Rattan, Archivist (Literary Papers and Archival Collections) at the Thomas Fisher Rare Book Library, and photographer Paul Armstrong, Digital Scanner (Rare Materials). Both showed such patience and professionalism in providing material from their collections for *Where the World Was.* Michael Wurstlin and Laurie Maher prepared the photos for me, for which I am deeply grateful.

Over the years I have had exceptional editors. Iris Tupholme has been my editor from my first biography in 1991. Her loyalty, wisdom, and affection have proven boundless. Marty Gervais of Black Moss Press published my books of poetry and my children's book, which I hold close to my heart. The brilliant editor Claire Wachtel accompanied me on my journey in pursuit of Varian Fry and Svetlana Alliluyeva with enthusiasm and intelligence; Sara Nelson has been wonderful in her endless patience and engagement with the Anne Frank Project. I would also like to thank my lifetime agent Jackie Kaiser for her unfailing support. Her generosity and enthusiasm have carried me through the triumphs and trials of the writing life.

I would like to acknowledge my friends and readers: my sisters Colleen, Sharon, and Patricia; the author Plum Johnson, who was the first to read the manuscript and discovered its title; and the gifted poet and editor Karen Mulhallen, who read scrupulously (finding the errors) and enthusiastically supported the collection. I would also like to thank Barbara Gowdy and Linda Spalding for sharing their experience as young writers starting out. And finally, I thank Juan Opitz, my husband and enthusiastic partner in many of these adventures.

My thanks go to Goose Lane who took on the publication of *Where the World Was*; to Alan Sheppard at the helm who skillfully directed the project; to Erin Russell, design intern; to my editor Linda Pruessen who deeply understood the ambition of this book to illustrate a woman's writing life and helped me to shape it to that end; Jill Ainsley, the line editor on whose patience and generosity I came to depend; and Kristen Chew, who proofread the manuscript with an eagle's eye.

Rosemary Sullivan is the author of sixteen books of biography, memoir, poetry, travelogue, and short fiction. Her books include *Shadow Maker: The Life of Gwendolyn MacEwen*, winner of the Governor General's Award; *Villa Air-Bel: World War II, Escape and a House in Marseille*, winner of the Canadian Jewish Yad Vashem Award in Holocaust History/Scholarship; and *Stalin's Daughter*, which won the Hilary Weston Writers' Trust Prize, the BC National Non-Fiction Award, the RBC Charles Taylor Prize, and the International Plutarch Award in Biography, and was a finalist for the PEN/Bograd Weld for biography and the National Books Critics Circle Award. In 2012, Sullivan became an Officer of the Order of Canada for her contributions to Canadian culture.